PUBLIC ADMINISTRATION IN THE INFORMATION SOCIETY

Innovation and the Public Sector

The functioning of the public sector gives rise to considerable debate. Not only the efficiency and efficacy of the sector are at stake, but also its legitimacy. At the same time we see that in the public sector all kinds of innovations are taking place. These innovations are not only technological, which enable the redesign of all kinds of processes, like service delivery. The emphasis can also be put on more organizational and conceptual innovations. In this series we will try to understand the nature of a wide variety of innovations taking place in the public sector of the 21st century and try to evaluate their outcomes. How do they take place? What are relevant triggers? And, how are their outcomes being shaped by all kinds of actors and influences? And, do public innovations differ from innovations in the private sector? Moreover we try to assess the actual effects of these innovations, not only from an instrumental point of view, but also from a more institutional point of view. Do these innovations not only contribute to a better functioning of the public sector, but do they also challenge grown practices and vested interests? And what does this imply for the management of public sector innovations?

Series Editor:
Prof Dr Victor J.J.M. Bekkers
Erasmus University, Rotterdam, The Netherlands

Volume 11

Previously published in this series

Vol. 10. M. Veenswijk (Ed.), Organizing Innovation – New Approaches to Cultural Change and Intervention in Public Sector Organizations
Vol. 9. V.J.J.M. Bekkers and V.M.F. Homburg (Eds.), The Information Ecology of E-Government – E-Government as Institutional and Technological Innovation in Public Administration
Vol. 8. D. Ward, The European Union Democratic Deficit and the Public Sphere: An Evaluation of EU Media Policy
Vol. 7. M.M.J. van Klink and J.E.J. Prins, Law and Regulation: Scenarios for the Information Age
Vol. 6. I.Th.M. Snellen and W.B.H.J. van de Donk, Public Administration in an Information Age
Vol. 5. J.A. Taylor, I.Th.M. Snellen and A. Zuurmond (Eds.), Beyond BPR in Public Administration
Vol. 4. K.V. Andersen (Ed.), Information Systems in the Political World
Vol. 3. W.B.H.J. van de Donk, I.Th.M. Snellen and P.W. Tops (Eds.), Orwell in Athens. A Perspective on Informatization and Democracy
Vol. 2. P.H.A. Frissen, V.J.J.M. Bekkers, B.K. Brussaard, I.Th.M. Snellen and M. Wolters (Eds.), European Public Administration and Informatization
Vol. 1. P.H.A. Frissen and I.Th.M. Snellen (Eds.), Informatization Strategies in Public Administration

This series is a continuation of "Informatization Developments and the Public Sector" (vols. 1-9, ISSN 0928-9038)

ISSN 1871-1073

Public Administration in the Information Society

Essays on Risk and Trust

Edited by

Miriam Lips

Tilburg University, Tilburg, The Netherlands

John A. Taylor

Glasgow Caledonian University, Glasgow, Scotland, UK

and

Frank Bannister

Trinity College, Dublin, Ireland

IOS Press

Amsterdam • Berlin • Oxford • Tokyo • Washington, DC

ISBN 1-58603-597-5
Library of Congress Control Number: 2006920942

This is the book edition of the journal *Information Polity*, Volume 10, Nos. 1,2 (2005), ISSN 1570-1255

Publisher
IOS Press
Nieuwe Hemweg 6B
1013 BG Amsterdam
The Netherlands
fax: +31 20 687 0019
e-mail: order@iospress.nl

Distributor in the UK and Ireland
Gazelle Books
Falcon House
Queen Square
Lancaster LA1 1RN
United Kingdom
fax: +44 1524 63232

Distributor in the USA and Canada
IOS Press, Inc.
4502 Rachael Manor Drive
Fairfax, VA 22032
USA
fax: +1 703 323 3668
e-mail: iosbooks@iospress.com

PRINTED IN THE NETHERLANDS

Contents

Information Polity 10 (2005) 1–9
IOS Press

Editorial

Public Administration in the Information Society: Essays on Risk and Trust

Miriam Lips, John A. Taylor and Frank Bannister

1. Risk, trust and the state of public administration

Risk and trust are interlocking issues, thrown into the social, political and managerial foreground as governments pursue their responses to the development of the information society. Transformations in the ways in which information is gathered, stored, transmitted and shared throughout government and the wider polity raise a variety of concerns across the spectrum of scholarship and public commentary. As the use of ICT becomes virtually ubiquitous, debates about risk and trust have taken on deeper and broader dimensions, in part reflected in the growing interest in risk management, and more recently in trust management, in public administration.

Risk and trust must be acknowledged as central concepts in governments' ambitions to address the information society, therefore. As our societies, polities and economies become increasingly 'wired' and information intensive, the collection, management and development of information resources come more and more to the centre of attempts to control and regulate for risk and trust in and by public administrations. Flows of information deriving from new ICT applications pervade public administration and the wider polity, as the chapters in this book show. Indeed we are reaching a point where practising public administrators see remedies for major arterial blockages in the governmental body increasingly to be found in new forms of digital networking, of which the Internet perhaps provides the greatest opportunities. As these potential remedies are identified and implemented so it becomes ever clearer that governmental risk management is at the heart of many of them. Moreover, and as a concomitant of its management of risk, government is also seeking to manage trust, in particular the trust levels of citizens and consumers, not only of its own services, but those of the commercial world. As governments better manage risk so, it is assumed, the trust of citizens in those governments will rise.

Risks are omnipresent, both within the government machinery itself and externally to it. Government has a responsibility to deal with both. These risks can be macro in scale, such as the risk of losing public confidence in government, and micro, such as the risk of failure of a new government computer system. This macro/micro scale is a scarcely adequate bifurcation, however, for macro risks can have a myriad of micro consequences and vice versa. Moreover, management of these risks often can be reciprocally related to the management of trust, for to manage risk will contribute to increased trust and to manage trust implies the reduction of risk. Combining risk and trust management, opens up new management perspectives on emergent issues in the information society.

In the practice of public administration, risk and trust are pervasive and their management crucial. High quality information is critical to that management. To know more about these issues, to communicate more effectively about them and to implement far-reaching public policy measures, all require the further intensification of information management from which this enhanced risk and trust management can be realised. Yet, such information intensity in its turn introduces new risks. As the depth and breath of information passing through systems in public administration increases, new risks emerge and old risks can be amplified. Amongst these risks is loss of public trust. The management of risk and trust are crucial to effective public administration.

This volume explores a range of risk and trust issues emerging from contemporary developments in the management of information, information flows and resources in public administration. It does so in the form of a series of essays for which scholars were invited to explore widely, independently, uninhibitedly and even provocatively, the profound questions faced by both practice and discipline in public administration. As is clear from these essays, the challenges for governments are formidable, as is the search for effective solutions. These challenges must be confronted, however, if we are to have effective public administration within a society simultaneously labelled risk society and information society.

2. A collection of essays

By intention and design this volume of essays draws together perspectives on ICT developments with risk and trust management in contemporary public administration, perspectives that have either been largely ignored within the discipline or, equally inexplicably and unsatisfactorily, kept separate.

The origins of the book are to be found in plans laid in 2003 for the annual Study Group on ICT and Public Administration, held under the aegis of the European Group of Public Administration [EGPA] conference. For that meeting we encouraged scholars to try and fuse established perspectives on 'informatization' in public administration with emergent perspectives on the implications for public administration of societal, political, governmental and managerial risks and related issues of trust. The better the understanding that public administrators develop of the organisational, political and democratic impacts of e-government service delivery and the experience that consumers have of those services, the greater the chance of success of such systems and services. Equally if politicians, administrators and service professionals are to develop new ways of controlling external risks then better intelligence and information are essential. For governments to assess and manage the risks that arise as a result of informatisation requires that they have high levels of understanding of both internal and external operating environments and the relationships between them.

Clear perspectives informing both the conceptualisation and design of academic research and public policy formation, are crucial to influential research and effective public policymaking. Currently, however, in the discipline of public administration, major ambiguities, uncertainties and lacunae prevail in the key perspectives that concern us in this volume. From both the informatisation perspective, which must include the role of the Internet in modern government, and risk and trust-related perspectives, there is little agreed scholarly or practitioner understanding, leaving the discipline in a state of theoretical and conceptual incoherence and thereby limiting opportunities for useful, policy-informing research and improved policy implementation

This collection of essays is a first joint attempt of scholars in the broader field of ICTs and public administration to address these shortcomings. It is our hope that these essays will help both to develop our thinking and provide new insights which will in turn shine new light on the challenging, highly complex questions public administrations are facing in the developing information society.

3. Structure and contents

The contributions in this book fall into four sections, each of which we examine at greater length below. In the first of these our contributors examine issues of risk and trust. They do so by looking both at how government must understand the issues of risk and trust that it faces and also at how government finds ways of managing risk in its search for higher levels of trust. The second section looks at how information is being managed in new ways in different policy domains of government so as to mitigate risk, on the one hand, though introducing threats to personal privacy, on the other. The third section captures a further aspect of practice in contemporary public administration, that of the search for innovation. Information is a source of innovation, for government as well as for other sectors but, as government innovates in ways designed to reduce risks of failure, so new risks emerge – as these chapters show. The essays in the final section address overarching issues relating to Internet governance. How is the Internet governed, and how adequate is that governance? Is the formal governance of the Internet suborned by the *de facto* governance of what are fast becoming the world's largest companies – the computing and media industry giants whose own technical standards may be acquiring the status of universal industry standards, with far-reaching consequences both for the industry itself and for individual and collective forms of government?

3.1. Risk and trust

Issues of trust, including the lack of popular trust in government, have always been an important consideration in shaping the structures and practices of governance. It is therefore not surprising that the impact of information and communication technology (ICT) applications on public trust – what Dutton et al. in this volume refer to as 'cyber trust' – is a crucial element in the take-up and effectiveness of e-government services. The continuing debate about identity cards in the UK provides an example of widespread, identifiable public concern about the degree to which government can be trusted with the stewardship of information, including personal data, about its citizens.

At the heart of these concerns about trust in e-government is a 'trust tension' caused by the simultaneous need to collect data on individual citizens as the basis for providing public services, such as health and taxation records, and fears of data surveillance, including the inappropriate secondary use of personal information held in these records. Thus, according to these authors, governments must engage in 'trust enhancing strategies' that include the provision of 'learning opportunities' in cyber- service consumption for citizens and the establishment of clear guidelines for public service organisations that will reassure citizens, thus enhancing rather than undermining trust.

The gaining of citizen trust by government may, however, be more a matter of political rationality than logical prescription. In their contribution to this volume Taylor and Burt take us to what they call the 'trust diamond', a two axis, four point diagram. On one axis we see the relationship between government, at one point, and non-governmental agencies producing and providing electronic services on behalf of government, at an opposite point. On the second axis lie trust and blame. The authors argue that government may simultaneously reduce the negative consequences of assigned blame deriving from service mistakes and failures whilst raising up their trust level amongst citizens by off-loading high risk service delivery to non-governmental providers. This strategy for simultaneous blame avoidance and trust enhancement is most likely to succeed where such non-governmental providers are from the highly trusted voluntary sector. Here we have risk management through 'government by association'. Enlisting respected and trusted bodies from the charitable and voluntary sectors associates trust-starved government with highly trusted organisations, with the additional advantage that if mistakes and failures do occur within these transferred service arrangements, the blame does not fall directly upon government.

This essential social and political relationship between risk and trust is explored further by Bekkers & Thaens. Following Castells' analysis of the network society they argue that the mutual dependencies by which the information society is characterised are seemingly sustained by the existence and development of forms of social capital and the reciprocal trust relationships that derive there-from. Yet this perspective holds major problems within itself, as a further characteristic of the network society is the breaking down of the social identities from which social capital derives. Thus the socio-economic benefits that derive from the enhanced flexibilities and fluidities of the network society are set in counterpoint to the atomising tendencies of such a society with its consequent reduction of socially value- adding reciprocities and trust relationships. In this interconnected world of the network society, government must contend with risk that is both broadened and deepened, with events occurring that 'spin' and 'snowball' around these networks, including internationally, and thereby beyond the control of any single node [or government] on the network. Powerfully and persuasively, these authors argue that the governance of risk in this complex interconnected world has to be pluriform in nature. Differentiated, though interconnected, networks and infrastructures are cut across by differentiated policy regimes, themselves characterised by varied governance strategies. Models of risk management must take into account this mosaic. Prescriptions based upon a single focal point are highly vulnerable to failure.

3.2. Risks to privacy in new forms of information management

How can government secure its citizens and make them safer and at the same time shore up their rights to enjoying a private domain? This is a crucial question in an era in which government has to recognise the need for new forms of information management that seem to have diametrically conflicting goals. Enhanced informationabout service consumers, particularly consumers vulnerable to forms of criminal or anti-social or personal threat, provides government with new high order moral opportunities: as information is gathered, managed and used in new ways governments can choose to intervene in ways that protect citizens. Yet to know more about the citizen, in particular to focus holistically upon the citizen through the medium of information, is also to run into dilemmas about what government needs to know about the individual citizen. Is there a point in the gathering of information about citizens beyond which governments should not go if they are to avoid unnecessary intrusion into that citizen's personal sphere?

The two chapters in this section cover these and other related questions. Bellamy et al. address how government agencies pursue their goals through the development of enhanced information resources gathered through new forms and intensities of information sharing. So-called 'multi-agency' initiatives have been formalised across a host of social policy arenas, initiatives whose 'glue' is information exchange and sharing. The authors refer to the increased surveillance capacity of government that this information sharing represents, though they are hesitant about the extent to which one might argue that such sharing reduces personal privacy. The key to this plethora of initiatives is a form of risk management that the authors refer to as *"precautionary intervention"*. To step into a particular private situation before a public offense or misdemeanour arises is laudable, working as it does with the grain of the age-old question of how to deliver the theoretical efficacies attaching to joined up government. However, can such precautions lead to an undesirable increase in 'false positive' identifications with the numerous unfortunate possibilities that might accompany them? The risks here therefore are to be found in the possibility that more and more individual citizens will find themselves under a public spotlight that may prove unjustified or unwarranted. Risks are also evident in the loss of professional judgment implied by these shifts. As professional work becomes increasingly 'information driven' does the essence of professionalism, the ability and willingness to offer expert judgment, become reduced?

Bannister's contribution to this volume comes to the dilemmas raised over informational privacy in the context of the search for enhanced security in a more full-on way. Risk and privacy are to be found on the opposite scales of the balance. To raise up and seek to resolve issues of enlargement in the perception of social risk may well result in the relative lowering in importance of the protection of personal privacy. To raise up issues relating to the primacy of personal privacy may well result in the lowering in importance of risk assessment and risk management. A society that places primary importance on personal privacy can be expected to be one that is more risky whilst one that attaches larger significance to the management and reduction of risk may well be one in which the citizen is more constrained – more 'watched', more 'intercepted', more 'dossiered' or 'read about', as Bannister says, and more the subject of the softer side on information monitoring, that of intelligence with its strong requirement for the interpretation of personal data.

Looking through the lens of risk assessment Bannister offers up *"a number of mechanisms for achieving a better balance between the right to individual privacy and the need for communal security in an information society"*. Governments should introduce a 'privacy council', made up of societal stakeholders, whose specific function would be to manage on society's behalf the balancing between risk related encroachment into the personal sphere, on the one hand, and the 'palisading' or enlargement of the personal domain, on the other. Such a council would be sensitive to the core substantive point, but would be so whilst recognising its role in specific historical, socio-economic and political contexts. Secondly, Bannister calls for legislation and regulation that has potentially injurious consequences for personal privacy to be time limited in its force, thus requiring regular re-thinking of the imperatives under which such legislation is established. He links this point too to a third proposal, that of the need for improved forms of monitoring of government practices that impose themselves upon personal privacy. Fourthly and finally Bannister proposes more and better research and social debate on these matters so that they might be better informed. The essence of the call therefore is that personal privacy as with any 'currency' can be traded, but that trade is sufficiently significant from a societal perspective that it must be proportional. As in any regulatory regime therefore the principle of proportionality must be invoked repeatedly in a period in time and between such periods. To lose a sense of proportion in balancing risk and privacy is to risk the loss of deep social value and for citizens to find themselves subsequently unable to restore such value, able only to lament its passing.

3.3. *Information, innovation and risk*

We stated earlier in this opening chapter that *prima facie* information is a resource whose possession and management enables the mitigation of risk. Information is the balm applied to the risk society, a transcendent ameliorative that can in one application reduce the riskinesses of the modern polity. We now look again at this proposition through lenses provided by our contributors to this volume within this third section and conclude that the proposition does not indeed hold up under scrutiny. Searching for new ways of using information, as well as for new ways of enabling it to be communicated, often brings its own risks, whether through failures in the vast investments made in the development of new information systems, through overly simplistic appreciation of what is made possible by new flows of information in the democratic arena or through too little attention being paid to the unintended consequences of innovative information systems.

In her contribution Margetts revisits issues relating to the uptake by government agencies of new information systems and the dismal performances of so many agencies in their commissioning and subsequent adoption of new systems. These failures sit as a backdrop raising up a plethora of performance risks as well as risks that follow from public perceptions of 'failing government'. Margetts identifies three main ways in which many of these risks might be grouped. First are the risks that follow from government lagging behind in what Margetts calls the 'smart society' – failing to keep up with the business sector and an increasingly sophisticated and demanding citizenship thereby failing also to adopt the business imperative of 'knowing your customer' and being inflexible in the face of growing demands for more shaped and customised services. Secondly she discusses the failure to understand the complexities of new system building with 'third party' partners, failures that introduce new risk elements including those attaching to the nature of the partnerships involved. Thirdly, she examines the failure to recognise the embeddedness of information technology and systems in public policy to the point where policy and systems failures (and successes) are utterly interwoven. All of these failures, and indeed the risk of failure so inherent in new large-scale systems developments, can only be mitigated by new strategic understandings. New modes of contracting, new approaches to government learning and strong forms of within-government leadership are required.

In his contribution, Coleman takes us to an area that historically, in academic writing at least, was a progenitor for discussions of IT in the polity – that of 'electronic voting', now though, mostly thought of in terms of 'on-line' voting. The field remains, as it always has been, divided into the zealots, the believers in the power of technology to record and sort the citizen vote accurately and efficiently, and the sceptics pointing to the array of risks and pitfalls which always accompany technological solutions to the long standing problem of how to engage the *demos* in democratic societies. Coleman takes us away from this confrontation into an array of questions that are central to any evaluation of the risks of such developments as voting on-line. Let us be clear, he argues, about who is at risk, about the sort of democratic outcomes that are at risk. Let us ask whether the risks are purely technological or whether there are other matters at stake. We also need to ask 'in which spatial sphere is the risk greatest?' For the bulk of his essay Coleman takes us through these questions helping us to analyse and clarify the issues raised by on-line voting. Indeed he takes us further by asking what risks attend inaction, i.e. what are the risks in remaining with traditional methods of recording the vote? The rich tapestry woven by Coleman in this volume helps both to sort out the multitude and differentiated nature of perceived risks attaching to on-line voting and to open the debate about this aspect of modern democratic expression., a debate which he believes needs to be more widespread.

Meijer's essay examines, in very grounded ways, how the Internet can help mitigate risks in the everyday life of the citizen. His concerns are less about offering prescriptions for improvement or in sorting out the nature of high level democratic debate. Rather his paper asks an immediate question about whether in the specific case of offering neighbourhood detail in the form of a map to be found by citizens on the Internet, what might be termed 'social transparency' can be enhanced, thereby leading on to assuaging risk for the individual and the family in the neighbourhood? Meijer is especially interested in government responses to this new form of transparency and whether new forms of risk management by government accompany these maps as a consequence of real or presumed pressure from individual citizens and citizen groups. In his own country of The Netherlands, as in many other countries, local factories have suddenly and entirely unexpectedly been the cause of local tragedy. So how does new risk mapping, and the transparency that accompanies it through Internet access, affect these locally hazardous activities? Skilfully in seeking an answer to this question, Meijer invokes the rule of 'anticipated accountability' and shows how both governments and private companies react to this new form of transparency despite little demonstrable public or citizen concern being expressed. Here, he argues, public transparency and accountability are enhanced because of these reactions and the risk management measures taken. Thus the citizen is safer. A paradox exists within this reaction, however, as increased safety may coincidentally lead to lower security as, for example, terrorist groups also use this mapping data to identify potential targets. Thus the risks related to safety of the citizen, the family and the neighbourhood may reduce whilst the security risks to those same agents rise.

3.4. Risks to Internet governance

The final section in this volume takes on a series of macro issues relating both to *de jure* and *de facto* ways in which the governance of the Internet takes place, issues that are, at the time of writing this particular chapter, being debated publicly, not least in respect of the influence of a single country, the US, in the regulation of this vastly important global network.

Lips and Koops trace the short history of Internet, from early public utterances that seemed to interpret it as a phenomenon amenable to unique regulation in single countries, to the current recognition of its global ascendancy and the need for regulatory bodies and instruments to be similarly placed on a global footing. Their concern is to locate the debate about Internet governance within a clear understanding of the democratic and legal risks that this medium introduces. To do so they concentrate in their essay on the layers of Internet governance made manifest in a plethora of organisations and suggest that *"not only is [the well known] ICANN's situation unclear regarding the transparency of authority and related decision making powers. Other Internet organisations also have organisational structures and arrangements which make it difficult to grasp where responsibility and accountability lie"*. The authors conclude that the current modes of Internet governance are unsatisfactory, placing as they do so much power over Internet architecture and rules in the hands of scarcely understood bodies with at best fuzzy forms of public accountability.

Prins and Schellekens focus upon crucial, legally-derived issues of Internet governance in their essay. As they explain, the Internet consumer is often at the end of a long chain of Internet actors with each of these actors in some [weak or strong] sense responsible for content. At each link in the chain however is the potential for legal challenge as links such as Internet Service Providers (ISPs) or Payment Systems seek to 'regulate' Internet content or process. The authors cite a recent case involving PayPal – *"On September 13, 2004, Internet Law News reported that the US financial intermediary PayPal was going to levy a 'fine' of up to $500 on customers who violate its use policies – i.e. on those customers who use PayPal to pay for gaming, pornography ('adult content') and pharmaceuticals from unregistered pharmacies [2]"*. This initiative they argue is *"a clear sign of the growing pressure on Internet intermediaries to introduce enforcement policies against bad and/or untrustworthy Internet content. And this in turn raises the interesting question of what exactly 'bad' or 'untrustworthy' Internet content is."* The establishment and verification of high levels of trust, enforced under law, is therefore crucial to the effective operation of the Internet. But how is this best achieved given the legal risks that inhabit so many of the links in the Internet chain? The authors point to the insufficiency of the liability approach to the proffering of unreliable information on the Internet. Rather, they argue, a new approach must be found, one based firmly in the principle of self-regulation. Criteria for establishing the reliability of information on the Internet must be established and enforced, though this is much easier to write than to enforce. As they write, [we have shown] "... *that the step from reliability criteria to enforceable norms that regulate the behavior of the providers of information appears far from trivial. The very characteristic of information is that it is so flexible and diverse that it seems to resist every attempt to* *regulate it.*" Here, then, is yet another layer of risk in the governance of the Internet. As new codes and regulatory instruments are developed and supported by parliaments so the core of the problem, the nature of information itself, may indeed prove beyond robustly enforceable regulation.

Finally in this volume we have the essay from Hoff and Bjerke which raises major concerns, including new risks, relating to their development of the concept of 'media citizenship'. In an era where political life in all its forms is intensely mediated for the citizen by many media outlets and in which the facility for expression, involvement and engagement can be made more possible through these multiple media channels, a new form of citizenship, media citizenship, seems applicable. As the authors state "*[media citizenship] should function as a democratic norm alongside and in addition to the form of citizenship we normally associate with the fundamental rights in Western welfare democracies, i.e. civil, political and social rights*". But, do the de facto governance structures of the Internet severely inhibit and distort such citizenship? That is the question to which Hoff and Bjerke devote their essay.

At the core of the concerns about Internet governance and the realization of a strong media citizenship is the suffusion into everyday life of computer programmes through which information is stored, structured and presented. Control of both software development and its deployment become crucial therefore to the ways in which information comes to be handled and comprehended. Social discourse in its myriad forms can be highly structured by this deep communications infrastructure, therefore, with 'ways of seeing and doing' in large part pre-determined by it. They argue that copyright protection is currently one way in which such pre-determinations occur. Major companies in the media industry are now trying to create software platforms designed to protect commercial interests that simultaneously and necessarily exclude other market entrants and thereby other consumer choices. Following the well-known work of Lessig, they argue that legal code and software code are becoming synonymous, thus enshrining and realizing the commercial interests of some over others and unintentionally restricting other forms of creativity from which the citizen might otherwise benefit. Thus the mitigation by large media industry companies of commercial risks relating both to copyright and competition results in their replacement by profound social and political risks. Implied in the developments that they write about is high level control over the citizen when using the Internet. In 'western democracies' the Internet is becoming more and more the access point for news, entertainment, information, political discourse, and many commercial products and its regulation, particularly perhaps more hidden or *de facto* aspects of that regulation becomes of crucial social significance. As the world's largest media companies shape the Internet through new software solutions to 'problems' of copyright and competition, and as legislatures create rules and laws that sustain the interests of these giants of the information age, so the idea of media citizenship within the idealised forms that many have expected and wanted is not only put at risk, but perhaps lost forever.

4. Conclusions

Of course, conclusions to this volume are to be derived by readers. We asked our scholars to write in the form of essays so as both to provoke the reader's interest and to be highly accessible in explaining the positions that the authors take. We believe that authors have succeeded in meeting these goals. These essays should provoke us into thinking more deeply about the risks inherent in an information society, at so many levels of that society, and to realise how closely related to the management of trust these matters are. Their scope encompasses the management and governance of risk and trust: from risks affecting a single country to those that are global; from risks to the individual citizen, to those to society as a whole; from risks that can be narrowly defined and responded to, to those that relate in complex ways to other conceptual domains that have major importance in democratic societies, such as trust.

What we might describe as an information society could also be called a risk society, as the essays here show. By fusing these two perspectives in eleven scholarly essays we hope to have contributed both to a vital debate and to advanced scholarly and popular understanding.

Risk and Trust

Information Polity 10 (2005) 13–23
IOS Press

The cyber trust tension in E-government: Balancing identity, privacy, security

William Dutton[a,*], Gerardo A. Guerra[b], Daniel J. Zizzo[c] and Malcolm Peltu[a]
[a]*Oxford Internet Institute (OII), University of Oxford, Oxford, UK*
[b]*EGADE, ITESM, Monterrey, Mexico*
[c]*School of Economics, University of East Anglia, Norwich, UK*

Abstract. The growing use of the Internet and other information and communication technologies (ICTs) in e-government services raises important new issues of 'cyber trust' that could have a significant influence on governance structures and practices in the future. This paper argues that at the heart of debates about cyber trust in e-government is a 'trust tension' between the need to collect data on individuals as the basis for providing services and fears about the inappropriate use of personal information gathered, stored, and analysed using ICTs. It draws on studies of experiences in e-commerce and e-business, as well as e-government, to illuminate the nature of cyber trust and its wider social dimensions, including the main related challenges faced in e-government and some strategies, products and services for dealing with them.

1. Introduction: The importance of cyber trust in E-government

Issues of trust, and the lack of trust, have always been a strong ingredient in shaping the structures and practices of governance. It is therefore not surprising that the impact of information and communication technologies (ICTs) on trust – 'cyber trust' – is a crucial element in the take-up and effectiveness of e-government services (e.g. [31,36]). Debates about ICT-based identity card systems also illustrate widespread concern about the degree to which public agencies can be trusted as information on citizens become more integrated.

At the heart of concerns about cyber trust in e-government there is a 'trust tension': between the need to collect data on individuals as the basis for providing services, such as health records and voter registration, and fears of data surveillance or the inappropriate secondary use of personal information in computer databases. An absence of data impedes trust because accountability is limited, but data gathering creates trust anxieties regarding the use of that data.

This trust tension can be affected by the two-edged nature of ICTs, which can bring potential disadvantages as well as benefits in most application areas. For instance, many initiatives for national identification cards are motivated in part by a desire to enhance the efficiency and trustworthiness of e-government services. However, they raise concerns over unintended implications for the surveillance and sorting of citizens [24]. Likewise, the US Help America Vote Act of 2002 provided $4 billion to overcome problems with a more primitive voting technology that delayed a decision in the 2000 US

*Address for correspondence: William Dutton, Oxford Internet Institute, University of Oxford, 1 St Giles', Oxford OX1 3JS, UK. Tel.: +44 1865 287 210; E-mail: Director@oii.ox.ac.uk.

Presidential election. Nevertheless, some computer experts and civil liberty groups contend that these machines are 'black boxes' unable to provide a clear audit trail where discrepancies can be checked or to offer strict safeguards against fraud [22]. High-profile public sector computer failures, such as widely publicised failures with immigration and Child Support Agency computers in the UK, can also undermine confidence in the 'e-' in e-government.

'Cyber trust' may be a new term invented for the cyberspace of the Internet, but the issues it raises date back to the introduction of computer mainframes in the 1960s and anxieties about the Orwellian 'Big Brother' potential of centralised databases [38]. In Europe, those initial cyber trust debates led to the formulation of international data protection guidelines and national legislation in many countries that sought to allay concerns about holding information about citizens in electronic media (e.g. [26, 28]). The rapid growth since the 1990s of Internet-based e-commerce online services and e-business networks encompassing supply-chain and electronic payment systems has been facilitated by efforts to address consumer trust concerns. These include Privacy-Enhancing Technologies (PETs), such as data encryption and access controls for credit card information used in online transactions.

Pressure to improve the quality and efficiency of public services has led governments around the world to look for assistance from the more advanced experiences in e-commerce and e-business to help move government into cyberspace successfully. For instance, enterprise-wide Customer Relationship Management (CRM) software is being adapted to e-government requirements as 'Citizen Relationship Management' systems, as indicated by the Scottish Executive's introduction of a CRM programme to 'transform' Scotland's public services by putting the 'Customer in Focus' (see www.scotland.gov.uk).

This paper similarly draws on studies of experiences in e-commerce and e-business to explore how much – and how little – is known about the role of cyber trust in e-government. After defining the concept of trust and discussing evidence that can help to illuminate the nature of cyber trust and its wider social dimensions, it examines the main related challenges faced in e-government together with various strategies, products and services for dealing with them.

2. Defining 'trust'

Definitions of 'trust' vary greatly across disciplines. For example, Pettit [30] makes a distinction between the attribute of trust and the behaviour of trust. Kini and Choobineh [21] make a distinction among three different perspectives on trust: individual, societal and relationship. Baron [4] identifies trust as a good, a belief and a behaviour. These examples indicate that there is no commonly agreed definition of trust.

Nevertheless, one key factor is present in most definitions: *uncertainty* [19]. Without uncertainty, trust is not a significant issue because certainty means the outcome will be the same whether or not a trusting act was involved. But there are significant factors other than uncertainty which affect trust.

For example, a consumer may choose to enter into a transaction to buy a good of unknown high or low quality. By purchasing from the seller, the consumer is not necessarily signalling trust in the seller; if the price of the good is lower than the buyer's reservation price for a low-quality good, from the perspective of pure self-interest buying it becomes a rational choice, not a trusting act. It could also be argued that all that is necessary for trust to occur is that the people displaying or acting in trust – the trustors – perceive a risk to themselves, even if the people they trust – the trustees – are not aware that they can benefit from abusing that trust. However, whether or not the trustor's model of the decision problem is correct is not relevant in terms of this behavioural view of trust. It is critical only that the trustors believe they are playing a trust game.

One example of a definition of trust adopted by some economists states something like: 'a person trusts someone to do X if she acts on the expectation that he will do X when both know that two conditions obtain: if he fails to do X she would have done better to act otherwise, and her acting in the way she does gives him a selfish reason not to do X' [2,19]. Within this definition, the trustors must put themselves in a position where they would be worse off should their trust be violated. Furthermore, the people they trust should have some temptation to violate that trust.

This highlights two trust factors in addition to uncertainty: exposure from the trustor (by allowing the trustee to make her worse off) and temptation for the trustee (as he can profit from violating trust). However, common understandings of trust that confront e-government do not conform to such specialist definitions – and there are many – because people define trust to suit their own perceptions and needs. The most conventional usage of trust is defined in the Oxford English Dictionary as '... a firm belief in the reliability or truth or strength etc. of a person or thing ... a confident expectation ... reliance on the truth of a statement etc. without examination.' For example, when people say they do not trust what a politician says or a newspaper reports, they might mean that they are uncertain over the truthfulness of the statements or that they are certain that the statements are biased or otherwise misleading – and so not to be trusted. Trust may be a problem of judgement about the situation (e.g. [15]).

Given that uncertainty is a common theme in trust definitions, it might be thought that trust will necessarily be enhanced as a person learns more about the technology. However, information can create as well as reduce uncertainty. This is the hypothesis of a curvilinear relationship between information and certainty posited by MacKenzie [25], which he called a 'certainty trough'.

At one extreme of that trough, those most socially distant from the Internet, with no knowledge of the technology or its use, are likely to be alienated from the technology and least certain about its role. Thus, as people gain more experience in using a technology like the Internet, they might gain a higher level of certainty and trust in it. However, those who are most socially proximate to – less distanced from – the technology are likely to gain knowledge about the inner-working of the system that increases their level of uncertainty.

In e-government, it is important to recognise a possible difference between trust in the technology of the Internet – the array of equipment, people and techniques used to gain access to an e-government service – and trust in the people using and communicating through it for the provision of a particular government service. For example, significant ICT failures in government services could affect perceptions of risk in specific ICT-based public services, like Internet-based voting, but not trust in Internet service provision per se. Alternatively, general online problems with spam or viruses could undermine trust in using the Internet, even if a person trusts e-government services. As this illustrates, people can be simultaneously involved in multiple trust games.

3. Emerging evidence on key elements of cyber trust

A number of studies identifying a lack of trust as one of the main constraints on e-commerce (e.g. [5]) have highlighted three main dimensions of cyber trust: identity, privacy and security, which are also of relevance to e-government. The difficulty of establishing the authenticity of individual or organisational identity online, for instance, is a distinctive characteristic of cyber trust. Some research (e.g. [37, p. 51] [5, pp. 25–26]) also indicates that the Internet might undermine trust by making it harder to observe the vital non-verbal physical cues that have generally been the prime means of detecting deceit, such as through facial expressions and body language. This reduced communication channel could make the Internet a place where it is 'easy to lie and get away with it' [37, p. 51]. It may also reduce the willingness of consumers to provide personal information, as such disclosure is considered particularly vulnerable to exploitation [29].

On the other hand, early experiments comparing face-to-face with mediated communication failed to substantiate many conventional expectations about the superiority of face-to-face interpersonal communication [35], and the debate has continued since. Some now contend that trust can be enhanced by making effective use of the greater availability of high-quality information via the Internet, for example through platforms for Internet content selection (PICS), online product comparisons and specialised expert chat rooms (e.g. [5, pp. 14–16][33]). The 'comparisons' and 'experts' accessed via the Internet can be deceiving, for instance if they are posted by fraudsters mimicking genuine sources. Increasing the overall trustworthiness of people may require a long-term cultural change, possibly involving a change in preferences [39] or through a change in the way that agents perceive the decision problem [3,18].

4. The influence of social and digital divides on cyber trust

Survey research by the Oxford Internet Surveys (OxIS) on the use and public perceptions of the Internet in Britain [14] identified two distinct empirical dimensions of cyber trust: confidence in the information and technology of the Internet ('Net confidence') and perceptions of risks in being online ('Net risk'). Analyses of the OxIS data show that the Internet is an 'experience technology', as levels of confidence and risk tended to be positively associated with an individual's patterns of use (or non-use) of the Internet over time. Experience with the Internet tends to foster a learned level of trust (ibid.).

Following the pattern of MacKenzie's certainty trough, this shows that experience tends to engender a higher level of Net confidence as people gain experience and skills. However, there is a countervailing impact of experience. Those who use the Internet more, and in more ways, are also more likely to be exposed to more negative experiences, such as computer viruses and unwanted e-mail (spam). Negative experiences tend to undermine trust [14]. Although this gives users a more realistic and watchful view of the Internet's pitfalls and benefits, in practice it seems to increase perceptions of risk to their privacy and exposure to poor quality services and products. The study by Olivero and Lant [29], with fairly experienced subjects, seems consistent with this view.

The concept of the certainty trough would indicate that those most proximate, such as Web content producers and ICT professionals, could be the most sceptical because they understand the complexities involved in establishing reliable online identity, privacy and security controls. However, within the range of experience captured by the OxIS survey, there was a more consistent pattern of experience engendering a learned level of trust, mitigated by exposure to negative experiences online.

Non-users are the most distrustful of the Internet, uncertain of its value, concerned about the potential risks, and have least confidence in the people, services and information that can be accessed online. This view of the Internet as an experience technology has important implications for e-government because it highlights how social distance and know-how contribute to the shaping of cyber trust perceptions and, therefore, the use of e-services. It also reveals how inequalities across social and digital divides can influence cyber trust and thereby constrain initiatives to narrow divides.

People with the appropriate skills to collate and interpret online information can enhance their ability to authenticate the value of e-government information, services and products. Others with less expertise could remain offline and alienated from the technology, or go online and get drowned in a flood of information and be more vulnerable to online deception. For example, OxIS found lower levels of cyber trust among the elderly, the less affluent and other social categories with less access to the Internet. It is within these groups that experience in using the Internet could have a particularly disproportionate positive impact, by increasing their trust in the Internet while lessening their concerns over its risks.

These survey findings underscore the potential value of trust-enhancing technologies and services – from firewalls to personal identification and authentication systems – that might decrease exposure to negative experiences online. However, these innovations need to be approached with an understanding of the tensions between privacy, security and identification.

5. Seeking a framework to resolve the trust tension

The trust tension between collecting personal data to deliver services and worries about data surveillance and how databases are used has led to considerable efforts in public and business ICT-enabled services to develop technical, legal and social approaches to enhancing cyber trust. There is much agreement about the elements that contribute to enhancing trust, such as PETs and data protection guidelines, but there is still much debate over whether certain strategies are likely to enhance or undermine trust in different circumstances. The growth of e-government could be inhibited, for example, if the strengthening of privacy protection is achieved using methods that create unacceptable increases in costs or operational burdens. A widespread belief that increased trust will reduce overall transaction costs and risk is countered by alternative views of the relationship between trust and traditionally-interpreted transaction costs [23].

Finding a balance between the need for both personal data collection and privacy protection requires a framework that addresses uncertainties affecting the many interrelated economic, psychological, social, institutional, technical, legal and other ingredients integral to the co-evolution of human, organisational and technological systems [12,13]. For instance, uncertainties created by the reduced communication channel provided by online interactions make the establishment of identity especially important in e-government transactions. Well-managed data collection can help to create trust, for example by establishing a verifiable audit trail between the parties using a PET capability like 'non-repudiation'. This provides the sender of data with proof of delivery and the recipient with assurance about the sender's identity.

6. Trust-enhancing strategies and tools for e-government

Arrow [1] recognises that, in order to improve efficiency, trust can be enhanced via non-market controls. These can be endogenous (the inherent qualities of individuals) or exogenous (provided by third parties). Bacharach and Gambetta [2] identify two types of endogenous trust properties of an individual: krypta (unobservable) and manifesta (observable). The reduced channel of electronic communication is likely to make it more difficult to detect facial expressions and other non-verbal manifesta that are important in establishing trust and guarding against 'mimics' who pose as something they are not. This section looks at three particularly important strategies that can address these and other cyber trust issues in e-government: identity establishment; guidelines and legal frameworks; and third-party certification.

6.1. Establishing identity

Given that imitation in electronic media is inexpensive, it is vital to gain effective assurances regarding the identity of the individual, group or organisation involved in an online e-government transaction such as filling in a tax return, requesting a welfare payment or ordering a publication. Establishing trustworthy identification in online systems has been a prime driver in the development of PETs. These now cover a wide range of capabilities, such as 'digital signatures' providing a special code that can be attached to an electronic communication to identify the sender, in a similar way to a handwritten signature. The adoption and exploitation of digital signature technology by public administrations in Europe is being promoted in EU-funded projects such as SPES (www.spesproject.org). In the US, the Office of Management and Budget (OMB) has issued e-authentication guidelines to Government departments and public agencies which include four levels of identity assurance relating to the validity of an asserted online identity for e-government transactions, ranging from little or no confidence to very high confidence [7].

E-government packages and infrastructures combining more comprehensive identity, privacy and security checks include the US Government's Access Certificates for Electronic Services (ACES) programme, administered by its General Services Administration (GSA). This incorporates digital signatures in providing: *authentication* of identity for each part in an electronic transaction; *access control* to help protect and streamline security; *data integrity* to ensure data has not been changed or corrupted during electronic transfer; *technical non-repudiation* to validate a user's identities; and *confidentially* to protect information from interception during electronic transmission.

Although such approaches can help to reduce the key trust factor of uncertainty in many respects, they can also potentially raise the threat to privacy because authentication checkers have to record a 'trail' of detailed personal information requests for verification, in case a dispute arises. Many privacy and security experts believe PETs can greatly help to overcome such concerns because they enable advanced mathematics to be applied to the protection of privacy in ways that 'disrupt the conventional pessimistic association between technology and social control' [20, pp. 4–5]. PETs generally achieve this through four core capabilities (ibid. 5–9): *anonymity*, where an online service is used without the identity of the user being known, for example where a third-party assures authenticity of the anonymous user; *pseudonymity*, where a verifiable consistent online identity, such as a nickname, is used without revealing the person's actual identity; *unlinkability*, to ensure use of different online services cannot be connected; and *unobservability*, to guard against use of an online service being observed by others.

The European Commission recommends that PETs should be favoured in supporting trusted e-government services [10, p. 14]. But Rand Europe [32] draws valuable lessons from interviews with e-government experts to warn of some key obstacles likely to constrain PET use in e-government: lack of financial resources; high perceived risks; lack of knowledge about PETs; insufficiently mature PET technology; a perceived need for greater standardisation; decision makers not feeling the need for technical reinforcement to improve privacy protection; institutional preferences to keep current methods; and insufficient demand from within institutions for privacy protection.

6.2. Guidelines and legal frameworks

Regulation and legislation reduce temptation to break cyber trust by making illegal or undesirable activities expensive. For example, privacy concerns about computer-based Big Brother databases led to the development, initially in 1980, of OECD [26,28] guidelines including eight basic Fair Information Practices (FIPs) for personal data. These aim to ensure: limits are set on the nature of data gathering; there is accurate, complete, up-to-date and relevant data quality; the purposes for data collection are specified; limits are placed on the use of data, including the time it is held for the specified purposes; data are securely protected; there is openness about related developments, practices and policies; individuals participate in obtaining and challenging personal data; and accountability for compliance is vested in a data controller. These guidelines have contributed to data protection legislation and guidelines in many countries and regions, including EU Directive 2002/58/EC of July 2002.

Computer-related laws, for example the US Electronic Funds Transfer Act, have been enacted to guard against fraud and other cyber crimes, such as identity theft (use of someone else's personal information to pose as them) or infringements of privacy (use of personal data provided *bona fide* for uses different to those intended when the information was first provided). A legal framework can also reduce uncertainty by establishing an Alternative Dispute Resolution (ADR) strategy for resolving online disputes [27].

Other forms of legislation also have an effect on e-government. The US Paperwork Elimination Act, for instance, requires that people and organisations are given an option to submit or maintain information to the government in an electronic form when practicable, including provisions for a digital signature and information safeguards. The diverse nature of e-government activities also means guidelines or legislation could be needed for a variety of specific contexts. For example, the Information and Privacy Commissioner for Ontario has issued a model access and privacy agreement for use when a government function involving citizens' personal data is transferred to the private sector [8], as well as privacy guidelines relating to Radio Frequency Identification (RFID) technology: small radio-emitting tags that can transmit information about the person associated with an RFID-tagged library book or other object [9].

The difficulties of translating privacy guidelines or legislation into appropriate actions was dramatically highlighted after the murder of two ten-year-old girls in Soham, UK in 2002. One regional police force claimed that a reason for deleting records on the person subsequently convicted of the killings was its interpretation of the UK Data Protection Act. Although this interpretation was questioned by many privacy experts, a public inquiry recommended the establishment of a new Code of Practice for record creation, review, retention, deletion and information sharing among police forces [6].

6.3. Third-party certification

Certification by trusted third parties can provide information that goes beyond just the identity of an agent, for instance using products that signal external approval (e.g. 'quality seals' and 'trustmarks' for Web sites, such as the VeriSign secure seal and TRUSTe privacy mark). The main objective of such certification is to reveal information about characteristics that cannot be otherwise observed by individuals [17]. This can reduce both uncertainty and the temptation to violate trust, for instance by reporting whether or not trust is warranted on the basis of the reputation of the individual identified. However, privacy concerns can be raised about the use made of confidential information by the trusted third party. The UK government's e-Envoy [16] has developed 'trust services' guidelines for use by 'certification authorities' to assist in raising levels of cyber trust in e-government, for example by ensuring that commitments made electronically can be supported by technical evidence if there is a dispute.

Another form of third-party certification comes in the form of consumer forums where consumers may provide advice about the quality of sellers to other consumers [34]; second-order certification about the quality of buyers' advice may also be given in some cases. eBay is a classic example of a consumer forum, the rules of which are set by eBay but which otherwise is run by consumers for other consumers. The certification system may allow the building of reputation by trustworthy sellers and buyers. It is possible that similar forums may be profitably used in some e-government settings.

7. Assessing trust-enhancing approaches

Strategies, products and services to enhance trust can be evaluated along the 'who, where, when and how much' dimensions discussed in the following subsection, each having its own important implications for trust and privacy.

7.1. Participation

Participation focuses on the participant who is covered by a particular approach to trust enhancement, for instance legal frameworks must be universal while different types of certificates and authentication can be either universal or restricted. When there are several market providers of a trust-enhancing product, such as third-party certification, those being monitored could go 'shopping' for the best one they can obtain, thereby diminishing the informative value of that certificate. One way to avoid this problem would be to monitor third-party certification agents. However, the implied non-voluntary involvement in this monitoring could result in an infringement of privacy that raises important policy issues.

7.2. Depth

Depth refers to where the boundaries are set for a PET or other trust-enhancing mechanism. For instance, variations in the scope of a PET are indicated by the amount of information disclosed in establishing the identity of an agent, which may be restricted just to whether that person is who he she claims to be, or could be extended to include personal demographics (e.g. age, sex, race) and preferences (e.g. welfare requirements, consuming habits). Trust-enhancing legislation is likely to be most effective when its depth has a well-delineated focus that avoids being so broad as to allow many loopholes, or so narrow that it may be restricted to very particular cases.

The greater the information required by a PET, the higher is the risk of invading the privacy of individuals, although its value in trust enhancement could also be higher. Depth is well defined for personal authentication, as it generally tries to answer the question 'Is this who the person claims to be?', which could be carried out through the use of a personal identification number (PIN) and other personalised information when logging into an online service. Depth is less clear in other areas, such as security and privacy quality seals for Web sites.

7.3. Publication

Publication addresses the timing of *when* aspects covered by a PET, legislation or other trust-enhancing approach, need to be made available or released. For instance, information can be made available on demand (e.g. from a third party) or can be shared publicly with all potential participants at the same time. An individual may be willing to share sensitive personal information with one government agency but reluctant to make that information available to other government units.

The significance of the effects of this dimension can be seen when trying to understand the differences in the regulation of privacy in the USA and Europe. Interpretations of the US Constitution protect citizens against government invasion of their privacy. The US legal system protects consumer privacy but considers data to be corporate property with respect to private corporations: once a person voluntarily discloses information, that information is no longer considered private. Market and public relations concerns are the primary protection for consumers. European regulations, on the other hand, tend to focus on preventing the secondary use of data, which must be collected for a specific purpose and cannot be used for a different one (with the exception of historical, statistical or scientific purposes). This has implications for some widely-implemented FIPs, such as time limits on data retention.

Legislation and loss insurance clearly have to be made public before they can be applied. Authentication and certification, however, can be made public on application or on demand. The benefits and shortcomings of both approaches have to be taken into account to optimise their use.

7.4. The payer

The payer is who should be charged for the trust-enhancing product or service. When a product is a public good, in that its use by one agent does not prevent other agents from using it, the socially optimal approach may be to have the whole society pay for it. Coestier [11] proposes public financing of certification, given its public-good characteristics, as otherwise there could be too little supply of the certificates that are required. Consumer forums, of course, have the advantage of minimising the cost of certification, though the quality of the certification may also be lower.

7.5. Price

Price obviously focuses on *how much* is charged to obtain a trust-enhancing product or service, such as certification. This depends on the characteristics of the payee. For instance, if the owner of a Web site pays for some form of quality mark or other certification, the exposure factor of trust may be increased. This can produce undesirable effects as there is a risk of moral hazard, in which the supplier of the mark who verifies the system might charge a higher price for a better outcome, thereby increasing uncertainty among consumers when they see the mark.

8. Conclusions

This paper has highlighted the complexities of trust both as a concept and in its role within e-government. It has also identified a number of potentially valuable trust-enhancing strategies, products and service that could help to meet key cyber trust challenges for e-government:

1. Enable citizens to gain experience with the use of the Internet-based services in order to overcome the predispositions of those who have not used the Internet by engendering a learned level of trust.
2. Manage the trust tension between citizens' privacy/security concerns and their rights to receive efficient e-government services requiring the collection of personal data in order to be able to operate effectively. This requires an understanding of the relationships and cross-impacts between trust and its three principle aspects: identity, privacy and security.
3. Establish agreements, guidelines and frameworks to enhance cyber trust.
4. Ensure such agreements are implemented in ways that enhance rather than undermine trust, for example through the use of appropriate PETs.
5. Design, build, run and evolve sustainable ICT systems that deliver reliable and appropriate public services to all those who could make use of them.

According to the European Commission [10, p. 14], a failure to 'always guarantee secure interaction and access for citizens and businesses' in e-government may entail significant social and economic costs, in addition to breaching the law. Further research in the following key areas will help to develop effective e-government policies and practice to avoid such failures:

- *The broad effects of ICTs on trust.* Establish more empirical evidence on how trust can be enhanced in online environments, for example by complementing online service with offline contacts.
- *Influence of social contexts on trust perceptions.* Understand how issues relating to cyber trust and trust-enhancing solutions are shaped by institutional, cultural, educational, generational, geographical, gender and other contexts.

- *Effectiveness of different trust-enhancing strategies and tools.* Investigate actual uses of different approaches and develop evaluation aids in comparing PETs and other options.
- *Addressing social inequalities.* Gain a better understanding of how cyber trust perceptions and e-government outcomes are affected by the availability of skills in accessing, managing and interpreting information through the Internet and other ICTs.
- *Learning global lessons from local contexts.* Find out more about how networks of innovation can be developed to assist in transferring knowledge and lessons gained about what works, or doesn't work, in one context to help those developing e-government policies and practices in other situations.

Acknowledgement

We thank Alexandre Gaudeul and Frank Bannister for feedback; the usual disclaimer applies.

References

[1] K.J. Arrow, *Essays in the Theory of Risk Bearing,* North-Holland, Netherlands, 1971.

[2] M.O.L. Bacharach and D. Gambetta, Trust in Signs, in: *Trust and Social Structure,* K. Cook, ed., Russell Sage Foundation, New York, 2001, pp. 148–184.

[3] M.O.L. Bacharach, G.A. Guerra and D.J. Zizzo, *Is Trust Self-Fulfilling? An Experimental Study,* University of Oxford, Department of Economics Discussion Paper 76, 2001.

[4] J. Baron, Trust: Beliefs and Morality, in: *Economics, Values and Organization,* A. Ben-Ner and L. Putterman, eds, Cambridge University Press, Cambridge, 1998, pp. 408–418.

[5] A. Ben-Ner and L. Putterman, Trust in the New Economy, *HRRI Working Paper 11-02,* University of Minnesota, Industrial Relations Center, 2002.

[6] M. Bichard, *The Bichard Inquiry Report,* The Stationery Office, London, 2004.

[7] J.B. Bolten, *Memorandum to the Heads of all Departments and Agencies: E-Authentication Guidance for Federal Agencies*, Washington DC: Executive Office of the President, Office of Management and Budget, December 16. www.whitehouse.gov/omb/memoranda/fy04/m04-04.pdf, 2003.

[8] A. Cavoukian, *Model Access and Privacy Agreement,* Ontario Information and Privacy Commissioner, Toronto, February 1997, www.ipc.on.ca/docs/model-ag.pdf.

[9] A. Cavoukian, *Tag, You're It: Privacy Implications of Radio Frequency Identification (RFID)Technology,* Ontario Information and Privacy Commissioner, Toronto, February 2004, www.ipc.on.ca/docs/rfid.pdf.

[10] CEC, Commission of the European Communities, *The Role of eGovernment for Europe's Future,* COM(2003) 567, CEC, Brussels, 2003, http://europa.eu.int/information_society/eeurope/2005/doc/all_about/egov_communication_en.pdf.

[11] B. Coestier, Asyméetrie de l'information, Reputation et Certification, *Annales d'économie et de Statistique* **51** (1998), 49–78.

[12] W.H. Dutton, *Society on the Line: Information Politics in the Digital Age,* Oxford University Press, Oxford, 1999.

[13] W.H. Dutton, *Beyond the Information Society,* UNESCO Publications for the World Summit on the Information Society, UNESCO, Paris, 2004, forthcoming.

[14] W.H. Dutton and A. Shepherd, *Confidence and Risk on the Internet,* Science Review for Foresight Cyber Trust and Crime Prevention Project, 2004, www.foresight.gov.uk/cybertrust.html.

[15] C.C. Eckel and R.K. Wilson, Is Trust a Risky Decision? *Journal of Economic Behavior & Organization* **55** (2004), 447–465.

[16] e-Envoy, *Trust Services: e-Government Strategy Policy Framework and Guidelines,* The Stationery Office, London, September 2002, http://e-government.cabinetoffice.gov.uk/assetRoot/04/00/09/68/04000968.pdf.

[17] G.A. Guerra, *Certification Disclosure and Informational Efficiency: A Case for Ordered Ranking of Levels,* University of Oxford, Department of Economics Discussion Paper 64, 2001.

[18] G.A. Guerra and D.J. Zizzo, Trust Responsiveness and Beliefs, *Journal of Economic Behavior & Organization* **55** (2004), 25–30.

[19] G.A. Guerra, D.J. Zizzo, W.H. Dutton and M. Peltu, *Economics of Trust: Trust and the Information Economy,* DSTI/ICCP/IE/REG(2002)2, OECD, Paris, 2003.

[20] HiSPEC, Human Issues in Security and Privacy in E-Commerce, *Privacy Enhancing Technologies State of the Art Review,* University of Manchester Institute of Science and Technology (UMIST), Manchester, February 2002, www.hispec.org.uk/public_documents/7_1PETreview3.pdf.
[21] A. Kini and J. Choobineh, Trust in Electronic Commerce: Definition and Theoretical Considerations, in: *Proceedings of the 31 Annual Hawaii Conference on System Sciences,* (Vol. IV), W. Blanning and D. King, eds, IEEE Computer Society, 1998.
[22] T. Kohno, A. Stubblefield, A.D. Rubin and D.S. Wallach, Analysis of an Electronic Voting System, *IEE Symposium on Security and Privacy,* IEEE Computer Society Press, Piscataway, NJ, 2004.
[23] E. Lorenz, Trust, Contract and Economic Cooperation, *Cambridge Journal of Economics* **23** (1999), 301–315.
[24] D. Lyon, Identity Cards: Social Sorting by Database, *Internet Issue Brief No. 3,* Oxford: Oxford Internet Institute, University of Oxford, 2004.
[25] D. MacKenzie, The Certainty Trough, in: *Society on the Line: Information Politics in the Digital Age,* W.H. Dutton, Oxford University Press, Oxford, 1999, pp. 43–46.
[26] OECD, *Guidelines on the Protection of Privacy and Transborder Flows of Personal Data,* OECD, Paris, 2002.
[27] OECD, *Resolving E-Commerce Disputes Online: Asking the Right Questions about ADR,* OECD, Paris, 2002.
[28] OECD, *Guidelines for the Security of Information Systems and Networks: Towards a Culture of Security,* OECD, Paris, 2004.
[29] N. Olivero and P. Lunt, Privacy versus Willingness to Disclose in E-Commerce Transactions: The Effect of Risk Awareness on the Relative Role of Trust and Control, *Journal of Economic Psychology* **25** (2004), 243–262.
[30] P. Pettit, The Cunning of Trust, *Philosophy and Public Affairs* **24** (1995), 202–225.
[31] PIU, Performance and Innovation Unit, *Report: Privacy and Data-Sharing: The Way Forward For Public Services,* The Stationery Office, London, April 2002, www.number-10.gov.uk/su/privacy/index.htm.
[32] Rand Europe, Technological Solutions to Protect Privacy in eGovernment, *RE: view* **2**(3) (2003), www.rand.org/randeurope/review/2.3-horlings.html.
[33] P. Resnick, Filtering Information on the Internet, *Scientific American* (March 1997), 106–108.
[34] P. Resnick and R. Zeckhauser, Trust Among Strangers in Internet Transactions: Empirical Analysis of eBay's Reputation System, in: *The Economics of the Internet and E-Commerce,* M.R. Baye, Elsevier, Amsterdam, 2001, www.si.umich.edu/~presnick/papers/ebayNBER/.
[35] J. Short, E. Williams and B. Christie, *The Social Psychology of Telecommunications,* 1976, John Wiley and Sons, London, 1976.
[36] P.S. Trimble, A Question of Trust, *Federal Computer Week* (22 May 2000), www.fcw.com/fcw/articles/2000/0522/pol-trust-05-22-00.asp.
[37] P. Wallace, *The Psychology of the Internet,* Cambridge University Press, Cambridge, 2001.
[38] A.F. Westin and M.A. Baker, *Databanks in a Free Society: Computers, Record-Keeping and Privacy,* Quadrangle, New York, 1972.
[39] D.J. Zizzo, Empirical Evidence on Interdependent Preferences: Nature or Nurture? *Cambridge Journal of Economics* (2003), 867–880.

Information Polity 10 (2005) 25–35
IOS Press

Managing trust, generating risk: Incorporating the voluntary sector in UK e-Government

John Taylor[a,b,*] and Eleanor Burt[c]
[a]*Caledonian Business School, Glasgow G4 0BA, Scotland, UK*
[b]*The Oxford Internet Institute, University of Oxford, Oxford, UK*
Tel.: +44 1413313000; E-mail: jta@gcal.ac.uk
[c]*School of Management, University of St Andrews, The Scores, St Andrews KY16 9AL, Scotland, UK*
Tel.: +44 1334 462804; E-mail: eb19@st-andrews.ac.uk

Abstract. As the UK government seeks to (re)-establish a high-trust relationship with citizens, voluntary sector organisations (VSOs) are being incorporated within the state in ways that are designed to shift blame and risk away from government. This is not a straightforward process: as the government seeks to manage trust relationships through this engagement with VSOs, significant new risks are being generated for e-government. In conceptualising this emerging relationship between government and VSOs as concerned with trust, blame, and risk, this essay brings fresh perspective to the deepening debate about how government and voluntary sector are re-positioning their relationship.

1. Introduction

In this essay it is the 'political rationality' of blame and risk, in the context of the search for high levels of public trust in government, that is our paramount theme; though we acknowledge that risk is also to be understood as a phenomenon susceptible to more techno-rationalist forms of management, including those most clearly epitomised within compliance and new electronic regimes.

We set this essay against a backcloth in which concerns with the 'democratic deficit' and diminishing levels of public trust in the institutions of the state are persuading Government to seek closer engagement with the voluntary sector. More highly trusted than Government, the incorporation of the voluntary sector within the state brings new opportunities to shift responsibilities away from Government towards the voluntary sector. At the same time and resulting from this re-direction of responsibility, with its potential also for the re-assignment of blame, opportunities emerge for the migration of trust from the voluntary sector towards Government. This is not a straightforward 'trade-off' for, as one set of risks is off-set following this trust migration, we argue that significant new risks are being generated. The electronic mixed economy of welfare services is the major e-government policy initiative against which the emergent new risks within this evolving relationship are set out in this essay, and against which the 'political rationality' of risk and its management are played out.

*Corresponding author.

Our aims in writing this essay are twofold. Firstly, we aim to conceptualise how Government is seeking to regain public trust through closer engagement with the voluntary sector; including, in particular, through the laying-off towards the voluntary sector of potential blame for policy failure. Secondly, and grounded within scholarly understandings of the unique roles and contributions of Government and voluntary sector within society, our aim is to set out the new risks that the incorporation of the voluntary sector within the electronic mixed economy will generate.

2. Trusting government

Evidence has been growing in many national political systems, including the UK, of citizens disengaging from the formal governmental and democratic institutions at the centre of the polity. There has been marked decline in political party membership and activism; diminishing electoral turnouts; and mounting evidence of reduced (and reducing) public trust in politicians and the institutions of government. Opinion polls and other research consistently point to low trust of politicians, governments, and parliaments amongst citizens. Furthermore, the substantive levels of trust enjoyed by governmental and democratic institutions have fallen catastrophically. One study [1], drawing on findings from the Henley Centre and MORI, shows that public confidence in the civil service fell from 46% of respondents expressing confidence in 1983 to just 17% in 2000. In the same period, confidence in the legal system has fallen from 58% to 22%, and confidence in parliament from 54% to 14%. The Citizen Audit survey [33] broadly confirms this trend with 46% of citizens scoring the government and 55% scoring politicians within the range 0 to 3 on a ten point scale where ten is the highest level of trust.

Evidence of this disengagement sits alongside other evidence pointing to citizens searching for alternative forms of political activity [6]. 'New social movements' and other forms of mass mobilisation, such as the anti-capitalism movement, are taking place within the space vacated by formal politics. Citizens are increasingly voicing their concerns through the signing of petitions, or taking part in public demonstrations, also [21,28,30]. Swelling membership levels within environmental voluntary sector organisations (VSOs) may also further indicate shifting preferences in modes of political engagement [30].

These issues of trust in government, the so-called 'deficit' in formal democratic practices, together with the engagement of citizens in alternative outlets for democratic 'voice', sit powerfully behind governments' interest in new forms of engagement with VSOs, not least in the UK. VSOs are commonly perceived as high trust organisations [22,23,27] and as positive contributors to the polity from social, economic and political perspectives. The UK Government's enthusiasm for communitarianism [9] and the enhancement of 'social capital' [29], are also powerfully driving the government's interest in engaging this sector in the shaping and delivery of public policy. Added to this mix, and of particular importance in the context of e-government and the delivery of services through the electronic mixed economy, is the perception that VSOs are highly appreciative of the needs of their customers and sufficiently flexible to deliver services closely attuned to their requirements [13].

3. Managing trust

This incipient desire to incorporate the myriad of organisations that comprise the UK's voluntary sector into mainstream public service provision has been a highly distinctive aspect of UK central government in the period from the late 1990s to the present day. Whilst many of these organisations have been major providers of services to the public for many decades, hitherto they have done so largely outwith the

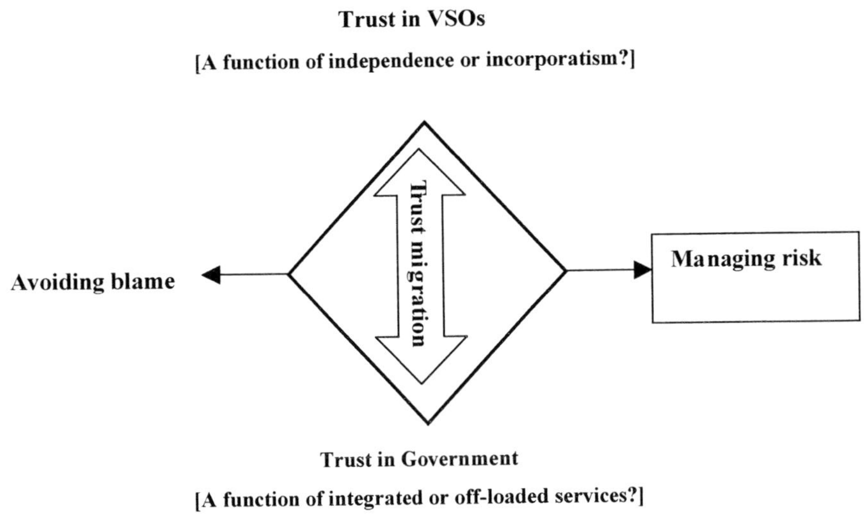

Fig. 1. The trust diamond.

mainstream. From the mid to late 1990s their contribution to the provision of public services has been actively sought by government, with the development of the electronic mixed economy being the most recent manifestation of this engagement. As we shall set out, the growing urgency within government to realise step increases in the consumption of electronic public services has further sharpened government focus on the role of the voluntary sector in the delivery of public services.

It is against this broad policy thrust that we shall discuss risks attendant for both sides in this relationship as trust is managed. We shall do so in the context of Fig. 1, and its depiction of what we call the 'trust diamond'.

The location of 'trust in government' and 'trust in VSOs' as respectively the lowest and uppermost points of the trust diamond indicates the potential for an oppositional or zero sum relationship between them. Integrated government carries high potential for blame when policies and management practices fail. By off-loading activities from government to VSOs so, we suggest, high trust levels that currently adhere to VSOs may well begin to migrate to government as VSOs are held by customers to be directly responsible for service failures. Moreover, where services are successfully delivered through VSOs, we can also anticipate the migration of trust to government as the acknowledged author of the particular policy environment. Indeed it is a proposition of this essay that such trust migration is sought by government and that its strategies for blame avoidance are largely to be explained in the context of its search for enhanced public trust and reduction in the democratic deficit. If enhanced public trust is the goal, then incorporatist strategies such as the electronic mixed economy are providing government with opportunities for its achievement. Moreover, with higher public trust the goal for government, the avoidance of blame coupled with successful risk management are combined means by which it can be achieved.

But, how should we consider risk management in government? Is risk management best crystallised by Kasperson [18], for example, when he writes "risks are trade-offs between potential losses occurring from uncertainty and potential benefits that should outweigh the losses"? Or should we look at government through less techno-rationalist lenses and instead address risk management in government as springing from an altogether different motivation, in summary perhaps best described as the 'management of blame'? As Hood [16] has written "... *the blame game shapes the risk game ... the study of blame and its management is one of the central and perennial themes of political analysis*".

In combination, these quotations provide a *leitmotif* for the study of risk in public administration. They point out that those of us involved in the study of this field must in part see risk as a substantive, technical reality that can and must be managed by practising public administrators in their rational pursuit of effective public policy implementation as they face deeply uncertain operating environments. The objective of technical risk management is to identify, control, and minimize the impact of events that, at their least, contain uncertainties and, at their greatest, cannot be closely specified at all. Equally, in the world of public administration, we must study risk and its management as the surface manifestation of deeply imbued cultural norms of British public service organisations, such as the anonymity and risk aversion of their officials. It follows from this latter perspective that the actions of public administrators must in part be understood as responses to their cultural disinclination to be exposed as responsible for taking risky decisions linked to their consequent inclination to offset risks by involving third parties. From these two perspectives, public administrators are to be studied as simultaneously pursuing forms of technical and economic rationality in their careful management of risk, on the one hand, and as in pursuit of political rationality in their playing out of the "blame game" [12,16].

In this essay it is the 'political rationality' of risk that is the paramount theme, with techno-rationalism as a sub-text. Government, we argue, is seeking to manage blame in part through its engagement with third parties such as organisations from the voluntary sector.

The electronic mixed economy, providing the policy focus here, specifically involves government in a developing relationship with the UK voluntary sector within which new arrangements for 'co-producing' electronic public services are being formed [4,31]. This initiative is one aspect of the profoundly intimate relationship that is emerging between government and voluntary sector organisations (VSOs) wherein lie considerable opportunities as well as deep risks for both sides. For VSOs, these opportunities include the creation of a more sustainable funding base and the stronger realisation of organisational vision and mission, whilst the risks are most in evidence over threats to organisational independence and public trust, for it is from each of these latter that the voluntary sector draws considerable strength and unique 'voice' [10]. For government, opportunities include off-loading responsibility for services that are under-performing, whilst risk attaches mainly to the capabilities of VSOs to take on these service provisions as well as in establishing clarity over the locus and process of public accountability.

Moreover, there is a level of risk that goes beyond this analysis of each side in the relationship, risk that may be best described as 'polity-wide'. To what extent do systemic changes, such as the ones we review here, have far-reaching systemic consequences? As the voluntary sector is drawn into government, is the independence that these organisations have historically brought to the polity being compromised and, with that, the strength of politics as a whole diminished? As government seeks this new engagement with the voluntary sector so some voluntary sector organisations will come more closely than ever into the 'shadows of the state' [34]. As they become intermediaries in the delivery of e-government services, their guardianship of an independent 'public space' is made increasingly vulnerable.

4. Rescuing e-government

Implementing e-government services has proved to be a slower and more difficult process than UK government anticipated; particularly when measured against take-up by citizens though also against broader benchmarks. Proposals by UK government to bring about an 'electronic mixed economy of public services delivery' are expected to speed the scale and scope of e-government, to reduce the investment costs and risks to government, and to lead to enhanced take-up by citizens [24]. The electronic mixed economy will see public services delivered through intermediaries that include voluntary and private sector organisations. Their closeness to the citizens they serve and their reputation for creativity and innovation suggest that VSOs are well positioned to deliver e-enabled public services that will be extremely attractive both to their existing customers and to potential new markets. Under the recently announced policy for the development of an electronic mixed economy of service delivery, nine priority areas have been identified within which 520 public services are targeted for potential delivery through 'intermediary' organisations [24–26]. These services will include VSOs taking on public services that 'fit' with existing online 'product ranges', as well as the customisation and personalisation of government services in ways that make them more attractive and accessible to citizens. Intermediary organisations, such as VSOs will also have the option of charging premium rates for 'value-added' service of this type. Thus, an organisation such as the Citizens Advice Bureaux that has specialist legal expertise available to it might, for example, offer a 'plain English' interpretation of an Act of Parliament or a concise summary of its message and implications. Equally, it will be possible within these proposals for VSO intermediaries to offer up quantitative opinion sampling in addition to direct service delivery. Thus, hypothetically, the Royal National Institute for the Blind might undertake surveys of those with sight impairment in respect of proposed new policy directions as well as taking on public services for the blind community directly.

The process by which VSOs will be contracted to provide these services will be competitive. To be successful VSOs will need to present a strong business case that demonstrates that the services are financially viable, that they can be provided on a sufficiently large-scale, and that they sit within the existing portfolio of services offered by the organisation. There will be no direct financial transaction between government and a VSO intermediary in support of e-service delivery though government may offer a VSO a percentage of demonstrable cost reductions on a case by case basis. In short, the proposition from government is that intermediaries will own these services and thereby carry responsibility for their successful delivery and for subsequent innovation.

5. Managing the transition to achieve public trust

From the perspective developed in this essay the electronic mixed economy initiative is to be understood as part of an underlying government strategy to (re)establish public trust in the institutions of the state. This initiative will allow government to offload services in the under-performing domain of citizen-centric electronic government to high trust, customer sensitive voluntary sector organisations. The rules of the 'blame game' will thereby be changed and subsequent risks attaching to service delivery standards *et cetera* will be borne by the new, wholly owning intermediaries.

The mixed economy initiative marks down a bold transition within the system of government. It raises many challenges within that transition, challenges attaching to the nature of universal service, the nature and method of public accountability and the capabilities, legitimacy and appropriate independence of intermediary organisations. It is not surprising therefore within this milieu to see that government has taken significant steps to prepare the way for the changes that it is seeking and to manage the risks involved in this transition.

6. Managing the transition: Establishing a new management climate in the voluntary sector

Whilst still in opposition, the Labour Party signalled its intention to develop a 'compact' with the voluntary sector that would position it to play a central role in the generation of 'active citizenship', social capital formation, and community cohesion. It has done so since achieving office. And through the compact and other measures the voluntary sector has become an accepted player in 'democratic renewal', not least through the locus the sector is achieving within the public service mainstream, including as 'intermediary organisations' through which citizens can receive services directly or be facilitated in doing business with government.

The 'compact' between government and voluntary sector is a mutually agreed expression of roles and responsibilities that serves as a guiding framework through which partnership is to be taken forward. It also marks a paradigmatic shift on the part of government in the nature of government-voluntary sector relationships in the UK. For here, is strong, forthright acknowledgement by government '*to recognise and support the independence of the sector, including its right within the law, to campaign, to comment on Government policy, and to challenge that policy, irrespective of any funding arrangement that might exist, and to determine and manage its own affairs*' [14]. At the same time, the compact is also the marker for the broader 'responsibilisation' [20] of the voluntary sector as other measures are brought through in its wake that will more closely guide the behaviour of these organisations. Thus, the broad defining principles of the compact are being more closely specified within sets of guidance notes that are beginning to address how to embed democratic arrangements within the voluntary sector so as to demonstrate their transparency, legitimacy, and accountability. For example, the voluntary sector has committed to defining individual organisational constituencies, to showing how these constituencies are represented by the organisation, and to showing how they are engaged in the processes associated with public policy shaping. The recently proposed 'Compact Plus', if implemented, will award a kitemark to organisations that achieve minimum agreed commitments in partnership working [15]. Other ways in which 'responsibilisation' is being managed by government include, for example, the proposal to introduce a quality standard and brand for social enterprises that conform to minimum behavioural standards. '*This would be particularly important were social enterprises to be delivering public services or using community and public money and assets*' [8].

Moreover, government is seeking simultaneously both to manage and to liberalise the voluntary sector through regulatory changes. Two recent major reviews by government have examined the conditions under which charitable status is conferred upon VSOs and the constraints that this places upon their political engagement. Measured in tone, the intention is clearly to generate a more supportive regulatory climate for VSOs. In particular, the government supports the recommendation put forward in 'Private Action, Public Benefit', '*That the Charity Commission guidelines on campaigning should be revised so that the tone is less cautionary and puts greater emphasis on the campaigning and other non-party political activities that charities can undertake*' [5].

Furthermore, government is seeking simultaneously both to manage and liberalise the voluntary sector through enhanced financial independence. The vision here is of 'social enterprises' that, unlike their more traditional counterparts within the voluntary sector, are considerably less dependent upon grant income, for example; and more open to, and able to access, forms of funding that are typically under-utilised, such as loans from 'charity banks', commercial banks, and investments. As well as reducing the cost to government and the wider public sector if VSOs could access funding in this way, the greater financial independence that would ensue for VSOs would be wholly to their benefit as democratic actors.

Finally, government is seeking both to manage and liberalise the voluntary sector by enhancing the sector's electronic capabilities, so positioning it to take on a closer relationship in its business with the state. Here, VSOs are being drawn into a world of uniform technical standards and technological platforms such as the electronic government interoperability framework (e-gif) that will entail investments in compatible operating systems, meta-data standards that will shape the ways that information is managed and controlled, and the use of Government Gateway through which 'business-to-business' exchanges will increasingly be undertaken. The significant investment costs attached to this will 'lock-in' VSOs to new modes of compliance, raising issues associated with the control of information as it does so. This change may simultaneously enhance the influence of VSOs within government as they gain access to information that was previously resident within the sealed information domains of the State.

In practice, the government's optimism may be misplaced however. Several recent, independent, research studies have pointed to high levels of technical incapacity throughout the voluntary sector from which the large national and international VSOs that will in principle be able to deliver the high-volume services required of intermediaries are not immune [2,3,11,32]. Initiatives on the part of government and the voluntary sector that attempt to resolve the problem through the establishment of a hub body providing dedicated technical support to VSOs, or through increased funding in the form of the *futureBuilders* initiative, for example, will have a limited effect given the scale of the problem. Research has also shown that the failure of senior executive managers within the voluntary sector to adopt a visionary approach to ICTs and to be at the forefront in leading e-enabled transformations in the way they organise and do business is also of critical importance.

7. Managing the risks of implementation

These managerial, financial and ICT-related interventions by government provide a broad framework of compliance from which proposals for e-service provision from VSOs can be judged. In these respects therefore government is managing the risks associated with this transition to intermediary-based service provisions. Services will be released to VSOs able to demonstrate that they have the managerial, financial and ICT-related capabilities that will support the provision of e-government services. Significant new risks are generated, however, as implementation occurs, and it is to these risks that we now turn in this essay. We have grouped these risks as: risks to VSOs; risks to the system of government; and risks to the political system as a whole.

7.1. Risks to VSOs

The enlargement of the role of VSOs as public service providers brings forward opportunities to provide a more streamlined, comprehensive and complete range of services to existing clients. Moreover, alongside these opportunities are others such as the attraction of new clients, thus increasing both market share and public profile of the organisation.

Whilst the mixed economy initiative has strong allure, VSOs must also weigh its risks:

- The mixed economy business model suggests that costs attaching to the provision of electronic public services will largely be borne by the new provider. Only in exceptional circumstances will government offer financial support and only then by offering a proportion of savings to the public purse that derive from the shift in service ownership. The challenge for the voluntary organisation is to re-model their own value-positions and business development opportunities as they take on these services so as to reduce these immediate business risks whilst remaining true to their charitable objectives.
- The mixed economy model will require opening up and sharing information between government agencies and VSOs. VSOs, such as the Citizens Advice Bureaux, have built up high levels of trust amongst their members and wider client base and such data sharing runs the risk of jeopardising

this trust, as both the uniqueness and discreteness of VSOs is perceived to be compromised. The challenge to VSOs is to enhance their service quality and range under this initiative in ways that do not lead to diminished public trust.

- The mixed economy model will provide some VSOs with 'insider status' within the polity, a status that will require compliance to government-established performance criteria, operating standards, and technical specifications. Even VSOs that have traditionally been insiders, working closely with government and preferring a more collaborative and consensual style of engagement, are likely to find risks inherent in this new regime as their resources are diverted away from policy-influencing activities and towards compliance-based administrative activities.
- A related risk for VSOs, deriving from the emergence of an elite of 'insider VSOs', is that the sector will become increasingly rationalised as government engages more selectively. There is a view at the centre of government that lead organisations need to be cultivated within this sector. Such sectoral engineering could be of particular detriment to the myriad of small, local, community-based VSOs as they seek access to public funding and also to retain a political voice within the polity. The sector-wide challenge is to find ways of sustaining and enhancing the range, diversity and relative independence of VSOs in this new context and ensuring that some interests of VSOs are not systematically favoured over others.
- VSOs that engage more closely with government risk finding it increasingly difficult to distance themselves from public policy decisions that prove disadvantageous to the constituents they serve. Where VSOs are engaged in the co-production of public policies they must ultimately bear some responsibility for policy outcomes of those policies. The challenge for VSOs here is the retention of client and public trust and the nurturing of the willingness of citizens to engage within the public space provided by them.

7.2. *Risks to the system of government*

As we have argued, the attraction for government in engaging with VSOs lies in the prospect that services can be delivered more efficiently and effectively and that, where performance breakdowns occur, these will become associated with VSOs and not with government. We have seen too that government has been developing the capability of VSOs so as to reduce managerial risks attaching to this transition. The 'management of trust' through the avoidance of blame carries further, deeper risks for government however:

- Can government departments and agencies be persuaded into this new system for service delivery? Already, one leading commentary is suggesting that perhaps the biggest risk facing this mixed economy initiative is that departments and agencies will fail to embrace the intermediaries initiative [17]. For government departments and the public sector more widely, co-produced e-government is a process that challenges existing patterns of policy control as information that was previously held within deeply institutionalised 'information domains' and protected by the associated professions, is opened up and shared within the polity.
- Can VSOs take on the requirements to adopt the new governance arrangements that will make these organisations more internally democratic and thereby more legitimate as providers of public services? Moreover, to what extent do VSOs derive democratic legitimacy from the 'mandate' of their constituents. Whilst there are VSOs whose internal governance arrangements are supportive of high levels of internal democracy these are exceptional. Clearly, the types of compliance measures that are beginning to require VSOs both to demonstrate who their constituents are as well as how their

constituents are actively engaged in the democratic process, are a response to this issue. However, the extent to which VSOs will be able to implement these measures in practice will be highly variable.

- VSOs derive their legitimacy as democratic actors in large part as a result of their autonomy and independence from government. Whilst government is clear that intermediaries will act on behalf of the citizens to whom they are providing public services under the mixed economy initiative, this focus may prove difficult to achieve in practice and could compromise public trust as a result.
- A further issue to arise in relation to legitimacy concerns the representativeness of the intermediaries. VSOs will be engaged as intermediaries within the mixed economy initiative on the basis of their organisational and business fitness for the task, and not on the basis of democratic criteria. This is likely to mean that some causes and groups will be better represented within the democratic polity than others.
- The arm's length relationship that government will have with intermediaries makes it uncertain if not improbable that citizens will have equality of access to services of equal quality. By relinquishing ownership and control of services, provided hitherto on universalist principles, government is fundamentally shifting the criteria against which public accountability can be secured. If electronic services are fragmented within the mixed economy then it follows that standards and quality of service will be varied. What is not clear within this co-production initiative is to what extent and in what ways mechanisms for public rather than market accountability for these services will continue to exist.

7.3. Risks to the political system

As we have suggested above in this assessment of the risks involved in pluralising e-government, delivering public services through a (quasi) market in the ways that government proposes, places the principle of universal service at considerable risk. It is not clear how government will ensure equality of access to public services or equality in the standards of provision when these services are delivered through intermediaries over which it has limited direct control.

- Pluralism and diversity are great strengths within liberal democracy. The mixed economy initiative appears severely to jeopardise these strengths as compliance and selectivity lead to an unprecedented degree of rationalisation within the voluntary sector. Such rationalisation might severely limit the oppositional voices that inhabit the sector and the democratic opportunities that it makes available to citizens. As government engages VSOs more closely within the shadows of the state, will it result in the further 'decline of the public', as Marquand [19] has called it? As the political voice that is perhaps the clearest indication to citizens of the autonomy and independence from government of these organisations becomes increasingly sanitised, and as citizens thereby perceive VSOs to be less willing to challenge government, so public trust in these organisations to represent the public interest may diminish.

8. Concluding comments

Popular disengagement with the formal democratic process, together with diminishing public trust in Government are issues of profound importance for society. Government in the UK is responding to these challenges in part by seeking to manage trust; to establish conditions for public services that will permit the laying off to VSOs of responsibilities for their successful delivery. By so-doing Government may simultaneously escape blame in the event of service failures and improve the degree of popular trust that it enjoys. Equally, it will expect to gain kudos from well-delivered policy successes.

As we have set out in this essay, however, significant new risks are attendant on these changes. These new risks emerge for both the voluntary sector itself and for government, but can they be managed without damaging beyond repair the political system that currently exists? Indeed, by seeking to tackle these emergent risks, does each party, government and voluntary sector, exacerbate to breaking point the risks to the political system that we have highlighted here?

If the voluntary sector is to manage its finances better [and to be supported by government in so-doing]; if it is to do business with government through the exchange of data on the personal circumstances of clients; if it is become 'quieter' by accepting that its political voice must be more in line with that of government; and if it is to be rationalised in ways that create a *de facto* organisational hierarchy, then does it from all of this inevitably and inescapably risk putting the virtues of the pluralist political system as a whole in jeopardy, as we suggest above?

The same question can be asked of government too. If it can bring its constituent Departments, Ministries and Agencies into the electronic mixed economy; if it can 'force' the necessary reforms of governance in the voluntary sector; if it can persuade voluntary organisations that their traditional independence can be sufficiently conserved within the electronic mixed economy because they will be providing e-government services in response to client needs, nonetheless, functionally crucial balancing forces within the pluralist polity will be severely eroded, if not lost.

The blame game is superior to the risk game. Re-aligning the risks of being blamed so as to enhance trust brings new risks that at immediate levels can be managed, as we see above. At a deeper level, however, to manage such risks suggests long term change in the political and governmental system and, with that change, come commensurately profound new forms of risk not amenable to management. Thus we conclude by asking whether the incorporation into the State of the voluntary sector will breathe new life and confidence into ailing governmental institutions within the polity or whether in the longer term it will serve to damage profoundly those same institutions?

References

[1] B.T. Government, *eGovernment. Ready or Not?*, Issue 1, July, 2000.
[2] E. Burt and J.A. Taylor, *Information and Communication Technologies: Re-shaping the Voluntary Sector in the Information Age*, The Centre for the Study of Telematics and Governance, Glasgow Caledonian University, 1998.
[3] E. Burt and J.A. Taylor, *VSOs in the Electronic Polity: Technical Capacity, Organisational Capabilties, and Competitive Edge*, Department of Management, University of St Andrews and The Centre for the Study of Telematics and Governance, Glasgow Caledonian University, 2002.
[4] E. Burt and J.A. Taylor, Drawing VSOs into the Information Polity: Information Resources and Macro Politics, *In Public Policy and Administration* **19**(1) (2004), (66–81).
[5] Cabinet Office, *Private Action, Public Benefit*, Strategy Unit, London, 2003.
[6] B. Cammaerts and L. Van Audenhove, *ICT-usage among transnational social movements in the networked society: to organise, to mediate, and to influence*, University of Amsterdam, Amsterdam, 2003.
[7] J.D. Clark, *Worlds Apart: Civil Society and the Battle for Ethical Globalisation*, Kumarian Press, Bloomfield, 2003.
[8] Department of Trade and Industry, *Social Enterprise: A Strategy for Success*, London, 2002.
[9] A. Etzioni, *The New Golden Rule. Community and Morality in a Democratic Society*, Profile Books, London, 1997.
[10] R.E. Goodin, *Reflective Democracy*, Oxford University Press, Oxford, 2002.
[11] A. Hall, *E-enabling the voluntary and community sectors*, Final report, London, 2003.
[12] R. Hartwig, Rationality and the problems of administrative theory, *Public Administration* **56** (Summer, 1978), 159–180.
[13] H.M. Treasury, The Home Office, DTI *Exploring the Role of the Third Sector in Public Service Delivery and Reform: A discussion document*, London, 2005.

[14] Home Office, *Compact on Relations Between Government and the Voluntary and Community Sector in England*, CM 4100, London, 1998.
[15] Home Office, *Strengthening Partnerships: Next Steps for Compact*, London, 2005.
[16] C. Hood, Managing Risk and Managing Blame: Political Science Perspective, in: *Risk, Democratic Citizenship and Public Policy*, A. Weale, ed., The British Academy Occasional Paper: Oxford University Press. Oxford, 2002.
[17] I. Kearns, *Intermediaries and the Electronic Delivery of Public Services. A Mixed Economy in e-Government: A Public Response to the Government Consultation*, IPPR, London, 2004.
[18] R.A. Kasperson, Introduction: the Trouble with Risk, in: *Risk and Responsibility*, W. Leiss and C. Chociolko, eds, McGill-Queen's University Press, Montreal, 1994.
[19] D. Marquand, *Decline of the Public*, Cambridge, Polity Press, 2004.
[20] J. Morison, The government-voluntary sector compacts: Governance, governmentality, and civil society, *Journal of Law and Society* **27**(1) (2000), 98–132.
[21] T. Munton and A. Zurawan, *Active communities: Headline Findings from the 2003 Home Office citizenship survey*, London.
[22] NCVO, *Blurred Vision – Public Trust in Charities*, Research Quarterly, January, 1998.
[23] NCVO, Coming Apart – or Coming Together?, *Research Quarterly* **11** (2000).
[24] Office of the e-Envoy, *Policy framework for a mixed economy in the supply of e-government services: a consultation document*, London, 2003.
[25] Office of the e-Envoy, *Policy framework for a mixed economy in the supply of e-government services*, Official response to public consultation, London, 2003.
[26] Office of the e-Envoy, Policy framework for a mixed economy in the supply of e-government services, *Implementation Guidelines* **1** (2003), London.
[27] A. Passey and F. Tonkiss, Trust, Voluntary Association and Civil Society, in: *Trust and Civil Society*, F. Tonkiss, A. Passey, N. Fenton and L. Hems, eds, Macmillan, Basingstoke, 2000.
[28] D. Prime, M. Zimmeck and A. Zurawan, *Active Communities: the Home Office Citizenship Survey*, Initial report, London, 2001.
[29] R. Putnam, *Bowling Alone*, Simon and Schuster, London, 2000.
[30] Social Trends, London: Office of National Statistics, 2003.
[31] J.A. Taylor and E. Burt, VSOs as e-Democratic Actors: Political Identity, Legitimacy and Accountability and the Need for New Research, in *Policy and Politics*, Forthcoming, 2005.
[32] P. Ticher, A. Maison and M. Jones, *Leading the Way to ICT Success*, The Worshipful Company of Information Technologists, London, 2002.
[33] P. Whiteley, The state of participation in Britain, *Parliamentary Affairs* **56** (2003), 610–615.
[34] J.R. Wolch, *The Shadow State: Government and Voluntary Sector in Transition*, The Foundation Center, New York, 1990.

Information Polity 10 (2005) 37–48
IOS Press

Interconnected networks and the governance of risk and trust

Victor Bekkers[a] and Marcel Thaens[b]
[a]*Erasmus University Rotterdam, Department of Public Administration, P.O. Box 1738, 3000 DR Rotterdam, The Netherlands*
E-mail: bekkers@fsw.eur.nl
[b]*Ordina Public Management Consultancy/Tilburg University, P.O. Box 7101, 3430 JC Nieuwegein, The Netherlands*
E-mail: Marcel.Thaens@Ordina.nl

Abstract. Interconnected networks constitute the backbone of our society and bring many advantages to our daily life and activities. At the same time, however, our dependence on these networks and the fact that they are all interconnected makes our society vulnerable. Risks emerge from these interdependencies. How can society deal with these risks? To answer this question we first explore the closely related concepts of risk and trust. These explorations enable us to understand the implications of interconnected networks in terms of governance challenges. On the basis of this insight, we conclude that it is impossible to define risk as a 'general' policy concept. A major policy challenge in the governance of risk is not only the interplay of all kinds of networks and infrastructures, but also the interplay between diverse policy regimes with different governance models. We have discerned a number of specific governance models that can be used to handle the risks resulting from interconnected networks and infrastructures. Following Ashby's law of requisite variety, the variety of risks in the network society asks for a variety of risk governance models, in which different values are attached to the role of government, the private sector and the civil society.

Keywords: Risk, trust, interconnection, networks, governance

1. Introduction

In our society, often characterized as a network society, everything is connected to everything else. This is especially true for networks and infrastructures. When we look, for example, at ICT-networks and infrastructures, we see that they are interconnected with at least two other types of networks and infrastructures. First, there are social and organizational networks of groups of people and organizations, located in a specific area (for instance, in the business area of Manhattan). These groups of people and organizations use ICT-networks to exchange and share information as well as to communicate with one another. Second, ICT-networks are interconnected with physical and logistical networks and infrastructures that are used to transport commodities like gas, electricity, water, goods, but also people. Often ICT-networks are embedded in these logistical networks, for instance, to control the delivery of energy or to monitor the movements of these commodities during their transportation.

These interconnected networks constitute the backbone of our society and bring many advantages to our daily life and activities. At the same time, however, our dependence on these networks and the fact that they are all interconnected makes our society vulnerable. According to the domino principle, a disturbance in one of these networks could spread relatively easily to the other networks. A multiplying effect and increased vulnerability to disturbances could bring our daily activities to a standstill.

1570-1255/05/$17.00

In the summer of 2003 the lights went out in New York City. Due to a power outage trains stopped, elevators got stuck, computer networks shut down, traffic lights did not work, water supplies were affected because water is distributed through electric pumps and airports experienced delays and some were shut down. The normal flow of work and life was disrupted. In New York City 40,0000 police officers and the entire fire department were mobilized. Not only New York City was struck, but also dozens of other cities in the United States and Canada – like Cleveland (Ohio), Detroit (Michigan) and Toronto and Ottawa in Canada – became victim. This 'cascading blackout' left 1.4 million customers without power at its peak. In just three minutes, starting at 4:10 P.M, 21 power plants went off line. The original failure took place in Ohio, but the grid of computer and computer network as well as energy transmission lines initiated a system-wide snowball effect.

We will investigate the interconnection and interdependence of different kinds of networks and the risks that emerge from these interdependencies. The main question we want to answer is how society can deal with these risks. We will start by exploring the network society concept because this can be regarded as the basis of interconnected networks. This concept will show that in a network society, interconnection of networks lead to patterns of reciprocity. Reciprocity means that the parties involved in a network accept that, at least for a part, they become dependent on each other. This dependency implies a risk for those parties, which is only acceptable to them if there is a certain amount of trust between them. So, the concepts of risk and trust can be perceived as two sides of the same coin when it comes to the question of dealing with this reciprocity.

In section three we therefore try to grasp the process of risk definition and in section four we will address the issue of trust. These explorations will enable us to understand the implications of interconnected networks in terms of governance challenges. On the basis of this insight, we will then reflect on four different governance models which can be used to deal with the vulnerabilities of the network society.

2. Background: The network society

Before turning to crucial concepts such as risk and trust, we will first take a look at a number of theoretical notions to achieve a better understanding of the network society. The concept of the network society is the basis of interconnected networks. We will see how the interconnection of several networks shapes the network society and, we will show the kinds of vulnerabilities that emerge.

2.1. A new technological paradigm

Castells is a leading author on the subject of the network society. He sees this type of society as the result of a fundamental change in the dominant production technology of capitalist economies and modern (western) societies: "a technology based primarily on cheap inputs of energy to one predominantly based on cheap inputs of information derived from the advances of microelectronic and telecommunication technology" [7, p. 61]. He describes five reasons why this change has happened. First, all of these new technologies act on information, not just information acting on technology, as was the case in the industrial revolution. Second, because information is an integral part of all human activities, all the processes involving our individual and collective existence are directly influenced by ICT. ICT has penetrated every domain of human activity, not as an exogenous source of impact, but as a fabric in which such activity is woven [7, p. 31]. Third, the morphology of the network seems to be well adapted to the increasing complexity of interaction and to the unpredictable patterns that emerge from this interaction. Network technology and the digitalisation of commodities and processes [17], make it possible, for instance, to create flexible connections between people and organizations that cross traditional geographical, temporal and functional boundaries. Flexibility is therefore the fourth reason for this shift to a network society, while the convergence of specific technologies into a highly integrated system is the fifth and last reason. Microelectronics, telecommunications, bioelectronics, opto-electronics, and computers are now all integrated into comprehensive systems and part of ambient intelligence i.e. the interaction between human beings and digital information technology.

The resulting 'technological paradigm' leads to social and economic conditions in which the nature of the production is focused on the production of information processing itself, the production of information processing devices and on the management of information processing [7, p. 67]. Moreover, the economy of the information society is a global economy; it is an economy with the capacity to work as a unit in real-time on a planetary scale, which uses ICT-networks to create new production and competition conditions that are based on the creation of information spaces [7, p. 92]. To describe the creation of informational spaces on a planetary scale, Castells [7, p. 412] uses two notions: 'space of flows' and 'timeless time'.

2.2. *Space of flows*

Space of flows refers to, "the material organization of time-sharing practices that work through flows" (of capital, words, images, sounds, interactions etcetera). This space of flows is a combination of at least three layers of material that support its constitution:

- The circuit of electronic impulses, the network of interconnected technological systems themselves like, for instance, microelectronics, telecommunications, computer processing and broadcasting systems [7, p. 412].
- Its nodes and hubs. An electronic network is always linked to specific places, with well-defined social, cultural, physical and functional characteristics [7, p. 413]. Some places are exchangers and function as a communication and coordination hub to facilitate the smooth interaction of all the elements integrated into the network. Other places are nodes of the network, that are the location of strategically important functions that build a series of locality-based activities and organizations around a key function in the network. The location in the node links up the locality with the whole network. Wall Street can be seen as a node in the highly computerized global financial market system.
- The spatial organization of the dominant, technical, financial and managerial elites [7, p. 415] who, through hubs and nodes, have access to the space of flows.

2.3. *Timeless time*

The second notion Castells uses to describe this new informational space is that of 'timeless time'. He describes this notion as, "the systematic perturbation in the sequential order of phenomena performed (...). Perturbation may take the form of compressing the occurrence of phenomena, aiming at instantaneity, or else by introducing random discontinuity in the sequence eternity" [7, p. 464].

3. Reciprocity and local and global risks

Based on the previously mentioned concepts, ICT, social, and organizational networks are, for example, becoming increasingly interconnected. This leads to patterns of reciprocity that make people, groups, organizations, or even states more and more mutually dependent on each other. This reciprocity also creates vulnerabilities (after all, a chain is as strong as its weakest link), that become manifest in the location of certain 'hubs' and 'nodes' in the space of flows. It is within these 'hubs' and 'nodes' that the interconnection of networks is organized. A power plant is an example of such a node. If disturbances appear in the global space of flows of timesharing activities and interactions, this reciprocity can, at the same time, also lead to local and global risks. The late eighties crash in Wall Street called Black Monday is an example. This had enormous local and global effects because of the connections between electronic bidding systems through network technology. That is why it is important to look at the nature of risk in the network society.

4. The concept of risk and the risk society

4.1. Risks and 'reflexive modernization'

According to Beck, our society is a risk society. This is the result of a process that he calls, 'reflexive modernization'. This means that the transition from the industrial to the risk epoch of modernity occurs unintentionally, unseen, compulsively, in the course of a dynamic of modernization which has made itself autonomous, on the pattern of unintended consequences [4, p. 73]. The risk society is not an option that can be chosen or rejected in the course of political debate. It arises through the automatic operation of autonomous modernization processes that are blind and deaf to the consequences and dangers. In total, and latently, these produce hazards which call into question the basis of industrial society. In contrast to earlier industrial risks, new risks occur, for example biological risks such as the rise of BSE disease; chemical risks, such as the explosion of a dioxin plant in Seweso, Italy; nuclear risks, such as the explosion of a nuclear plant in Chernobyl; environmental risks such as, diminishing of the Ozone layer; and, genetic engineering risks, such as DNA manipulation and food production. These kinds of risks share some characteristics:

a) they cannot be limited in terms either of time or place;
b) they are not accountable according to established rules of causality, blame and liability, because of their complexity, dynamics and the overwhelming number of actors involved;
c) they cannot be compensated or insured against [4, pp. 54, 77].

4.2. The dominance of a social engineering approach of risks

Before the industrial revolution, in the eighteenth century, confrontation with risks was a confrontation with the will of God [4]. Our assessment of risks and dangers changed in the nineteenth and twentieth centuries. Since then, risky behaviour is considered to be dangerous and it can be traced by looking at the decisions that have been made. These decisions may have intended and unintended consequences that produce specific risks and dangers. As a result of this changing perspective on risk assessment, the 'calculus of risk' was introduced. The idea is that risks can be calculated and can be (statistically) described as events. This makes them, to a certain degree, understandable and manageable. Moreover, the calculation of risks makes it possible to buy-off a risk by taking out an insurance policy and/or by taking countermeasures, like technical adjustments. A 'calculus of risk' means that the governance of risk is seen as a process of social engineering that permits a type of 'technological moralization' [2, pp. 51–52]. Technological moralization refers to a process in which paying an insurance premium can lay off risky behaviour or it can be neutralized by reducing the risk to a minimum percentage of occurrences. The result is a monopolization of the way modern societies define and deal with risks, of the way knowledge about the causes and effects of potential risks is presented, and the way in which actions are or will be taken [4, p. 59]. The assessment of risk and risky behaviour is no longer the subject of moral, ethical and individual considerations; it de-individualizes and is not the subject of political debate. This can be seen a one-dimensional, techno-economic definition of risks and risk avoidance [3]. Risk management is predominantly seen as 'social engineering'. An example of a social engineering approach of risk avoidance is defining risk management as the management of the safety chain. Effective management can then be seen as establishing a smooth coordination of separate activities which together constitute the chain.

4.3. The need for increased reflexive capacity

As a result of the previously described characteristics of the 'new' type of risks, these risks become an event with a beginning and no end; an open ended festival of creeping, galloping and overlapping waves of destruction [5, p. 54]. Beck sees only one way out. We need to create a process of self-confrontation with the consequences of the risk society by increasing the reflexive capacity of the modernization process itself [5, p. 73]. In order to create the necessary conditions to establish this reflexive capacity, we need to rupture the monopoly of the way risks are being defined and perceived. In a self-identified risk society, it is important to break up the one-dimensionality of risk management policies. The critique should be democratised in such a way that alternative risk definitions can compete with the existing ones [5, p. 79]. Social self-criticism is needed which can overcome an industrialized society with a 'truncated' democracy, in which questions of the technological change of society remain beyond the reach of political-parliamentary decision-making [5, pp. 70–71]. This can be established by a further separation of powers between the political and economic-technological powers, and by the creation of a free public sphere, in which an open and public debate can be organized.

4.4. The cultural biases of risk assessment

Beck's notion of a 'truncated' democracy implies that there is a bias in the dominant assessment of the vulnerabilities of our network society. To learn more about this bias, we turn to the work of Douglas and Wildavsky on risk and culture. According to them, risk and uncertainty are two of the same thing. Knowledge about risks is surrounded by uncertainty and they point out that the assessment of risks is a highly subjective matter. It is a process that not only takes place on the individual and micro-level, but also on a meso, group and macro societal level. The assessment of an event considered as risky is a joint product of knowledge about the future, and consent about the most desired prospects. In Douglas and Wildavsky's [10, p. 4] perspective the ultimate challenge in the process of risk assessment is to create a common perception, which is an understanding of a definition of risk, and thus an agreement upon it. In most cases, knowledge is uncertain and/or the criteria and norms people use to assess these risks also differ. The process of the selection and definition of events considered to be risky is about acceptability, which is always a political issue. There is no single, correct concept of risk; there is no way to get everyone else to accept 'it'. Therefore, risk assessment should be seen from a cultural perspective, looking at cultural bias. This bias is embedded in each social arrangement, for instance in a group, in an organization or in a society. The choice of risks and the choice on how to live are taken together. Each social arrangement has its own risk portfolio, in which common values lead to common fears and vice versa. As Douglas and Wildavsky [10, p. 8] put it "risk taking and risk aversion, shared confidence and shared fears, are part of the dialogue on how to organize social relations. For to organize, means to organize some things in and other things out". This notion implies that a cultural analysis of risk assessment, risk taking and risk avoidance is a meaningful way of looking at risks. How do actors or social institutions define risks? Which norms and values does this definition conceal? What interests are at stake, and how do actors communicate their definition of risk in order to create a shared understanding of certain events? It is the social environment that defines which dangers are worthy of attention [10, p. 9].

4.5. The institutional bias of risks: Regulation regimes

Following the opinion that risk assessment is a cultural phenomenon, it is interesting to look at the way society handles the occurrence of risks. Hood et al. [15, p. 6] introduce the concept of a regime. They analyse the definition of risks and the measures which are taken to control the emergence of these risks from an institutional perspective. They look for the 'rules' that influence the definition of risk and risk policies. Rules are "the routines, procedures, conventions, roles, strategies, organizational forms, and technologies around which ... activity is constructed ... We also refer to the beliefs, paradigms, codes, cultures, and knowledge that surround, support, elaborate and contradict these roles and routines" [16, p. 22]. These rules reflect the institutional bias of how organizations, systems of organizations, or even policy sectors define the nature of the risks which they see as crucial for their survival and the actions and measures they take. Hood et al. [15, p. 6] focus on the question as to how governments try to regulate societal risks. The result is a policy and intellectual archipelago, a myriad of risk domains isolated from one another, with different policy stances across them. Each domain has its own risk regulation regime, in which a specific institutional bias is dominant.

As stated before, the concept of risk is only one side of the coin when it comes to dealing with reciprocity as a result of the interconnection of networks. The concept of trust is the other side. In the next paragraph we will look at this concept more closely.

5. Trust as a lubricant of the network society

5.1. Trust as an indication of social capital

In the literature on the network society, a lot of attention has been paid to the notion of reciprocity as a product of economic, cultural, social and political specialization and differentiation, which can be described in terms of individualization, the decline of the great ideologies, the breakdown of hierarchy and authority, modernization or even post-modernization [12]. The fact that people, groups, and organizations, or even states have become mutually dependent and, the fact that socio-organizational, physical and ICT-networks have become interconnected, has created patterns of reciprocity. According to Fukuyama [12], and Putnam [18], trust and the social capital which is built on trust, can been as a natural way of dealing with the risks that emerge from the interdependencies within the network society. Risk and trust can therefore be perceived as two sides of the same coin: how to deal with reciprocity. Trust tells us something about the integrity and vulnerability of the functioning and behaviour of other persons, groups, organizations, institutions, networks on which we rely, and about the quality of the interactions between these persons, groups, organizations, institutions and networks. It tells us something about their willingness to cooperate and to organize collective action on the basis of commonly shared norms, for instance, by dealing with the problem of interconnected risks. The existence of trust is an indication of the social capital within a group, a network, a community or even a society. Fukuyama [12, pp. 7, 33] claims that a nation's well-being, as well as its ability to compete is conditioned by the level of trust in a society and this depends on the 'crucible of trust': social capital. Fukuyama [12] and Putnam [18] are rather sceptical about the potential of social capital in the network society, although both see the re-discovery of trust and social capital in social and political thought as an alternative governance strategy which could be used to face the risks that emerge from the interconnection of networks and infrastructures.

5.2. Identity politics as the heart of the political system

Castells relationship with trust is ambiguous. On the one hand he sees the emergence of the network society as ad hoc, temporary, and flexible co-operative arrangements which are the outcome of reciprocity and trust. Networks produce social capital in order to meet the societal, economic and political challenges. On the other hand he observes that the nature and dynamics of the network society (e.g. globalization and fragmentation) threaten the natural identity of established institutions, like the sovereign entity of a nation-state as a source of meaning which influences the trustworthiness (and thus legitimacy) of these institutions [8, p. 6]. At the same time, the network society produces new identities, which are more fluid and flexible. Moreover, they can easily be constructed by the combination of images, words, sounds and symbols. And, in a world in which images, icons and symbols play an important role, identity politics is at the heart of the political system [9, p. 347].

The implication of the above observation on trust for government is that the natural identity and trustworthiness of government, as the natural and sovereign institution which organizes collective action in order to meet risks, is under pressure, due to the nature of these risks. At the same time, risk policymaking has become highly symbolic implying that the governance of risk is increasingly becoming more of a challenge to society. In the following section we will explore this challenge in more detail.

6. Risk as a governance challenge

6.1. Dimensions of risks resulting from interconnected networks and infrastructures

When we look more closely at this governance of risk, and especially those risks resulting from interconnected networks and infrastructures, we can see that we are dealing with a 'wicked problem'. We have a limited understanding of the variety of potential risks emerging from the interconnection of ICT-networks, socio-organizational networks and physical networks. However, some dimensions of risks resulting from interconnected networks can be discerned:

- *The broadening of risks.* The interconnection of networks and existence of interconnected risks can lead to spill-over and snowball-effects, which will penetrate other domains and activities.
- *The deepening of risks.* Events can hit a node in the networks, which can be seen as attacking the heart of the network and will lead to a severe crisis. This can be illustrated for example, by the attack on the Twin Towers in Manhattan that as a result of that incident also hit the heart of the financial system.
- *The acceleration of risks.* The real-time or timeless nature of the network society can generate harmful effects within seconds. Computer viruses prove this time and time again.

- *The glocalization of risks.* Disturbances in interconnected networks, which support worldwide economic, financial, military, and other operations and activities, do not only have global effects, but also have local effects that can vary in intensity. At the same time, local disturbances can be spread, using these networks and generate effects all over the world. The SARS virus is an example of a local disease which originated in China and has spread via global air traffic infrastructures to Hong Kong and Canada, for example.
- *The subjectivity of risks.* Risks in the network society are culturally and institutionally biased and this can lead to different perceptions of risks and different risk avoiding or risk taking activities by the nodes in the network or the different parties that are gathered around a node.
- *The fragmentation and interdependency of risk regimes.* A government's capacity to anticipate or to deal with interconnected risks is fragmented in different policy domains and regimes. Within these domains the institutional biases compete which each other. However, at the same time the nature of interconnected risk demands coordination and integration.

6.2. Resultant problems for governance

Because of the different dimensions, clear causal relations cannot be discerned. We also do not know whether the measures which have been taken to avoid possible risks, are sufficient. Moreover, we do not know how we should assess these risks politically. The normative framework to assess the measures to be taken is constantly under discussion, for instance, in relation to privacy issues. At the same time, we see that a broad variety of public, semi-public and private organizations are tackling this problem, and this brings about all kinds of multi-layered and multifunctional communication and coordination problems.

7. Addressing the challenge: Different risk-governance models

The governance of risks can be seen as a wicked problem with multiple dimensions and different kinds of problems. Based on this understanding, we have identified four different governance models that can be used as a perspective on how to address the problem of the governance of interconnected risks. There is a dominant coordination mechanism in each model, which has different implications for the relationship between government and citizen.

7.1. The cybernetic state: Command and control

The potential disturbing impacts of interconnected risks on the integrity and stability of society are important drives for strong and intensive government intervention in terms of 'command and control'. Indeed, this is the 'raison d'état'. There are two distinguishable variations of this command and control model of governance. First, risk management can be viewed as a managerial-administrative problem where the major issue is the enforcement of rules and regulations. Second, risk management can be seen as a technological challenge. ICT's can be used to monitor people's behaviour, organizations and groups, and flows of commodities in order to make them visible. This improves the response and quality of the necessary government interventions.

A cybernetic governance model [14] was the dominant model behind these two command and control approaches. At the centre of this model is the idea that government is situated at a central point above society and is capable of performing preventive and corrective interventions. The legitimacy of these interventions is based on legally defined competences to exercise administrative pressure, such as the closing of hazardous buildings, the withdrawal or suspension of permits, the enforcement of fines and the distribution of warnings. Processing feedback information is crucial for this model to function and to be able to assess whether the defined security standards have been met. The activities in the following order: inspection, monitoring, and supervision are important to gather the necessary feedback information.

In this model safety risks are control issues. Strengthening central control is seen as a way of improving the supervising ability of government. In the practice of public administration this can be carried out in four ways:

a) Integrate inspection agencies. Such an integration can strengthen problem-solving and the governance capacity of these agencies in order to deal with the interconnectedness of risks, and thus with the reciprocity of different policy domains.
b) Support supervision by improving the information supply of an inspection agency. For example, by developing monitoring systems based upon 'the will to know' [6].
c) Extend and refine legal competences to intervene, especially from the viewpoint of administrative and criminal law.
d) Develop 'safety enhancing technologies', which are based on the detection ability of new technologies. A well-known example is the use of video-surveillance in buildings and public spaces, and in streets.

New technology and, especially the new detection abilities, offer possibilities for enhancing control. These growing detection abilities are the result of new technological developments, such as computer technology which is becoming smaller and smaller, more mobile, and wireless. One of the results is often the application of a chip in devices for people, buildings, goods, appliances, and animals. Local intelligence tools are being installed to detect these devices from a distance. These detection infrastructures are the product of 'ambient technologies', based on the sophisticated integration of ICT and other networks (such as television), which foster a cybernetic governance model. They make it possible to centrally monitor the behaviour and movements of people, and vehicles for example, and to intervene if necessary. Usually, this 'command and control' model evokes doubts about people's privacy. This is because detection technology calls to mind the idea that 'Big Brother is watching you'. At the same time however, the introduction of this sort of technology often involves the introduction of new networks. This leads to an interesting paradox. To reduce the safety risks that result from the interaction and the interconnection of different kinds infrastructures, a new infrastructure is connected to the existing infrastructures. As a result, the complexity and the accompanying risks will increase.

7.2. The market: Quality assurance and certification

This model recognizes that our society is an 'open society', in which government plays a dominant role as the guardian of society's stability. This puts the government's role into a certain perspective and indicates the limits of central government intervention. Governance of risk is seen as governance at a distance. Within legal frameworks, the care for safety is seen as a delegated responsibility of citizens and companies. Since these frameworks contain standards for processes rather than standards regarding the content of the safety measures to be taken, citizens and companies have the freedom to develop their own ways of meeting their own responsibilities. Some examples are: compulsory third-party liability insurance for citizens and motorists, and internal company-wide sustainability programmes.

A radical critique on the command and control model leads to the opinion that corrective and preventive government interventions cannot succeed in order to handle risks. It is up to individual citizens and companies to raise their own awareness of risks and to take care of them. Safety risks then become liability problems that have to be solved by private law. The assumption behind this line of reasoning is that the possible financial consequences of such a liability, work preventively. When accidents or incidents occur the consequences are covered by compensations and insurances against the damage caused. The problem with this model is that 'new' risks can no longer be insured (see [4]). Their effects are so massive, disastrous and radical that they would cause the bankruptcy of the insurance branch. Since the attacks on the WTC in New York on the 11 September 2001, this is why insurance companies have changed their insurance contracts so that now damage as a result of terrorist attacks is no longer covered.

Private companies can prevent the occurrence of risks by developing a quality assurance system which is coupled to a system of certification. It raises the quality-level within the company, but more important, it can also lead to the prevention of various liability claims. A well-known example in the Netherlands concerns an international supermarket chain, Albert Heijn. The supermarket demands a certain standard of quality from their suppliers for their fresh foods (such as meat). These demands are imposed by certification. If a supplier cannot or can no longer meet the required demands, they will lose their certificate and as a consequence their returns. So, safety risks are not covered by the government, but by private enterprises.

7.3. Civil society: Civic competence

In the next model risk management is seen as a joint responsibility of the State, private companies and society. An attempt is made to involve citizens and groups of citizens in safety-issues. Therefore, these safety issues become a societal issue. This applies to the public debate about safety but also to the (mostly preventive) approach towards vulnerabilities that are the result of interaction and interconnectedness of social-organizational, physical and technological networks.

Beck [4] pointed out the importance of organizing a public debate about the nature and the effects of 'new risks'. He questioned a risk management approach in which the nature and the effects of these risks were over-rationalized in econometric models, and in measures for prevention and correction based upon these models. This suggested an illusion of controllability. As a result, certain groups of scientists monopolized the diagnosis of risks. These groups also monopolized the way in which knowledge about the risks was presented and the way in which these risks were dealt with. Beck [4] also blamed politicians and administrators for following these groups of scientists. Occasionally, this led to an 'iron coalition' between scientists, politicians and administrators who each had an interest in cherishing the previously mentioned illusion of controllability. Therefore there is a plea to break-down this monopoly by introducing some alternative perspectives and by setting-up platforms for debate and dialogue. These platforms will be aimed at influencing opinions held by the public and by politicians.

Consequently, as a result of this criticism, it is important to involve citizens in (interactive) risk management policymaking, by seeing them as co-producers of risk management policies or by seeing them as co-supervisors together with inspection agencies. The introduction of citizens as co-producers can be considered as establishing an alternative perspective in the practice of risk management policymaking. Their introduction can also be seen as introducing new 'checks and balances' in the existing risk management systems in order to enhance their transparency. However, it is essential that these engaged citizens have access to the relevant information about the existing supervision processes, relevant quality standards, and relevant results. Access to specific monitoring information enables them to judge for themselves whether the quality of measures and actions taken by government live up to their own standards and interests. Internet and web technology cannot only provide the necessary access to monitoring information, but it can also function as a platform for communication and deliberation to facilitate citizen's self-organization as an interest group, and to make their opinions known. For example, in May 2000 a large firework warehouse explosion in the Dutch town of Enschede caused many deaths and devastated a complete residential area. As a result, many provinces have now developed risk registers that citizens can consult through Internet. Access is given to information about safety risks (related to vulnerable objects like plants), which are present in the neighbourhood in which a citizen lives and works. Citizens can also see what the safety requirements are for these objects and installations, and what measures have been taken by the local government to meet these requirements. Access to information is seen as an incentive to increase the public's pressure on local government, inspection agencies well as to private companies regarding risk management measures. Ironically, it is that same access to information that could lead to termination of the risk registers. In the light of the concept of 'risk', it was recently argued that these kinds of registers make it too easy for possible terrorists to plan their evil attacks.

7.4. The network: Self-organization and trust

Another governance model is the network model of the Internet itself. A characteristic of Internet's organization is its self-organizing capacity in order to manage complexity and turbulence. If one of the nodes or hubs in the network stops functioning, then other nodes and hubs will take over its functions. Evaluation of the power outage in New York in 2003 shows that Internet survived although slowed down by it. Other servers took over those servers that were hit by the outage [13]. Risk management strategies related to the breakdown of ICT and physical networks could be based on this principle. However, in this risk management model the notion of redundancy is critical. The only way to manage major catastrophes is through the introduction and maintenance of enough redundancy in critical networks. This is not always the most efficient way of organizing things. At the same time governments are constantly trying to reduce their operating costs and their risk management activities.

Self-organization as a governance model is also important in relation to the functioning of socio-organizational networks. However, as we have learned from the observations in a previous section, the self-organizing capacities of a socio-organizational network of people, groups and organizations also depend on trust. Hence, the development of trust and social capital in networks can be an important governance model in order to improve the self-organizing capacity of communities when they are confronted with possible risks and threats. For instance, in the Dutch city of Rotterdam, local government is trying to improve the self-organizing capacity of neighbourhoods. The quality of the social capital in a neighbourhood is being mobilized to improve social defence mechanisms in relation to the crime and degeneration of the neighbourhood.

In some cases the Internet is being used as an instrument to support and stimulate the emergence of social capital in the neighbourhoods of the city of Rotterdam. It offers people new ways of communication, participation and deliberation and stimulates trust in each other. Although Putnam [19] accepts that the Internet removes communication barriers and thus facilitates new social networks, he remains sceptical about its influence on the emergence of social capital. Fukuyama [12] even believes that the Internet erodes established relationships and thus social capital, while Castells [7] has the opposite view. For Castells, ICT is a central result in the creation of a new social space in which new local identities can emerge on the basis of new contacts, and also new values and relationships which challenge the rigid identities of industrial modernism, based on class and nation [11, p. 102]. In discussing the impact of the Internet on the development of social capital as a governance model, Field [11, pp. 102–106] argues that Internet use in general is associated with higher levels of participation in voluntary and political associations and that there is generally positive association between online and offline participation. He concludes that Internet promotes the reflexivity of individuals, groups and communities, which is an important incentive for self-organization.

8. Conclusion

We have explored the nature of the risks that emerge from the interconnection of ICT, and the socio-organizational and physical networks. We have also looked at some of the different governance models used in order to manage these risks. It is impossible to define risk as a 'general' policy concept. This is because of the complex nature of the interconnection of networks, and the cultural and institutional bias to define what risk is. The variety of possible risks and their unpredictable outcomes show that the notion of 'the risk society' (as an aspect of the network society) is too broad and too abstract [15]. Moreover, a major policy challenge in the governance of risk is not only the interplay of all kinds of networks and infrastructures, but also the interplay between diverse policy regimes with different governance models. We have discerned a number of specific governance models that can be used to handle these risks resulting from interconnected networks and infrastructures. We do not have a preference for any one model. Following Ashby's law of requisite variety [1], the variety of risks in the network society asks for a variety of risk governance models, in which different values are attached to the role of government, the private sector and the civil society.

References

[1] W. Ashby, *Introduction into Cybernetics,* Wiley, New York, London, 1965.

[2] U. Beck, The Reinvention of Politics, Towards a Theory of Reflexive Modernization, in: *Reflexive Modernization,* U. Beck, A. Giddens and S. Lash, Polity Press, Cambridge, 1994, pp. 1–55.

[3] U. Beck, The Politics of Risk Society, in: *The Politics of the Risk Society,* J. Franklin, ed., Polity Press, London, 1998, pp. 31–58.

[4] U. Beck, *Risk Society,* Polity Press, London, 1999.

[5] U. Beck, *World Risk Society,* Polity Press, Malden, 1999.

[6] V. Bekkers, New Forms of Steering and the Ambivalency of Transparency, in: *Public Administration in the Information Age,* I. Snellen and W. van de Donk, eds, IOS Press, Amsterdam, 1999, pp. 341–358.

[7] M. Castells, *The Rise of the Network Society, The Information Age: Economy, Society and Culture,* Blackwell, Cambridge, 1996.

[8] M. Castells, *The Power of Identity, The Information Age: Economy, Society and Culture,* Blackwell, Cambridge, 1997.

[9] M. Castells, *The End of the Millennium, The Information Age: Economy, Society and Culture,* Blackwell, Cambridge, 1998.

[10] M. Douglas and A. Wildavsky, *Risk and Culture, An Essay on the Selection of Technological and Environmental Dangers,* University of California Press, Berkeley, Los Angeles, London, 1983.

[11] J. Field, *Social Capital,* Routlege, London, 2003.

[12] F. Fukuyama, *Trust,* Hamish Hamilton, London, 1995.

[13] General Accounting Office, *Electricity Restructuring,* United States GAO, Washington, 2003.

[14] H. van Gunsteren, *The Quest for Control,* Wiley, London, 1976.

[15] C. Hood, H. Rothstein and R. Baldwin, *The Government of Risk. Understanding Risk Regulation Regimes,* Oxford Press, Oxford, 2001.

[16] J.G. March and J.P. Olsen, *Rediscovering Institutions,* Free Press, New York, 1989.

[17] N. Negroponte, *Being Digital,* Knopf, New York, 1995.

[18] R. Putnam, *Making Democracy Work,* Princeton University Press, Princeton, 1993.

[19] R. Putnam, *Bowling Alone,* Simon & Schuster, New York, 2000.

Information Management and Privacy

Information Polity 10 (2005) 51–63
IOS Press

Multi-agency working in British social policy: Risk, information sharing and privacy

Christine Bellamy, Charles Raab and Perri 6
E-mail: Chris.Bellamy@ntu.ac.uk

Abstract. Tensions between goals of integrated, seamless public services and of client confidentiality are increasingly important, as trends in public services require more extensive sharing of information about users of those services. This article identifies reasons why these tensions have become more salient under the Labour Government in the UK and the types of policy initiative that now give rise to them, before considering the development of the policy frameworks intended to strike settlements between these goals. In conclusion, the sustainability of these settlements is considered in the context of the trade-off between the risks of different types of judgment errors likely to be made by professionals providing public services in decisions on whether, when and how much to share client information.

1. Introduction

Surveillance techniques based on extensive gathering, processing and sharing personal data are now an essential element in the armoury of social policy. Yet governments must also defend and promote human rights, including the right to privacy. It can be argued that, in principle, these imperatives are not in conflict, especially if the accuracy, relevance, timeliness, security, proportionality and fitness for purpose of personal data – all important data protection principles – are considered to be equally important for effective government interventions into social problems. However, in practice, tensions and conflicts are often palpable, especially in the context of multi-agency working. In this article, we consider the nature of these tensions in relation to the commitment of the British Government to 'joined-up' working. We argue that much of this pressure currently stems from the government's anxiety to protect citizens from risk, especially from risks posed by terrorism, crime, child abuse, social care, debt and fraud. These are all fields in which public service workers are obliged to handle personal information of great sensitivity, often relating to vulnerable people, and to make decisions that, as we have seen in a number of recent high-profile cases, can result in life or death. Decisions – such as when to open a record about a particular individual (with risk of stigmatisation), when to share personal data (with risk of unwarranted incursions in privacy or breaches of professional confidentiality norms) and when to intervene aggressively in a case (with risk of unwarranted removal of freedoms or disruption to family relationships) – often need to be taken in the absence of decision rules that would be obvious and acceptable to all interested parties. Professional workers face continual dilemmas between the risk of 'false negative' error judgements (when no action is taken, but where it turns out later that it should have been taken) and the risk of 'false positive' judgements (where action is taken, although it turns out later that the risk was lower than would justify it). This article is concerned, then, to discuss how the British Government has sought to manage tensions between these different kinds of risk in the context of its parallel commitments, on the one hand, to joined-up government and, on the other, to protecting privacy and human rights.

1570-1255/05/$17.00

2. Joined-up government and privacy: A social policy issue

We locate much of the concern about privacy in information-age government in the domain of social policy, not – as is more conventional – in the policy field of e-government. This is because a host of recent social policy initiatives, sometimes involving new legislation, have brought the tension between data sharing and privacy to the fore, frequently but not always in the context of new innovations in information technology (IT) and information systems (IS). Most of these initiatives are being introduced specifically to support the shift to multi-agency working. Table 1 demonstrates this point systematically, by setting out a more or less comprehensive list of data sharing initiatives promoted by the present Labour Government in support of multi-agency approaches to the development and implementation of social policy. It has been compiled by means of a search of the relevant grey literature and government websites, supported by over 40 interviews with senior policy makers, as part of our ongoing research project on data sharing and privacy in British Government.[1] It refers mainly to England and Wales, although a similar (and overlapping) list could be compiled for the devolved Scottish government. Many initiatives (marked with *) are, at the time of writing, in the planning or developmental stages. Only national initiatives aimed at promoting multi-agency working have been included, but these encompass a wide range of government agencies and policy fields, including social care, health, policing, education and criminal justice.

By focusing exclusively on initiatives designed to support data sharing in multi-agency contexts, Table 1 certainly underestimates the sheer range and volume of new sets and flows of personal or micro-level data currently being created by British public services. If, however, as is often said, the significance of new information technologies lies primarily in their capacity for deriving new and better kinds of information from existing repositories, as much as in their capacity for processing higher volumes of information, then Table 1 captures the scale and range of the British Government's current aspirations on that score. It thereby offers some hard empirical evidence about the government's present ambitions for using the distinctive capabilities associated with the information age for enhancing the surveillance of the population. How far this surveillance invades privacy, and whether such invasions are justifiable in relation to the presumed benefits of the policies, are important questions requiring sector-by-sector analysis beyond the scope of the present chapter.

Why has the integration of social policy and public services under this Government led to such an unprecedented emphasis on collecting and integrating personal data, when previous attempts to place more emphasis on co-ordination have not? Elsewhere, we have offered a provisional explanation of this phenomenon by identifying five key drivers for data sharing in contemporary social policy [2,3].

3. Explaining the current policy emphasis on integrating personal and micro-level data

3.1. Citizen obligations

We share the view that much of the current Government's social policy reflects the strength of the communitarian streak in its thinking [11,14,15,32,44]. Anti-social behaviour, refusal to accept employment, abuse of welfare programmes and the shirking of parental obligations are considered to

[1] 'Joined-up Public Services: data sharing and privacy in multi-agency working', funded by the Economic and Social Research Council, award number RES-000-23-0158.

underlie many social ills, and public services are increasingly asked to identify those at fault or at risk of being so. Rights and duties are therefore perceived to be reciprocal elements in citizens' relationships with the state, and the subjecting of individuals' data to risk assessment techniques of various kinds is regarded as a fair return for benefiting from public services [19,20]. Likewise, the justifications given for introducing identity cards imply that residents in the UK have duties to identify themselves when reasonably required to do so by public officials [1].

3.2. *Resource rationing*

The Government's interventionist instincts have, however, created tensions with its public expenditure policies, especially in the first term (1997–2001) when it observed spending restrictions inherited from the former government. It has therefore sought politically acceptable ways to target resources on those deemed to be most in need, most at risk of harm or most at risk of harming others. The development of data-driven risk assessment techniques – for example: the use of the Offender Assessment System (OASys) by Multi-Agency Public Protection Arrangements (MAPPAs) to identify the most risky sex offenders; the use of the Young Offenders Assessment Profile system (ASSET) by Youth Offending Teams (YOTs) to identify young offenders most at risk of recidivism and harmful behaviour; the use of increasingly refined data matching techniques by the Department of Work and Pensions (DWP) and the Audit Commission to detect the most probable cases of benefit fraud – all offer apparently objective techniques for allocating scarce resources in the most efficient way, particularly when these techniques are validated by evidence from 'what works' studies, as they increasingly are (e.g. [5,25,35]).

3.3. *Combating social exclusion*

The pressure to target resources is reinforced by a growing view that poverty and other social ills are not to be regarded as states of affairs to be relieved by ameliorative care, but as the outcome of dynamic processes by which individuals and families become detached from social norms of work and self-reliance. It is believed, too, that these processes are capable of being inhibited by preventive interventions [18,37]. Many initiatives mentioned in successive Spending Reviews and allied policy documents therefore focus, for example, on identifying children and young people exhibiting known risk factors, such as inadequate parenting, unemployed parents, and chronic failure to maintain contact with the universal public services, especially schools and health agencies. This intelligence-led, proactive approach requires data about young people and their families to be integrated from a number of agencies; the Integrated Children's System (ICS) and the Children's Database listed in Table 1, as well as the records maintained by initiatives such as *SureStart* and *Connexions*, are all means to this end.

3.4. *Joined-up working at the micro level*

In this Government's view, then, the most significant problems are concentrated among defined groups of individuals (such as the small number of prolific offenders thought to be responsible for a high proportion of crime), certain high risk families, and a number of very small geographical areas that have been identified by local regeneration studies or crime mapping analysis to display high concentrations of social problems or particular types of crime [24]. For this reason, current policies target interventions at the family, client or neighbourhood level, in contrast to earlier approaches that focused on administrative co-ordination. This approach is epitomised in Table 1, for example, by the use of geographic information systems to identify crime hotspots by local Crime and Disorder Reduction Partnerships (CDRPs). Multi-agency 'zone' structures have been introduced in health, education, and employment, and a National Neighbourhood Renewal Strategy developed [42]. The Neighbourhood Statistics programme also reflects this drive [43].

3.5. Prevention and risk management

For these reasons, social policy and crime policy have acquired a marked preference for precautionary intervention over remedial action, and may, in large part, be analysed under the rubric of the 'risk society' [6,30,33] and the 'risk-based penology' [21,22,31]. They require the use of data-rich analytic tools and risk assessment techniques to identify people and neighbourhoods that are particularly at risk of high levels of unemployment, anti-social behaviour or criminality. Some of these tools and techniques – for example, those employed by the MAPPAs for identifying and managing violent and sexual offenders, by the proposed new national intelligence system for the police, and by child protection agencies – will be required to include 'soft' personal data, including data about people who have yet to be convicted of a criminal offence.

Our contention is that Table 1 broadly validates the importance of all five drivers, but what is particularly striking is how strongly it features initiatives designed to share information about individuals for purposes that relate as much, or more, to the common good, or at least to the interests of specific groups, as to the interests of the individuals described – a feature reflecting the strong communitarian strand in Labour's approach to social policy. Thus, the first category includes initiatives designed to provide integrated case information and electronic health records about patients in the NHS [12,13], and an integrated database of qualifications earned by all learners in the education system (MIAP), it also includes the universal database of children required by the 2004 Children Act, the specialist database of vulnerable children (Integrated Children's System, ICS) under the new Information Sharing and Assessment Initiative (ISA) [23] and the multi-agency programme, *Connexions*, which aims to reduce the risk of social exclusion amongst young people by enhancing their human and social capital. The second category includes a range of initiatives aimed at identifying, detecting, assessing and managing people posing various kinds of threat. It is not surprising, therefore, that initiatives in the former category tend to be primarily (though by no means exclusively) centred on the work of the universal services, such as the NHS and education, whereas those in the second category tend to be centred on special purpose agencies. It should be noted, however, that the boundaries between initiatives in these two categories are far from impermeable, as far as data sharing is concerned. Thus, the new, comprehensive, electronic patient records being developed for the NHS National Programme for IT and the Information for Social Care initiative will include those of people with mental health problems, and some of these records will contain data that may be shared between the NHS and social care agencies, as well with agencies such as the police, in the interests of protecting the public. Likewise, data kept on ICS under the ISA initiative may also, in certain circumstances, be shared with the police or criminal justice agencies in order to prevent child abuse or identify young offenders.

The growing interest in encouraging multi-agency collaboration, and thereby the sharing of personal data, between universal services and specialist, social control or penal agencies, itself underlines how strongly the list in Table 1 reflects the current policy emphasis on preventing harm and mitigating risk, rather than either the promotion of positive wellbeing or the remedy of harm that has actually occurred. After some thought, it was decided to place the government's ID Card initiative in the second category, even though the associated database will, by definition, be a universal citizens identity register. However, the government's latest statements in support of the introduction of identity cards have

Table 1
National initiatives for promoting data sharing in social policy in UK Government since 1997

PRIMARY PURPOSE	INITIATIVE	ORGANISATIONAL SCOPE	TARGET POPULATION	DATABASE	DEVELOPMENT TIMESCALE	FUNCTION(S)
Individual-focused for benefit of the individual	NHS National Programme for IT	Primary and secondary care trusts	Universal	NHS Care Records Service	Summer 2005 to 2010	Joint service delivery/ MIS (Mgt Info System)
	Information for Social Care (Social Care Quality Programme)	Social services/ health/eventually voluntary organisations	Selected – clients	Electronic social care record	Oct 2004– Oct 2006	Joint service delivery/ risk assessment/joint planning/MIS
	Children's Database	Health/Education/ social services	Sub population – all children	Children's Index or Database	Being piloted 2004–5	Registration/service delivery
	Information Sharing and Assessment	Health/Education/ social services/police criminal justice system	Selected – vulnerable/at risk children	Integrated Children's System (ICS)	ICS due late 2005	Needs/risk assessment/ joint planning/case tracking/MIS
	Management Information Across Partners (MIAP)	16+ education providers	Sub population – adult learners	Unique learner number service/national learning database	Fully operational 2010?	Registration/service delivery
	Connexions	13–19 education providers/social services/youth justice organisations	Sub population – all teenagers			
Individual-focused for benefit of the public	Identity Cards	Pan-government	Universal	National Identity Register		Registration/service entitlement/service-delivery
	Criminal Records Bureau	Police National Computer/ Depts of Health & Education and Skills/Home Office	Selected – people working with children and vulnerable adults	Police Local Cross Checking (PLX) to flag records in local police systems	2007	Risk assessment
	Phoenix	Police forces/ courts/ other criminal justice organisations	Sub population – convicted offenders	Police National Computer Nominal Index	Introduced 1996 but under development	Service delivery/risk assessment
	National Police Intelligence System	All police forces and policing partners	Selected – (suspicious persons and informants)	PNC – (PLX) interim measure pending development of IMPACT	Phased in aut 04 to spring 05	Service delivery/risk assessment
	CJS IT Programme	Police/courts/probation/ prisons	Selected – all offenders in criminal justice system	Hub for case records in criminal justice system	Access to all applications Mar-08	Case tracking/MIS

Table 1, continued

PRIMARY PURPOSE	INITIATIVE	ORGANISATIONAL SCOPE	TARGET POPULATION	DATABASE	DEVELOPMENT TIMESCALE	FUNCTION(S)
	Multi-agency Public Protection Arrangements	Police/probation/prisons/ social services/health and others	Selected – Sex and violent Offenders	VISOR (PNC)	phased in from spring 04	Registration/service delivery
	Offender Assessment System	National Offender Management Service (probation/prisons)	Selected – all offenders in the CJS	OASys – structured tool and database	all 42 NOMS areas live on e-OASys	Risk assessment/MIS
	Youth Offending Teams	Police/probation/education/ social services	Selected – all youth offenders			
	National Fraud Initiative	All public services covered by the Audit Commission	Sub population – customers/staff of public services	No permanent database	every 2 yrs since 1996	Risk assessment
	Dept of Work and Pensions fraud work	DWP/Inland Revenue customer accounts	Sub population – social security claimants	No permanent database	ongoing	Risk assessment
Area-focused for public benefit	Crime and Disorder Reduction Partnerships	LAs/police and others	Area – crime hotspots etc	Regional/local information hubs	ongoing	Risk assessment/MIS

placed such emphasis on their prophylactic use against identity theft, international terrorism and illegal immigration [27,28] that it is difficult not to read the whole initiative in these terms. Indeed, not for the first time in British history [4], a period of particular international disorder and political uncertainty has stimulated loud calls for the introduction of categorising devices to distinguish the enemy within and without from ordinary British citizens.

Many initiatives in this list have been galvanised by the series of high-profile tragedies in child protection, mental health and law enforcement that have occurred that have been explained, at least in part by the fact that agencies have palpably failed to trade off, in ways that turned out to be appropriate, the risks associated with the sharing of sensitive information with the risk of physical and other harm [40]. Much of the current investment in the development of a universal children's database and the ISA initiative can be traced to official responses to Lord Laming's Report on the death of Victoria Climbié [41], a report that was but the latest of a series calling attention to endemic failures to share data effectively among children's services. Similarly, the Bichard Inquiry [8] into why police and education authorities failed to prevent the employment as a school caretaker of Ian Huntley, the murderer of the Soham schoolgirls, has spread wide ripples into data management practices in many different fields impinging on both the protection of children and the effectiveness of the police [29]. While its most obvious outcome is the creation of the optimal intelligence system for the police, its effects are also being felt in social services departments. It may also enlarge the scope of the Audit Commission's National Fraud Initiative (NFI), which has unique access to public service payroll data, including extensive data about employees in services that engage with children and other vulnerable people.

4. The policy framework for data sharing and privacy

The sheer range and scale of the initiatives listed in Table 1 map the strength and scope of imperatives since 1997 for significantly expanding the sharing of personal data in social policy. What may be more surprising, perhaps, is the marked patchiness of political opposition on grounds of threats to personal privacy. The sharing of personal data between public services has long been a concern of civil rights groups such as Liberty, which was joined in the 1990s by other organisations in the privacy field. By contrast, consumer organisations have shown only occasional interest. Public pressure has also been weak and patchy: the risks and benefits of data sharing are borne by diffuse populations and those groups that apparently have most to fear – offenders, fraudsters and debtors, for example – are not regarded as having legitimate grounds on which to complain. Parliamentary interest has been sporadic, though it has increased markedly in recent years, more obviously in the House of Lords. Here, human rights issues associated, for example with the retention of communications data have been taken up with more gusto than in the House of Commons. The single prominent exception is the strong opposition in both Houses to the extension of the powers of the Department of Social Security (DSS, now the Department of Work and Pensions, DWP) to source data, first in 1997 from other public services for the purpose of anti-fraud data-matching exercises and then, in 2001, from private sector organisations for the purposes of investigating probable cases of fraud identified by these means [7]. It is difficult, however, not to draw the conclusion that this opposition may be explained as much by longstanding suspicions amongst welfare lobbies and certain politicians of the motives of the DSS as by special concerns about privacy. Certainly, the data-matching operations associated with the Audit Commission's bi-annual National Fraud Initiative, which are much larger in scope and scale and which are largely aimed at the same population, have never been the subject of political opposition.

Much of the burden of surfacing concerns has therefore fallen on the data protection regulator, a role first set up under the Data Protection Act 1984, and now represented by the Information Commissioner under the Data Protection Act 1998. The worries of successive holders of this role about government data sharing have focused much attention on possible breaches of the second data protection principle, which specifies that data can only be used for the purpose(s) for which they were collected. If it was ever true that the purposes for which personal information is processed by public services were defined in terms of the mission of the particular service-providing organisations responsible for collecting that information, then that principle has now been substantially breached in order to support multi-agency collaboration. The principle of the paramountcy of the protection of children, set out in the Children Act 1989, the Care Programme Approach protocols governing mental health and the duties placed on agencies to supply financial information to investigators that may be of future use in fraud detection, are all examples of ways in which very widely defined categories of functions (e.g., law enforcement, prevention of harm) now provide 'joined-up' purposes for processing data far beyond the boundaries of the organisations collecting those data. Specific powers having been put into primary legislation or enacted into secondary legislation, the Data Protection Act 1998 cannot now be used to constrain extensions of purposes under these powers. However, there has been little explanation given to the public of the nature of the change in the purposes for which their personal records are handled – nor has government been able to issue any clear statement of general principle of just how remote the potential usefulness of a piece of information for one of these 'joined up' purposes would have to be before it would be deemed inappropriate for sharing in all but the most pressing circumstances. The finality principle remains legally intact, but its spirit is being put under considerable strain. This situation may be politically sustainable during periods of grave public anxiety about child protection, identity theft and identity fraud, social security fraud, illegal immigration and terrorism. But when this anxiety begins to abate, the question may be raised as to whether it will, after all, be necessary to clarify the limits imposed by the concept of 'purpose' on the sharing of personal data in the content of multi-agency working.

In the meanwhile, the probability that data will be shared – that is, disclosed to other agencies – gives added importance to those data protection principles that lay emphasis on the sufficiency, currency and accuracy of data, and the fairness, proportionality and lawfulness of their processing. However, the questions raised by the first data protection principle and its elaboration in Schedules 2 and 3 of the Data Protection Act 1998 – what counts as consent to data processing?; how explicit does it have to be?; can consent be revoked having once been given?; how far can service users distinguish between types or pieces of information to the sharing of which they will and will not consent?; and when may data reasonably be shared without consent? – are key ones in the current climate of increasing political sensitivity to risk.

The regulator has pressed, for many years, for the adoption by the UK of a statutory code on data matching, on similar lines to statutory codes of practice introduced in the USA, Canada, Australia and New Zealand. Its introduction has been consistently resisted by Ministers on the grounds that such a code would be insufficiently flexible to cope with changing technologies and administrative requirements. Instead, the fuss over the Social Security Fraud Act 1997 prompted Ministers to promise that the new data sharing powers would not be used before the publication of a voluntary code of practice [17]. The code was to be agreed by the regulator, who also took the opportunity to issue a guide to the drafting of voluntary codes for data sharing and data matching by government departments and local authorities. Detailed voluntary codes of practice have subsequently been issued as standard practice by a wide number of public service organisations, and these codes have formed the backbone of the UK's system of practical regulation of data sharing in government: indeed, in her annual report of 2000, the then Data

Protection Commissioner declared, on the basis of research commissioned by her office, that they had been effective in ensuring compliance and building public confidence in the handling of personal data by government departments [16].

Despite this optimism, it was decided in the wake of the *Modernising Government* White Paper [39] that the UK needed a more authoritative settlement between imperatives for data sharing and the protection of privacy. The Government therefore commissioned the (then) Performance and Innovation Unit (PIU) of the Cabinet Office to analyse the issues and to make recommendations. We have speculated elsewhere why this study was set up [3]. Public opinion and media pressure, being both very limited, do not explain it, and indeed by drawing attention to the problem the Government risked increasing its political salience. Nor does immediate pressure from the Information Commissioner appeared to have been an important influence, though she co-operated actively with the production of the Report. It is much more likely that pressure came from within Whitehall, where departments had come to understand that they needed an overarching policy statement to cover their aspirations for the kinds of initiatives listed in Table 1. Although the 1999 White Paper asserted that 'data protection is an objective of information age government, not an obstacle to it' [39, p. 51], officials across Whitehall seem to have been less clear that, in practice, they knew how data sharing could be put on a 'proper and lawful basis' [39, p. 51].

The PIU Report, which was published only after a very long delay, sought to show, but failed to convince, that government could achieve a positive-sum relationship between data sharing and privacy [38]. It brought forward twenty-five recommendations, each with a detailed timetable for consultation and implementation and each with a nominated lead department. Each recommendation was designed to address the legal, political, institutional and managerial conditions for extended data sharing and to increase public confidence that privacy would be safeguarded.

The PIU's package of recommendations appeared to give great, and even preponderant, weight to privacy and transparency, possibly in a bid to compensate for the extension of data sharing proposed by the report. Indeed, it seems that Ministers and officials were initially taken aback at how much weight was given to privacy safeguards, having probably assumed that the purpose of the report was to find a way round data protection 'barriers' to joined-up government. Many recommendations were innovations to put data protection principles into best practice; to extend them across government would amount to truly joined-up privacy protection.

But the report also made nineteen proposals for the extension of data sharing in specific areas through 'gateways'; these proposals were far-reaching in terms of promoting more intensive and extensive information sharing. A number of recommendations were highly controversial. The privacy lobby was dismayed, for example, to find recommendations relating to the introduction of smart cards and oblique references to identity cards, along with proposals envisaging the extension of data sharing without consent. These recommendations staked out the ground for policy battles if the Report were implemented. Unease was fuelled, no doubt, by the increased powers of surveillance which had recently been brought forward in the face of considerable opposition in the Regulation of Investigatory Powers Act 2000 and the Anti-terrorism, Crime and Security Act 2001, and which were considered to have compromised the government's stance on privacy protection.

In the event, responsibility for implementing the Report passed to the Lord Chancellor's Department, subsequently renamed the Department for Constitutional Affairs (DCA). Following further delays, the DCA issued a 'toolkit' for data sharing, including guidance for establishing protocols between data sharing organisations and complaints procedures, together with a 'library' of examples [9]. A major effect of its work will probably be the institutionalisation of a wider plethora of controls, with much more attention being paid to data quality standards, protocols, training and complaints procedures, along with the possible introduction of privacy impact assessments. On the core issue of data sharing without consent, the DCA asserted that 'an appropriate balance must be struck in the specific circumstances that surround each service or policy' [10, p. 3]. The first question is whether an organisation has express or legal powers (*vires*) to perform a function necessitating data sharing: if so, officials should then ascertain that sharing would not violate specific statutory restrictions against sharing or violate laws on data protection, human rights or common law obligations of confidentiality. In this context, 'necessary' does not mean 'absolutely essential' but 'reasonably required or legally ancillary to' the accomplishment of the purpose in question [10, paras 6.11; 6.12]. On the vexed question of what might be considered to constitute consent, the DCA observed only that 'that most people (we imagine) would feel able to recognise it when they saw it' [10, para 6.21].

Although the clear intention was to provide legal cover for the expansion of data sharing and to obviate the need to take the politically thorny path of legitimising further data sharing by enacting primary legislation, it is difficult not to come to the conclusion that the practical effect was to put the core issue back where it was in 1999–2000. It placed the onus for judging the appropriateness of data sharing onto policy-makers, managers and professionals in the public services concerned. In so doing, it provided little institutional discipline for consistency between government services or between tiers of government, and no great security that decisions would be judged in the same way on different occasions. Before 2004, for example, the most rational choice for a risk-averse manager would be to refuse to share personal data without express legislative enactment: following the blame heaped by the Bichard Inquiry [8] onto the Chief Constable of Humberside for the failures of the force to retain data on the (then unconvicted) Ian Huntley, refusal to retain or share data no longer seems the most rational choice. Who is to say, however, that high-profile cases involving over-zealous data sharing, such as those that led in the mid-1980s to the wrongful removal of children from their families in Cleveland, Orkney and Nottingham following accusations of satanic abuse, would not swing the pendulum of public opinion back to favour a more conservative approach?

In the absence of a clear, stable settlement in the horizontal, cross-governmental dimension, between imperatives for data sharing and imperatives for privacy, we expect tensions between data sharing and privacy to be settled within the vertical, service-specific dimension, and that decisions will vary widely, service by service, initiative by initiative, and often case by case. We have already seen, in the case of the DSS's anti-fraud activities, that levels of political antagonism to data sharing exercises vary significantly from one department to another, for reasons to do with different levels of trust. Similarly, we have shown elsewhere in the case of the NHS [7], that personal privacy is a much higher value to a service that processes sensitive records relating to the whole population than to one dealing with fewer, less 'respectable' individuals.

Of most interest in relation to the management of risk are the increasing range of decisions made in the context of 'social sorting' initiatives in those fields and functions in which frontline, professional judgment necessarily plays a large part. We use this term, following Lyon [34, p. 13], to refer to initiatives designed to enhance planning, predicting and preventing by identifying, classifying and assessing individuals marked out for special treatment on grounds of enhanced need or risk. For our purposes, the term covers those initiatives where propensities for shaping the life chances of the most vulnerable citizens are currently being formed, including information sharing initiatives and assessment frameworks in child protection, mental health, the care of elderly people, multi-agency public protection, prolific and other priority offenders, as well as the national police intelligence service being developed in the wake of the Bichard Inquiry [29].

In all these fields, though to varying degrees, there has been a strong assertion of national policy in the direction of expanded data sharing. Moreover, national policy reflects three important aspirations that impinge potentially on settlements between data sharing and privacy in such fields. First, there is a clear policy thrust towards exerting managerial control over the quality and objectivity of professional judgements. This is to be achieved either by requiring the use of formal, highly structured, risk assessment techniques – as in the case of OASys and ASSET which probation officers are now obliged to use for all formal assessment purposes within the criminal justice system, from pre-sentence reports to post-custodial supervision of all adult and youth offenders from the most innocuous to the most risky [36] – or, more commonly across the caring professions, by means of initiatives, such as the new ICS in child protection work, designed to marshal case information in such a way that professionals arrive at more consistent and defensible decisions. Second, and paradoxically, however, the robustness of such assessments is known to be significantly increased by the inclusion of 'soft' data and by enlarging the scope for qualitative judgement. For example, one of the major claims made for the superiority of OASys over rival tools is that static 'actuarial' data, relating for example to the offending history and socio-demographic characteristics of offenders, is supplemented by dynamic 'clinical' data, relating to their current circumstances and frames of mind. It was known, however, at the point when OASys was introduced as the preferred tool for the new National Probation Service in 2001 that it had not been subject to post hoc tests of its accuracy as a predictor of 'risk of harm' [26, p. 5].

This graphic example reflects the fact that such tools cannot replace judgement. Professional decisions still need to be made on an everyday basis about the most sensitive issues relating to vulnerable and risky people: case management protocols, data sharing agreements and new data systems cannot substitute algorithms for judgment in decisions on whether or not to share data. However, driven as they are by political imperatives to manage and mitigate risk, current national initiatives may now be systematically encouraging bias to false positive judgment errors rather than false negative judgment errors. This proposition has still to be tested empirically, but if it is true, we would expect to find that the range of situations in which organisations are seen as having legitimate reasons for sharing data is expanding; that there is less active concern at policy levels (but perhaps more concern among local managers and professionals) that organisations might have access to excessive and irrelevant information; and that, overall, risk of unfairness and inaccuracy of personal data held about citizens is increasing. Moreover, we would therefore expect any challenges to these developments to be made under the Data Protection Act, if only because it is more difficult to use the growing body of substantive field-specific legislation for this purpose.

5. Conclusion

It remains to be seen how far the settlement between confidentiality and integrated working that ministers and senior civil servants have sought to strike will be followed in the judgments made by frontline workers in their processing of client records. While fear of sanctions, blame or public obloquy may indeed shift practice toward more sharing of data, even at the risk of false positive judgment errors, past history suggests that when those false positive errors are sufficiently widely publicised, politicians rarely defend public servants. This remains true, even when inappropriate decisions have been made by following the very bias in the decision rule previously preferred by those same politicians. Moreover, there are many organisational processes that have more to do with routines, professional boundaries, mutual distrust, and managerial autonomy than they have with either confidentiality or holistic working. These processes also affect the ways in which agencies do and do not share data, with whom, for what purposes, on what terms and at what stage in a case.

We have argued that central government policy reflects the wider climate of politics and policy-making associated with perceptions of risk and with the growing importance of a communitarian mindset in government. Nevertheless, it cannot be assumed that this settlement is entirely stable. Indeed, should the present levels of anxiety about risk begin to abate, or should scandals arise as an apparent result of excessive zeal in sharing personal information that may in fact be incorrect, or at least misleading, it seems likely that the present policy mix would have to change. In any case, in a number of critical dimensions such as consent, purpose and remoteness, policy on the management of personal information remains vague. The policy is therefore likely to prove unstable when cases arise to test the boundaries of the current policy bias.

It follows that we may expect a wide variety of practices to emerge in relation to the management of personal data in British social policy over the next few years, and, notwithstanding the energy currently being dedicated to the long list of initiatives developed in response to the high salience of risk, we may also expect that both policy and practices will change.

References

[1] P. 6, Should we be compelled to have identity cards? Justifications for the legal enforcement of obligations, *Political Studies* **52**(2) (2005), 243–261.

[2] P. 6 and E. Peck, New Labour's modernization in the public sector: A neo-Durkheimian approach and the case of mental health services, *Public Administration* **82**(1) (2004), 83–108.

[3] P. 6, C.D. Raab and C.A. Bellamy, Joined-up government and privacy in the United Kingdom: Managing tensions between data protection and social policy. Part I, *Public Administration* **83**(1) (2005), 111–133.

[4] J. Agar, *The Government Machine: A Revolutionary History of the Computer,* MIT Press, Cambridge Massachusetts, 2003.

[5] K. Baker, S. Jones, C. Roberts and S. Merrington, *The Evaluation of the Validity and Reliability of the Youth Justice Board's Assessment for Young Offenders. Findings from the First Two Years of ASSET,* Youth Justice Board, London, 2003.

[6] U. Beck, *Risk Society: Towards a New Modernity,* Sage, Thousand Oaks, CA, 1992.

[7] C.A. Bellamy, P. 6 and C.D. Raab, Joined-up government and privacy in the United Kingdom: Managing tensions between data protection and social policy. Part II, *Public Administration*, forthcoming.

[8] Sir M. Bichard, *The Bichard Inquiry Report,* HC653, The Stationery Office, London, 2004.

[9] DCA, *A Toolkit for Data Sharing,* Department of Constitutional Affairs, London, 2003.

[10] DCA, *Public Sector Data Sharing-Guidance on the Law,* Department of Constitutional Affairs, London, 2003.

[11] A. Deacon, *Perspectives on Welfare: Ideas, Ideologies and Policy Debates,* Open University Press, Buckingham, 2002.

[12] Department of Health, *Information for Health,* Department of Health, London, 1998.

[13] Department of Health, *Building the Information Core: Implementing the NHS Plan,* Department of Health, London, 2001.

[14] S. Driver and L. Martell, *New Labour; Politics after Thatcher,* Polity Press, Oxford, 1998.

[15] S. Driver and L. Martell, *Blair's Britain,* Polity Press, Oxford, 2002.

[16] DPC, *The First Report of the Data Protection Commissioner on the 16th Year of Operation of the Data Protection Act 1984,* HC 575. London: Stationery Office.

[17] DSS, *Code of Practice for Data Matching,* Department of Social Security, London, 1998.

[18] DSS, *Opportunity for All: Tackling Poverty and Social Exclusion,* Cm 4445. Department of Social Security, London, 1999.

[19] DSS, *Safeguarding Social Security: Getting the Information We Need,* Department of Social Security, London, 2000.

[20] P. Dwyer, *Welfare Rights and Responsibilities: Contesting Social Citizenship,* Policy Press, Bristol, 2000.

[21] R. Ericson and K. Heggarty, *Policing the Risk Society,* Clarendon Press, Oxford, 1997.

[22] M. Feeley and J. Simon, Actuarial justice, in: *The Futures of Criminology,* D. Nelken, ed., Sage, London, 1994.

[23] HM Treasury, *Every Child Matters,* Cm 5860. HM Treasury, London, 2003.

[24] J. Hills, J. Le Grand and D. Piachaud, eds, *Understanding Social Exclusion,* Oxford University Press, Oxford, 2002.

[25] Home Office, *Effective Practice Initiative. A joint Risk/Needs Assessment System for the Prison and Probation Services,* Home Office, London, 1999.

[26] Home Office, *Using Risk Assessment in Effective Sentence Management,* Report of a criminal justice conference held at Pendely Manor Hotel, Tring, March 2002, at www.homeoffice.gov.uk/docs2/riskassess4.html. Downloaded 27/12/2004.

[27] Home Secretary, *Identity Cards: The Next Steps,* Cm 6020, The Stationery Office, London, 2003.
[28] Home Secretary, *Legislation on Identity Cards: A Consultation,* Cm 6178, The Stationery Office, London, 2004.
[29] Home Office, *The Government's Response to the Bichard Inquiry,* 2004, http://www.homeoffice.gov.uk/crimpol/police/bichard/response.html.
[30] H. Kemshall, *Risk, Social Policy and Welfare,* Open University Press, Buckingham, 2002.
[31] H. Kemshall, *Understanding Risk in Criminal Justice,* Open University Press, Buckingham, 2003.
[32] R. Levitas, *The Inclusive Society: Social Inclusion and New Labour,* Palgrave, Basingstoke, 1998.
[33] D. Lupton, *Risk,* Routledge, London, 1999.
[34] D. Lyon, ed., *Surveillance as Social Sorting: Privacy, Risk and Digital Discrimination,* Routledge, London, 2003.
[35] M. Maguire, H. Kemshall, L. Noaks, E. Wincup and K. Sharpe, *Risk management of sexual and violent offenders: The work of Public Protection Panels,* Police Research Series Paper 139. Home Office, London, 2001.
[36] National Probation Service, *The New Choreography,* Home Office, London, 2001.
[37] J. Percy-Smith, (ed.), *Policy Responses to Social Exclusion: Towards Inclusion?* Open University Press, Buckingham, 2000.
[38] PIU, 2002, *Privacy and Data Sharing,* Cabinet Office, Performance and Innovation Unit, London, 2002.
[39] Prime Minister and Minister for the Cabinet Office, *Modernising Government,* CM 4310. The Stationery Office, London, 1999.
[40] C.D. Raab, P. 6, A. Birch and M. Copping, *Information Sharing for Children at Risk: Impacts on Privacy, e-Care Programme,* Health Department, Scottish Executive, Edinburgh, 2004.
[41] Secretary of State for Health and Home Secretary, *The Victoria Climbié inquiry: Report of an inquiry by Lord Laming,* Cm 5730, The Stationery Office, London, 2003.
[42] Social Exclusion Unit, *Bringing Britain together: A national strategy for neighbourhood renewal,* Cabinet Office, Social Exclusion Unit, London, 1998.
[43] Social Exclusion Unit, *Report of policy action team 18 on better information,* Cabinet Office, Social Exclusion Unit, London, 2000.
[44] S. White, *New Labour: The Progressive Future,* Palgrave Macmillan: Basingstoke, 2001.

Information Polity 10 (2005) 65–78
IOS Press

The panoptic state: Privacy, surveillance and the balance of risk

Frank Bannister
Trinity College Dublin, Dublin, Ireland
E-mail: Frank.Bannister@tcd.ie

Abstract. Advances in technology and changes in the way that we communicate and store information have steadily increased the vulnerability of informational privacy. This vulnerability is compounded by a combination of increased concerns about citizen security and developments in e-government designed to improve state services and reform the public sector. Starting from a statement of principle of the right to informational privacy, recent technological developments are surveyed, the dangers they pose to privacy and existing protections are discussed. The question of risk in this context is then explored and, resulting from this, a number of mechanisms for achieving a better balance between the right to individual privacy and the need for communal security in an information society are proposed.

1. Introduction

"Those that can give up essential liberty to obtain a little temporary safety deserve neither liberty nor safety." Benjamin Franklin.

Most people are probably at least dimly aware of the growing intrusion of the state into their lives. A lesser number would be more conscious of the extent of this invasion and the political, social and ethical issues that surround it. A small minority of citizens have an in-depth understanding of just how far the government, commercial companies and other organisations can pry into their private affairs and of the escalating scope of this phenomenon. Probably only the security forces know the full extent of the surveillance tools and information now at the disposal of the modern state.

Privacy, like freedom of speech and freedom of assembly, is a human right. A right to privacy is recognised in article seven of the European Charter of Human Rights [25] and in article 12 of the UN Charter of Human Rights [36]. Throughout recorded history, there has always been a tension between the right of the individual to privacy and the right of the state to protect itself and the community at large by inquiring into the lives and activities of individual citizens. The problem today is that technology is changing the scale and dimensions of the state's ability to do this at an alarming speed.

It is easy to become paranoid about the invasion of privacy. There are many pro-privacy organisations to be found on the Web and elsewhere which stoke up such fears and, as Ball [3] points out, much of what is published on this subject is uncritical and/or polemical in nature. Maintaining academic detachment, not to mention objectivity, in such a charged atmosphere can be a challenge. One way to try to reach an objective viewpoint is to look at the balance of risk in this context. Even this cannot be separated from philosophical and political stance. However looking at this as a question of risk offers some hope for arriving at a sensible framework for judicious management of privacy rights in an unsafe world.

1570-1255/05/$17.00

2. The right to privacy

Privacy, as Introna and Pouloudi [19] observe, is not a straightforward concept. Cate [9] suggests that privacy is an unusually broad term and has always been susceptible to many meanings. Consequently it has no universally accepted definition. It encompasses not just a right to freedom from intrusion into our lives, it can extend to concepts such as personal space, one's own body, or the right to marry, use contraception or have an abortion. Formal legal definitions have been extended and "*stretched in common parlance*" to encompass even ideas such as trust and freedom from crime. It can, Cate observes, "*mean almost anything to anyone*" [9, p. 35].

This article is concerned with a particular aspect of privacy often called *informational* privacy, i.e. the right to privacy of one's personal information, including information about one's actions, and the deliberate invasion of that privacy by the state. The right to informational privacy can be philosophically grounded in various ways, not least in the absence of any automatic right, or any basis for a right, by A to know about the affairs of B. Provided that what A does or is doing neither has, nor will have, any impact on B, there is no basis for B having a right to know what A is up to. [1]

The weakness in this argument is that what is true at the level of two individuals does not generally hold true in a social context. Being a member of any society or community requires some sacrifice of personal privacy. In a social setting, there are few things that A can do that does not affect *somebody* else, so part of the community or even the community as a whole will have some level of interest in knowing, if not necessarily a right to know, about much of what A is doing. This, in turn, raises many problems, one of which is how does society know when A is doing something about which it needs to know? If A is not reporting all his taxable income or is making a bomb in the basement with a view to blowing up the local police station, he is hardly likely to advertise either fact. In order to detect this, society has to take some sort of pre-emptive action such as accessing his bank records or breaking in to A's house. Given the legal principle that somebody must be assumed innocent until proven guilty it is easy to see how the question of a 'right' to informational privacy quickly degenerates into a grey area where delineation of clear and unambiguous laws or principles is exceedingly difficult.

Privacy is something most individuals value and seek to protect. Consequently, the circumstances under which a citizen's privacy may be invaded, like those under which her freedom of speech may be curtailed, need to be defined with great care. The ability of individual citizens to control this process of definition is one of the core questions that needs to be addressed. This is a problem which has been widely discussed in the context of establishing rights to, or guidelines for, privacy and data access for those data used by the state in its delivery of public services. The 2002 UK Policy and Innovation Unit (PIU) discussion paper [28] is typical of this type of approach. It provides a model which sets out in considerable detail the type of data the state can acquire, the extent and nature of the data it can hold, and the rules governing access to that data. Less easy to find is any definition of when privacy can and should be invaded. What constitutes an exception or, in extreme cases, a state right to break its own laws? Where such issues are addressed, it is usually at the micro level, for example, the specific circumstances or conditions under which a search warrant may be issued. The circumstances under which democratic governments are justified in taking on sweeping powers is less often discussed. [2]

The dangers to privacy come from three directions illustrated in Fig. 1.

[1] Western societies have gradually moved in the direction of recognising this principle, for example in recognising of the rights of consenting adults to certain forms of behaviour hitherto regarded as criminal offenses.

[2] The UK Prevention of Terrorism Act and the Patriot Act introduced in the US after the events of 9/11 are examples of such legislation. Developments in the US recent years have alarmed even friendly observers, see for example The Wall Street Journal (2001) [37] or 'America the scary' editorial, Financial Times, June 9th 2003.

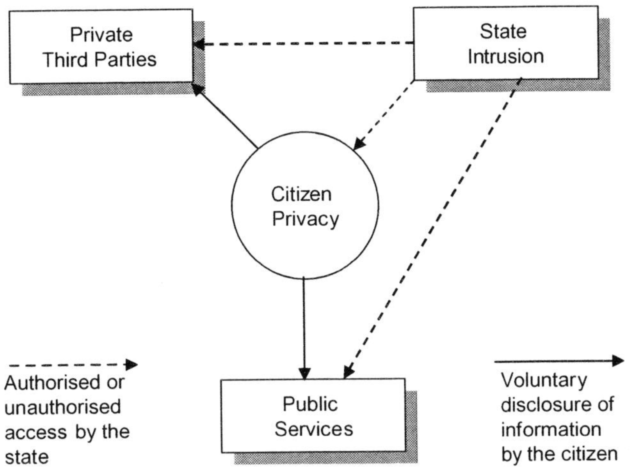

Fig. 1. Privacy: modes of intrusion by the state.

The state can, of course, invade individual privacy directly for security reasons. It can also misuse information supplied to the state voluntarily by citizens or acquired in the provision of state services (such as tax information or health records). Thirdly, many third parties legitimately hold private and voluntarily disclosed data into which the state can tap (legally or illegally). Increasingly institutions are required by law to report information to the state, for example banks must report cash transactions over a certain limit, airlines must report passenger details and so on.

Notwithstanding caveats about paranoia and conspiracy theories, the dangers of unwarranted intrusion are real. For example, it is now well established that the US National Security Agency (NSA) led Echelon system monitors the vast traffic of the world telecommunications systems [6,21].[3] In 2001, the EU Parliament became sufficiently alarmed about such developments to warn European citizens to encrypt their personal mail.[4] Where it is illegal for a state to spy on its own citizens, it can enter into a back-to-back arrangement with one of its close allies whereby each spies on the other's citizens and then exchanges information. The UK and USA have done this for many years in conjunction with a number of other countries including Australia and New Zealand [4]. This is by no means an Anglo-Saxon phenomenon [15]. For its part, the EU is currently working with the US Federal Bureau of Investigation (FBI) on implementation of its part of a system of global surveillance called ENFOPOL[5] 19 and so on. While threats to privacy from the state vary with country and culture and the degree of trust between government and citizens differs widely, there is ample evidence to conclude that use of citizen surveillance by some democratic states is both extensive and growing.

3. A taxonomy of intrusion

The technology enabled ability to spy on or invade the privacy of others has increased by orders of magnitude in the past two decades [23]. In considering the impact of technology on privacy, it is useful

[3]The extent of the agency's remit can be seen in its concern about the amount of telecommunications traffic now travelling by optical fibre rather than easily interceptable satellite or copper media. It has even been experimenting with undetectable ways of cutting its way into undersea cables (Wall Street Journal, May 23rd 2001).

[4]The Guardian, London, May 30th, 2001.

[5]Law ENFOrcement POLice matters. This is a generic title given to a number of documents and initiatives.

to classify invasions of privacy into four categories:

- Watching;
- Intercepting;
- Reading;
- Interpreting.

Each of these has its own characteristics.

3.1. Watching

The first category of privacy invasion is *physical observation/monitoring of what people are doing*. Physical surveillance is labour intensive and presents the state with difficult logistical and manpower problems if it is to be done on a large scale. Over the past decade developments in technology have considerably increased the scope of, reduced the cost of, and generally simplified, this process. The most obvious manifestation of this is the closed circuit television (CCTV) camera. The growth, impact and human rights implications of CCTV are discussed in some depth by Webster [38]. Advances in recognition technology may, in a few years, enable a sophisticated system to track the movements of individuals by recognising their features or characteristics when they come into camera view[6] [2]. Such systems can already recognise car number plates.[7]

Tracking the movement of citizens does not, of course, require cameras. Every time a citizen uses his credit card, buys an airline ticket or pays a parking fine, some computer somewhere is logging his location at that instant. Movements through cyberspace can be tracked using cookies and so-called spyware. In the UK, for example, the Regulation of Investigatory Powers Act (RIPA) [18] gives the authorities power to requisition personal data records from private organisations in order to establish the whereabouts of an individual at a given time.[8]

3.2. Intercepting

The second category of privacy invasion is *interception of communications*. This is as old as history itself. There is a long tradition of capturing couriers, steaming open envelopes and tapping telephone lines. An important strategy in most instances is to intercept information without the communicating parties being aware that their message has been read. As communication becomes increasingly electronic, so the potential for, and ease of, interception of communications between citizens and organisations has been transformed [21].

The authorities in most countries intercept e-mail and nowhere more so than in the United States and the United Kingdom (see above). As already noted, the Echelon system is alleged to read every single piece of e-mail traffic in the world or at least in and out of the USA. This might seem like a technological impossibility, but in theory there is no reason why it could not be done. Whether or not this allegation is true a vast volume of data is read and this raises the interesting (and important) question of how useful information is to be extracted from this (see below).

Counter-measures to interception are as old as interception itself [8,16,21]. The front line of defence is encryption where continual battles have been fought between the encrypters and the decrypters. From

[6]In the fictional BBC television series 'Spooks', MI5 uses CCTV to track people as they move around London.
[7]http://www.cctv-information.co.uk/constant2/numberplates.html.
[8]This can also be done on the word of a police superintendent.

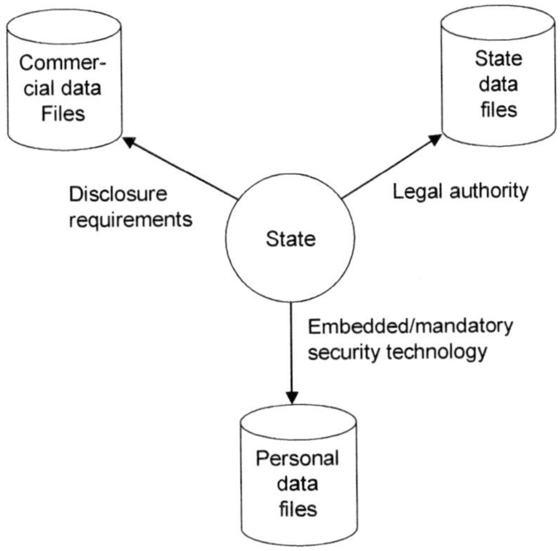

Fig. 2. State access to data.

the point of view of ordinary citizens, these battles are remote. The level of technology available to ordinary people for (say) encrypting their e-mail may be sufficient to deter even a fairly determined hacker, but it does not offer total protection against the security forces of the modern state.

3.3. Reading

The third type of privacy invasion is accessing *existing private data*, whether this data is publicly held (e.g. by a government department), privately held (e.g. by a family doctor) or personally held (e.g. on a home computer). The issues here are slightly different from those in the preceding two categories. Both physical surveillance and interception of communications involve data acquisition methods which are usually covert, sometimes illicit and over which the citizen has little control. Reading goes beyond this, accessing data such as private financial or health records. It also includes unauthorised access to data legitimately gathered by the state. For such data, the ethical and legal questions move from methods of acquisition to rights of access. Such data may be held privately by the individual themselves, by third parties/commercial concerns such as banks or medical practitioners, or by the state itself. This is illustrated in Fig. 2.[9]

There have been several developments which have raised the risks to privacy in this category. First there is ease of access. When the data was held in paper files it was hard work to locate, extract and collate it. Today, this can be done in seconds. Secondly there is a steady aggregation of data. One of the major objectives of e-government is joined up-government, a process whereby state service to the citizen can be made seamless. To achieve this requires, *inter alia*, a clear citizen identifier and demolishing the

[9]Embedded privacy technology is best explained by the a proposal made by the Clinton Administration that all telecommunications devices in the US use an common encryption standard (variously called the 'Clipper', 'Capstone' and 'Skipjack' algorithm). This would enable users to encrypt private conversations and/or data. However under the proposal, the state would retain a copy of the private key and thus be able to eavesdrop on any communication. The government claimed that this was necessary to fight crime. Civil rights groups claimed it was an infringement of privacy and civil liberties. For an interesting discussion of this of this see the testimony given by Whitfield Diffie to a US congressional committee at: archive.cpsr.net/program/clipper/diffie-testimony.html.

silo systems that have grown up over the years. Ironically, these very silos provide the citizen with a degree of privacy and protection. Modern society is rapidly moving towards a situation where, at the click of a mouse, a public servant will be able to access or assemble a wide range of information about a citizen.[10]

3.4. *Interpreting*

The fiasco over the non-existent weapons of mass destruction used to justify the 2003 Iraq war brought into public view the arcane and doubtful world of *interpreting intelligence data.* It was noted above that there is a simple logistical issue at the heart of all state intrusion into the private lives of individuals. Put in simple terms, there are many more of us than there are of them. One way to solve this problem is to encourage citizens to spy on one another. This has always been a favorite tactic of totalitarian states and is still to be found in some countries today. Where this is not possible, locating and tracking the movements of a single person by locating them on video tapes or DVDs could take several days. Scanning billions of e-mails each week by eye is just not possible. To overcome this type of problem, technologies such as data mining and artificial intelligence are used to try to identify mails or data which are of interest. If one is only looking out for certain key words or combinations of keywords, then it is relatively easy to process fairly large amounts of information quickly.

A second related issue is connecting data from various sources. Data from CCTV, credit card machines, medical or bank records and e-mail are captured in different ways, by different agencies, at different times and using different formats and technologies. To build up a picture it may be necessary to combine multiple sources. This implies first identifying the source, then working out a way to combine the data with that from other sources. The latter includes determining what exactly it is one is looking for. Much research continues into the problems of recognition and data mining [2]. An alarming development in this field was the Pentagon's Total Information Awareness programme[11] which sought to integrate all such information. The objective of such an exercise would be to spot potential terrorists (and presumably criminals) before they could act. While under current US law, this could only be done without prior judicial approval for non citizens, in January 2003 the US Senate voted to put limits on this type of data mining. Apart from the civil liberties implications of such a scheme, data mining is part science, part art and can sometimes prompt analysts to arrive at invalid conclusions. This type of invasion of privacy might be termed *implicit*, i.e. where existing data is combined to *infer* new information. The fact that such inferences are often wrong, is another concern.

4. Intrusion – a summary

Figure 3 summarises the taxonomy that emerges from the above discussion. It is clear that technology has not only greatly increased the ability of the state to acquire knowledge about its citizens, but also its ability to manipulate, manage and analyse the enormous volumes of data acquired. A traditional limitation on the power of the state to invade privacy was that there were many of us and few of them. It seems unlikely that technology will overcome this limitation in the immediate future, but there is no reason, in theory, why it should not. If and when it does, the panoptic state will become a reality and society will be left pondering Juvenal's question: "*Quis custodiet ipsos custodes?*".[12]

[10] This is not a problem that is restricted to public administration, but the concern here is with the state.
[11] See http://www.geocities.com/totalinformationawareness/.
[12] Who guards the guards?

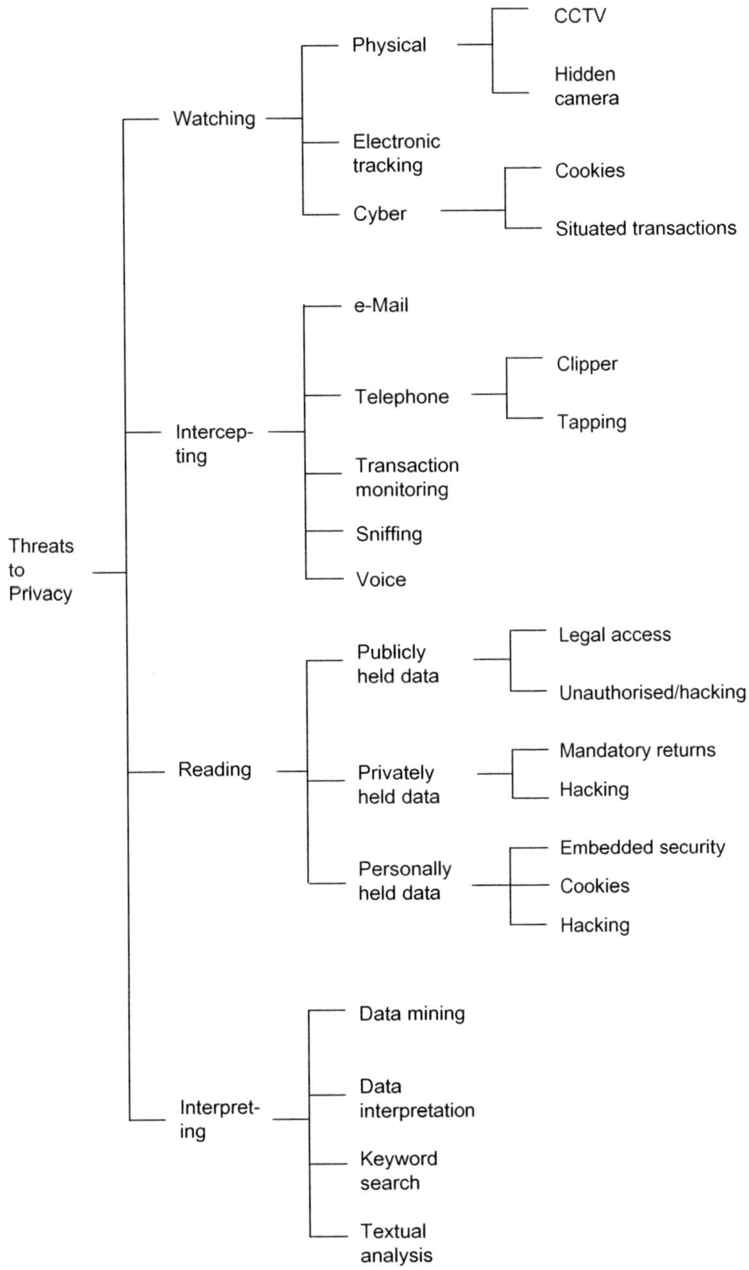

Fig. 3. A taxonomy of electronic threats to privacy.

5. Current protections

Protections of privacy fall into two basic categories: legal and personal. All democratic countries have some degree of privacy protection enacted in their legislation. At the apex of privacy protection is the UN charter of human rights. However charters, even those which have more official backing, such as the EU charter of human rights, need to be enacted into law to have an assured effect.

There are two types of legal protection of privacy. The first form of protection resides in data protection and freedom of information legislation. Under a 1995 Directive, all EU countries are obliged to have data protection acts [26]. Many, though by no means all, have freedom of information acts (see [31] for an overview of the position in Europe). While a data protection act entitles a citizen to know what data the state hold about her, there are some (understandable) restrictions when it comes to police and security matters and these are sometimes sufficiently vague to allow the authorities to claim information as privileged when it is not so. Freedom of information acts have proved a more powerful tool, particularly in the US. But this type of legislation is, at best, a back-handed protection of privacy. The citizen has to know what to look for and where to look for it.

Secondly there is legislation which entitles the state to invade a citizen's privacy, but specifies the terms and conditions under which this may be done. This includes, for example, warrants to search a private premises or tap a private telephone. These laws are extensively supplemented by legislation designed to counter/combat organised crime, illegal immigration and, most important, terrorism. In recent years, there has been a noticeable increase in the police powers in this regard, often in the form of a reduction in current constraints. In the UK and Ireland, these powers have led, if sometimes indirectly, to major injustices.[13]

With this background in mind, we can now turn to the question of risk.

6. The calculus of citizen risk

At the centre of any discussion of citizen privacy *vis a vis* the state is the question of individual and societal risk. While risk is not as difficult to define as privacy, it too contains subjective dimensions which mean that perception of risk varies with personal, social and cultural context. In simple terms risk can be defined as a combination of an undesirable event and the probability of that event occurring.[14] However, in public life the *perception* of risk is usually politically more important than the mathematical reality. Irrational fear, especially on a mass scale, can lead to all sorts of undesirable outcomes, not least a public willingness to cede important freedoms and civil rights in response to what may be an imagined, or even a manufactured, myth of danger. Such behaviour creates a different type of risk, that of misuse by the state of its powers. In this context, two pertinent questions are:

- how real are each of these risks?

and

- what constitutes a balanced risk management policy in the specific area of informational privacy where the answer to the above question is not clear?

6.1. The perception of risk

There are several aspects of risk that are important in any consideration of infringing human rights in general and privacy in particular, in the name of community risk reduction. The first, and most important, is that human perception of risk is often wildly wrong. Human risk perception is biased by a whole

[13]The most notorious example being the 'Birmingham Six' case where innocent people were jailed for over 16 years for a bombing atrocity they did not commit.

[14]How this combining should be done is a good question, but one which is outside the scope of this discussion.

series of cognitive and informational biases [5,20,24,27,30,35]. Misjudgment of risk frequently leads to poor decision making. One of the most common sources of biases, and one of the most important in the context of this discussion, is the phenomenon of availability. We tend to be influenced by information that is to hand or highly visible. It is well known that the risks of death in a road accident are significantly higher per kilometer when travelling in a car than in an aircraft. Yet far more people are afraid of flying than of getting into an automobile. Notwithstanding this, we are, as Adams [1] sardonically points out, all experts on risk.

6.2. The cost of risk reduction

The second point is that risk avoidance or reduction is rarely cost free. The cost may not be financial. It may be in terms of a loss of convenience, pleasure, time or more seriously freedom and control over one's life. The loss of psychological benefit arising from reducing one's intake of high cholesterol foods may be a minor price to pay for reducing the risk of heart disease, but this is only at the bottom of a long scale. A common fear in western society is crime and in particular personal assault. The risk of being assaulted can be severely reduced if not entirely eliminated by living in a gated estate and/or by employing a couple of large bodyguards. Unfortunately, many of the costs of security are be so easily perceptible because, for a majority of citizens, they are socially or temporally remote at the current time. In this context, weaknesses in human capacity to make judgments about the future is a critical problem [32].

6.3. Trading risks

The third characteristic of risk reduction is that reducing one risk often increases another. While putting multiple locks on the apartment door may reduce the risk of being burgled in the middle of the night, it also increases the risk of not being able to get out in time if there is a fire in the building. For certain types of risk reduction, a paradoxical outcome is that individual actions to reduce (real or perceived) personal risk can have adverse communal outcomes and communal actions to reduce risk can have adverse outcomes for individuals. An example of the former, which also illustrates the first characteristic of risk, is the mumps, measles, rubella (MMR) vaccine. Despite the fact that there is no proven link other than some questionable statistical evidence between MMR and autism in children [34] many parents refuse to give their child the MMR vaccine, preferring to take the risk of their child incurring measles, a dangerous and occasionally fatal disease. Similarly, decisions taken to reduce community risk can impact adversely on individuals. In Ireland, for example, the persistent failure of local authorities to get planning permission for waste disposal incinerators has increased the risk of diseases arising from landfill because of the potential for polluted ground water finding its way into drinking water in rural communities.

6.4. Communicating risk

A further problem is the communication of risk. This is an issue that continues to exercise the Royal Statistical Society (RSS) [33]. The Society devoted most of one of its journals to this issue in 2003 when it invited leading statisticians to examine the problems of conveying risk to the public in such areas as coronary heart disease [17], geo-hazards [29] and mobile phones [10].

Earlier, in 1996, this concern about communication, led the then president of the RSS, Adrian Smith, to initiate a project to come up with a method of measuring risk which was accessible to the public. The result was a concept called the 'Riskometer' [11–14]. In essence, the Riskometer endeavored to do for risk what the Richter scale does for earthquakes, i.e. put a complex phenomenon into a single metric which is meaningful to non statisticians/probabilists. The system takes into account both the size of the risk and its impact. The computation of the risk factor, which ranges on a scale from 0 to approximately 8, is moderately complex, but rigorous. The Riskometer tries to cope with widely diverse risks. For example, it attempts to enable a citizen to compare the personal risks arising from a nuclear conflagration with the risk from domestic accidents. It is possible that this approach could useful if adapted to social issues such as privacy and human rights although it has several limitations (see below).

6.5. *Summarising characteristics of risk*

In summary, when considering risk there are six important characteristics that must be borne in mind:

- People do not assess risks accurately;
- Risk reduction generally has a cost;
- Risk reduction in one area may increase risk in another area;
- Mass decisions to reduce individual risk may increase community risk;
- Decisions to reduce community risk may increase individual risk;
- Communicating complex risks to non-specialists is exceedingly difficult.

In a climate of fear, these can have a pernicious effect on privacy. With these characteristics in mind, how risks and privacy rights might be balanced can now be considered.

7. Towards a structural protection of privacy

7.1. *Balancing unknowns*

When it comes to informational privacy, citizens must make trade-offs. Willingness to cede fundamental rights, as opposed to some data, often occurs in a time of turbulence or public panic and the state can take advantage of such circumstances to advance other agendas. Many of the anti-terrorism and anti-crime measures currently on statute books today are there as the direct result of some major event. Often such legislation, rushed in in the aftermath of an atrocity, leads to bad law and serious injustice. The latter occurs because the framework within which such decisions are made is often ill-suited to take account of the long term interests of the community as a whole.

It is tempting to attempt to reduce the problem to a set of parameters, to develop a sort of 'Privometer' along the lines of Duckworth's Riskometer. However complex problems of this type cannot be reduced to simple parameters, to the tyranny of numbers [7]. Such an approach is replete with problems. Most people would prefer that the government was not able to follow their every movement, listen to their conversations or read their mail. At the same time they would like the government to capture terrorists or seize drugs before they cause public harm. Putting a value or measure on these feelings is hard. There are other, even less easy to quantify risks, for example that a future totalitarian government (or even an unscrupulous democratic one) could use personal information to harass or intimidate dissenters or that such information could fall into the hands of unauthorised individuals who could exploit it for blackmail, extortion or even legitimate, but unwanted activities (such as sending junk mail). Furthermore, as the great majority of the population are unlikely ever to be affected by these problems, so computing some sort of social cost becomes even more problematic.

The tendency for the 'right minded' is therefore to let it pass on the grounds that it will never affect them. An eloquent warning of the dangers of this type of thinking can be found in the words of freeborn John Lilbourne which resonate today as much today as they did in the 17th century:

> "... *for what is done to any one, may be done to every one: besides, being all members of one body, that is, of the English Commonwealth, one man should not suffer wrongfully, but all should be sensible, and endeavour his preservation; otherwise they give way to an inlet of the sea of will and power; upon all their laws and liberties, which are the boundaries to keep out tyranny and oppression; and who assists not in such cases, betrays his own rights, and is overrun, and of a free man made a slave when he thinks not of it, or regards it not, and so shunning the censure of turbulency, incurs the guilt of treachery of the present and future generations*".

(John Lilbourne (1614–1657) The Just Defence of John Lilbourne Against such as Charge him with Turbulency of Spirit (London: 1653)).

The problem can be summarised thus: notwithstanding the large number of groups monitoring and campaigning on this issue it is unlikely that *effective* initiatives to protect privacy will emerge from public concern through normal democratic channels. Governments cannot always be trusted to take such issues into account and even well-meaning politicians often overreact to extreme events with the result that existing legal protections are often subject to attack, even from the great and the good. History is littered with examples of the ability of politicians to exploit fear for their own ends and times when the great and the good stood idly by. It is well to remember Edward Burke's dictum that: "*all that is necessary for the triumph of evil is that good men should do nothing*".

7.2. Protecting privacy

A number of actions can be taken to improve the protection of individual privacy. The following are some suggestions.

First, a government could establish a standing body with sufficient collective expertise and a broad enough view to judge what should be permissible, where lines should be drawn *and to judge the balance of risks*. Such a body would need to both understand the human rights, political, security and risk aspects of privacy and be in a position to make balanced judgments. It is essential that this body have both political legitimacy, autonomy and authority. Current structures, such as data protection and freedom of information commissioners are useful, but their *raison d'être* is to ensure that governments and other bodies abide by the *established* rules. Consultation processes, such as the that undertaken by the UK PIU, are valuable, but they are, by definition, transitory. In the UK and Ireland, for example, once the law is enacted, interpretation becomes a matter for courts, public servants and commissioners who often assess the law on a case by case basis (although practice elsewhere in Europe varies). In the case of a court, its function is to adjudicate on facts of the case before it given the body of law, not to assess long term risks to the community. What is therefore needed is a standing body with democratic credentials, access to expertise and sufficient power to influence events and to prevent any government going beyond the limits of the reasonable.

One model for this might be a Privacy Council. This could be appointed, not by universal franchise (which would be too expensive), but, say, along the lines of the Irish Senate where different stakeholder groups (unions, employers, universities, local authorities, civil liberties groups and the government itself) have representation. The Council should have rights to scrutinise and make recommendations for changes in any legislation which is likely to affect the privacy of individuals.

Secondly, anti-privacy legislation and powers should never be permanent. State surveillance, data collection and retention powers should have to be renewed periodically by a full vote in the legislature. This would not only remind parliamentarians about these laws (which are often forgotten or misunderstood), but would also permit the different mores and circumstances of different times to be reflected in those laws. It is not inconceivable that at some more libertarian or less dangerous point in history, the community will come to regard many current practices as unacceptable. It also has the benefit of keeping the public aware of just what the laws are and what powers the authorities retain. Concomitant with this, anti privacy legislation should have clear procedures for appeals and complaints dealt with by an independent ombudsman.

Thirdly, there should be regular independent reviews and audits of 'routine' personal data used by the state. This is to ensure that there is a proven necessity to retain each item of data, that data which is temporary is duly erased and that access controls and security of data are watertight. Current data protection legislation requires much of this, what is often lacking is any routine audit of these procedures and controls to ensure that public servants comply with the rules.

Fourthly, there is a need for more research work on balancing the risks discussed in this paper and for a wider public debate on risk in this context. Much of the literature on privacy is about rights. Risks are less commonly discussed. The objective of such a discussion would not be to reduce the issue to a debate about cold-blooded utilitarianism, nor to rely on public opinion in a time of crisis, but to inform public and political discourse. If, ultimately, certain aspects of this debate have to be reduced to measurable parameters as an aid to decision making, so be it, but it should neither degenerate into a pure numbers game nor a politically driven agenda. This is not easy territory and takes the debate into areas that have taxed philosophers over three millennia. But what was, for John Lilbourne in the 17th century, a danger with no realistic prospect of realisation, is today a pressing problem and an all too real possibility. In the past, humanity could afford the luxury of contemplating these problems in the abstract. Now there is a need for action. The mechanisms to achieve this may need to be, in a certain sense, messy, but the principles underneath should be clear. A common criticism of utilitarianism is that dehumanises our humanity. If this be true, how much worse is an ill-informed utilitarianism?

8. Conclusion

Privacy, like freedom, is a valuable good which may be traded voluntarily for other goods or benefits. These benefits include both private goods, public services, security and membership of the community. The ability of citizens to judge collectively and correctly this trade-off is at the heart of a free society. This paper has argued that individuals and societies do not always judge this risk well and that one of the distorting factors is availability, the nature and impact of the information on different types of risk. Consequently societies face a structural danger of adverse consequences way out of proportion to the security and (less frequently) the service benefits gained. In the horror of seeing somebody live on TV jumping from the World Trade Centre, a minor step like requiring visitors to one's country to have their fingerprints in their passports seems such a small thing to ask and anyway, it only applies to foreigners. Yet it is precisely an accumulation of such small judgments that may, cumulatively, place the privacy of all in peril. If the US insists on all foreigners having fingerprints or retina scan data in passports, then the EU will probably follow suit as will Russia and China and other even less democratic regimes. And if for foreigners, why not for citizens? And if the constitution forbids us from spying on our own citizens, never mind, we can get the neighbouring government to do it for us and exchange data. In a short step society has moved from a state where only criminals or those accused of a crime can be fingerprinted, to a state where everyone is fingerprinted. Follow this logic, and it is only a matter of time before this is true of DNA. In such a world, the state would know the very essence of each citizen's genetic makeup.

"*Every man*", wrote the English poet John Donne, "*is a piece of the continent, a part of the main*". What is done to the privacy of one today may be done to all tomorrow. Against the risk of terrorism and crime, the risk to individual privacy must be re-balanced. A mechanism for balancing these risks which is accountable, understandable and understood is urgently required. This paper has proposed one such approach, but this issue needs more debate. Without suitable mechanisms to protect their long term freedoms, societies risk stumbling into a situation out of which it may be difficult to reverse and history offers some fearful lessons which must never be forgotten. Before ceding any freedom or right, it is always wise to remember the evocative words of Joni Mitchell: "*Don't it always seem the same, that you don't know what you've got till it's gone*".

References

[1] J. Adams, *Risk*, UCL Press, London, 1995.
[2] I. Amato, Big brother logs on, *Technological Review* **104** (2001), 7–58.
[3] K. Ball, Element of surveillance: a new framework and future directions, *Information, Communications and Society* **5**(4) (2002), 573–590.
[4] J. Bamford, *Body of Secrets: How America's NSA and the UK's GCHQ Eavesdrop on the World*, Century Books, London, 2001.
[5] M. Bazerman, *Managerial Decision Making*, (5th Ed.), Wiley, New York, 2002.
[6] J. Boag-Thomson, *Keeping Watch on the Watchers*, The Scotsman, June 20th, 2001.
[7] D. Boyle, *The Sum of Our Discontent: Why Numbers Make us Irrational*, Texere, 2001.
[8] J. Carroll, *Computer Security*, Butterworth-Heinemann, Boston, 1996.
[9] F. Cate, Principles for Protecting Privacy, *Cato Journal* **Spring/Summer 22**(1) (2002), 33–57.
[10] D. Cox, Communication of risk: Health hazards from mobile phones, *Journal of the Royal Statistical Society* **Series A, 166**(2) (2003), 225–232.
[11] F. Duckworth, Editorial: An RSS Riskometer? *RSS Newsletter* **24**(4) (1996).
[12] F. Duckworth, Editorial: A Lifetime of Risk, *RSS Newsletter* (October, 1998)
[13] F. Duckworth, The Quantification of Risk, *RSS Newsletter* (October, 1998).
[14] F. Duckworth, Editorial: Risk and Rationality, *RSS Newsletter* **27**(6) (2000).
[15] Federation of American Scientists, *Espionage: The French Listen In To Their Allies as Well*, http://www.fas.org/irp/news/1998/06/980606-sigint.htm, 1998.
[16] D. Gollmann, *Computer Security*, Wiley, 1999.
[17] I. Graham and E. Clavel, Communicating risk – coronary risk scores, *Journal of the Royal Statistical Society* **Series A, 166**(2) (2003), 217–224.
[18] House of Commons, *Regulation of Investigatory Powers Act, HMSO*, London. Available on-line at: www.hmso.gov.uk/acts/acts2000/20000023.htm, 2000.
[19] L. Introna and A. Pouloudi, Privacy in the information age: Stakeholders, interests and values, *Journal of Business Ethics* **22**(1) (1999), 27–38.
[20] D. Kahneman and A. Tversky, Judgment under Uncertainty: Heuristics and Biases, in: *Judgment under Uncertainty: Heuristics and Biases*, D. Kahneman and A. Tversky, eds, Cambridge University Press, 1982, pp. 3–22.
[21] S. Levy, *Crypto*, Viking (Penguin books), Harmondsworth, UK, 2001.
[22] J. Leyden, *Germany, Austria take stand against EU ISP data retention laws*, The Register, 21st November, available at: www.theregister.co.uk/content/6/28228.html, 2002.
[23] R. McArthur, Reasonable expectations of privacy, *Ethics and Information Technology* **3**(2) (2001), 123–128.
[24] D. Myers, *Intuition: Its Powers and Perils*, Yale University Press, New Haven, CT, 2002.
[25] Official Journal of the European Communities, *Charter of Fundamental Human Rights*, The European Commission, 2000/C 364/01, 2000.
[26] Official Journal of the European Communities, *Directive 95/46/EC of the European Parliament and of the Council of 24 October 1995 on the protection of individuals with regard to the processing of personal data and on the free movement of such data*, No L. 281, p. 31, 23 November, 1995.
[27] S. Plous, *The Psychology of Judgment and Decision Making*, McGraw-Hill, New York, 1993.

[28] Policy and Innovation Unit, *Privacy and Data Sharing: The way forward for public services*, www.strategy.gov.uk/2002/privacy/report/, 2002.

[29] M. Rosenbaum and M. Culshaw, Communicating risk arising from geohazards, *Journal of the Royal Statistical Society* **Series A, 166**(2) (2003), 261–270.

[30] P. Slovic, F. Baruch and S. Lichtenstein, Facts versus fears: Understanding perceived risk, in: *Judgment under Uncertainty: Heuristics and Biases*, D. Kahneman and A. Tversky, eds, Cambridge University Press, 1982, pp. 463–492.

[31] Sobotta, Christoph, *Freedom of Information in the European Union and Elsewhere*, http://www.rz.uni-frankfurt.de/~sobotta/FOI.htm, 2003.

[32] B. Schwartz, *The Paradox of Choice*, Harpur Collins, New York, 2004.

[33] A. Smith, Foreword to the papers on 'The communication of risk', *Journal of the Royal Statistical Society* **166**(2) (2003), 205–206.

[34] B. Taylor, E. Miller, R. Lingam, N. Andrews, A. Simmons and J. Stowe, Measles, mumps, and rubella vaccination and bowel problems or developmental regression in children with autism: population study, *British Medical Journal* **324** (2002), 393–396.

[35] A. Tversky and D. Kahneman, Availability: A heuristic for judging frequency and probability, in: *Judgment under Uncertainty: Heuristics and Biases*, D. Kahneman and A. Tversky, eds, Cambridge University Press, 1982, pp. 163–178.

[36] United Nations, *Universal Declaration of Human Rights*, Available at: www.un.org/Overview/rights.html, 1948.

[37] Wall Street Journal, *Tuesday's Attack Forces an Agonizing Decision on Americans – Government Eye Deters Terror but Can Exact A Terrible Price*, by Charles Goldsmith and David Pringle in London and Paulo Prada, September 14, 2001.

[38] C. Webster, Changing Relationships Between Citizens and the State: The Case of Closed Circuit Television Cameras, in: *Public Administration in and Information Age*, I. Snellen and W. van de Donk, eds, IOS Press, Amsterdam, 1998, pp. 79–96.

Information, Innovation and Risk

Information Polity 10 (2005) 81–94
IOS Press

Smartening up to risk in electronic government

Helen Margetts
Oxford Internet Institute, University of Oxford, One St Giles, Oxford OX1 3JS, UK
Tel.: +44 1865 287207; E-mail: helen.margetts@oii.ox.ac.uk

Abstract. This article identifies emerging risks in electronic government: the risk of government lagging behind a 'smart' society, where increasing proportions of citizens and businesses are accustomed to conduct their affairs electronically; risk involved in information technology outsourcing; and risk brought about by the integration of technology into governmental activities, particularly policy innovation. All three represent the introduction of risks more commonly associated with the private sector into government. For each of these three risk factors, the article suggests some potential strategies for dealing with them. First, government needs to use the capability of internet-based technologies to understand 'smart society' more fully. Second, the UK government in particular needs to develop a more relational style of contracting and learn from the sharp variations in contracting regimes across the world. Third, leaders of governmental organisations need to accept that digital technologies are now at the core of a wide range of their activities and adapt policy-making processes accordingly.

1. Introduction

At the heart of every definition of risk is the notion of uncertainty. For example, risk is given as 'a negative outcome that has a known or estimated probability of occurrence based on experience or some theory' [24]; 'the possibility of an adverse consequence causing loss, damage or injury' [9, p. 119]; or (more obliquely) 'the uncertainty of outcome, within a range of potential exposures, arising from a combination of the impact and probability of potential events' [18]. Contrary to all early assumptions about the rationalizing power of computers in administration, evidence from the last fifty years of computerisation in government leaves no doubt that technology has injected uncertainty into the heart of government [29] – with subsequently higher levels of risk for many public sector operations in the age of electronic government.

It has been accepted for over two decades that some degree of risk is involved in all information systems projects [31, p. 2]. Early studies of public sector risk engendered by information technology (IT) focused on the characteristics of specific projects and the technological capabilities of individual government organisations, delineating two key types: project risk and organisational risk. Project risk referred to requirements and specifications, the technical uncertainty of the technologies involved in the project and the commitment to and need of the project itself. Organizational risk referred to how equipped the organization was to implement the project in terms of personnel, skills and experience. These studies were generally applied to the development of information systems across both public and private sectors, although Margetts and Willcocks [31,32] examined the distinctiveness of risks involved in public sector IT projects. The UK government IT advisory body [5] adopted a framework developed by Parker et al. [37] with some modifications for public sector circumstances.

1570-1255/05/$17.00

Were there any doubt that information technology brings risk to public administration in the UK, it would quickly be assuaged by a number of high profile and expensive disasters over the last two decades. In the early 1990s Margetts and Willcocks [32] summed up some notorious IT projects of the time under the heading 'Information Technology in Public Services: Disaster Faster?' Since then the Passports Agency (in 2001, when a new system for allocating passports was paralysed), the Contributions Agency (with the second version of the National Insurance Recording System), the Child Support Agency (in 2002, when the cost of a new system rocketed to £200 million, £50 million over budget), the Immigration and Naturalisation Directorate (left with 12,000 letters unanswered after a new system was delayed and finally abandoned in 2001), the Benefits Agency (in a joint project with the Post Office to computerise the Post Office network and create a new benefits payment card system in local offices, finally cancelled with no result in 2001 at a cost of £1 billion) provide just a subset of examples of government agencies which have suffered major and costly failure of information systems or projects (for a list of 15 recent UK disasters see [36, p. 32]). Research evidence backs up politicians' views that in the UK, 'government + IT = disaster' (a claim made by Liberal Democrat MP Richard Allen at an Institute of Public Policy Research seminar, Westminster House, London March 2004) and *"Great big IT projects, databases and the rest of it have a horrible habit of going wrong"* (a depressingly frank comment made by then UK trade secretary, Patricia Hewitt on the BBC programme Question Time, in October 2003). For example, the UK scored badly against the US, Japan, Australia, Canada, New Zealand and the Netherlands for the scrap rate of government IT projects in a seven country study funded by the UK Economic and Social Research Council [13].

However, rather than go over the well-documented risks involved in large-scale computerisation projects the purpose of this paper is to investigate the extent to which the level of risk in government information systems development has increased with the rising pace of technological innovation, as claimed by Heywood [17, p. 203]: *"The accelerating rate of change means that each and every investment an organization makes becomes ever more risky"*. As use of information systems has become widespread throughout government, e-government, or electronic government – government which uses information technology internally and in its interactions with the outside world – has become a widely used term. For electronic government, traditional risks seem to have changed in important ways, perhaps even been superseded by new types of risk. This short essay identifies three emerging types of risk to which government agencies are prone through the development and use of information systems and suggests some strategies for risk mitigation for each of them.

2. Lagging behind 'smart' society

First, the increasing pace of technological change introduces the risk of not using technological innovation to achieve various benefits. The key breakpoint here is the widespread use of the Internet and web-based technologies. Earlier information technologies were largely internally facing, with few visible implications for the ways in which government agencies and citizens, businesses or agencies from other governments interacted. But rising use of the Internet by all sectors of society and the capacity of Internet-based technologies to link organisations and individuals brings in real possibility for transformation of the way that government interacts with the outside world. In a recent report on risk in government, the UK National Audit Office [34, p. 1] cites in particular the IT-specific risk of not using available technologies to increase efficiency of the public sector and allow access to public services more quickly, 24 hours a day: *"Citizens and businesses can lose out if departments are slow to adopt new forms of cost-effective service delivery made possible by innovation and technological advances"*.

In short, government runs the risk of lagging behind an increasingly 'smart' citizenry and business world. As citizens increasingly interact with shops, banks and travel agents on-line, they will increasingly question why they cannot do the same with government. Likewise, if businesses (as they do in most developed countries) undertake an increasing proportion of transactions electronically, dealings with government that have to take place on paper will begin to appear anachronistic. In fact government agencies do appear to lag behind the private sector and voluntary organisations in their development of e-based services (see [10,11]). The UK government seems particularly prone to this risk, lagging behind other developed governments in provision of e-government services comparable with UK e-commerce [13] and with a poor record of e-government usage in comparison with the e-economy; in 2003 18 per cent of UK adults had used some kind of e-government services (including merely seeking information on a government site), compared with 44 per cent in the US and 52 per cent in the Netherlands [38]. Likewise, by the end of 2003 only 3 per cent of UK income tax forms were returned on-line, compared with 58 per cent in the US. Some commentators have already suggested that in this way government can run the risk of experiencing a net loss of 'nodality' (defined as centrality in social and informational networks [21]) in the information age [34], thereby weakening one of the key tools of government policy.

The continuing 'smartness' in technology terms among citizens and the business world mean that this risk can only increase in countries where e-government has been slow to develop. Levels of Internet penetration in society have risen to over 50 per cent in the UK and well over that in many other countries, particularly the US, Canada and Scandinavian countries. By 2001, over 50 per cent of UK adults live in households with personal computers [6, p. 32], double the figure of a decade previously. The percentage of businesses on line is rising even more rapidly, 81 per cent of UK businesses in 2001 up from 63 per cent in 2000. Meanwhile, many UK government officials cannot see the web site of their own organisation while they are at work due to infrastructural problems and 95 per cent of VAT traders pay their VAT by cheque, while levels of on-line banking services among the SME sector soar [33]. It is possible to imagine a scenario in the near future where businesses maintain company chequebooks only to pay HM Customs and Excise and perhaps some other government bodies. At this point the banks themselves may start to question why they are keeping some paper-based channels open only for dealing with government. In this way, the increasing use of technological innovation by organisations outside government put pressure on government agencies to innovate, whether they feel like taking the risk or not. Private sector organisations are used to this type of risk, as competitive pressures mean they must always estimate the cost of not doing something. Airlines were early innovators for this reason, as if their competitors were developing on-line booking systems then failure to do so would run the risk of losing market share. But if usage levels of web-based technologies, mobile phones and other innovations in society continue to rise, then government could also find themselves having to develop on-line solutions in situations where the cost of not doing so becomes too great (if banks were to phase out cheques, for example). As Holmes [20, p. 11] put it, "Governments that stick to the old ways of doing business will further open themselves to ridicule and accusations of incompetence and corruption". And some commentators have started to suggest that citizens should be made aware of the differential costs of paper-based and on-line transactions and even compelled to use the latter in the name of transparency (see [7]).

In addition to the risk of not using technology in this way, there is of course the risk of using it unsuccessfully, in terms of value for money or reaching citizens and businesses. As NAO [34, p. 1] put it, *"there are risks involved with doing things differently and new forms of service delivery need to be implemented in a way that minimises the risk of them failing or the quality of public services not being maintained or improved"*. In addition to the by now familiar risks associated with IT projects, such risks include developing on-line services which citizens and businesses do not use: by 2003, the percentage of UK citizens filing taxes on-line, for example, had fallen way behind those of the US, Australia and other countries and the percentage of businesses using a pilot electronic VAT return system was running at 0.02 per cent while in Denmark (for example) take-up of the on-line VAT service was 29 per cent in 2002 and has been doubling every year since it was introduced in 1998 [33].

3. Tackling risks arising from pace of technological change: 'Smart' government

To minimise risk in keeping pace with technological development, government agencies should take advantage of the distinctive nature of new web-based technologies. The Internet and web-based technologies lend themselves to a 'build-and-learn' technique of administration (see [10]), while many government agencies are trying to apply techniques learnt on earlier information technologies; that is, large-scale long-term IT projects, requiring large scale capital investment and long payback periods. The UK civil service provides an example here. In 2002 the UK Customs and Excise department embarked on a long-term period of systems transformation, at a cost of £50 million per year, whereby its systems would be rationalized by 2009. Meanwhile it operated a poor web site and almost all small and medium-sized enterprises (SMEs) interacted with the organisation on paper. In contrast, during the 1990s the US Internal Revenue Service successfully developed an electronic filing service that ran in parallel with the expensive, problematic and as yet unfulfilled Tax Systems Modernization project to rationalize the agency's internal information systems. In general, as the pace of technological change speeds up, projects need to be of shorter duration, to avoid continual outdating of equipment and applications.

With respect to avoiding the risk of not entering 'smart society', government agencies need to use the key advantage of the Internet cited by e-business – the ability to know their customer base. As the director of Dell Computer's e-commerce put it, *"The Internet has turbocharged our ability to understand our customers"* [8, p. 1]. While companies use this characteristic of the Internet to reduce the cost of collecting buyer preference information and managing multiple prices to allow cost efficient custom product design [8], government agencies in the UK tend to be bad at understanding their customers' behaviour or researching what type of services they might use. Yet research of this kind is the key way that government agencies can minimise the risk of building on-line applications that citizens and businesses do not actually use. Obviously the reasons why citizens and businesses will use e-government are different from the reasons why customers will buy products. It is more difficult to introduce 'expressive' elements to the decision to file taxes on-line, for example, because basically there is little choice involved (although it might be the case that some technologically-minded citizens would gain a modernist satisfaction from dealing with government on-line). However, in obtaining information about what their customers would be likely to use, there is much that government agencies could learn from private sector companies. On-line banks, for example, use ethnographic research and stimulus based surveys to find out how prospective and actual customers respond to prototype web sites and on-line services. It is hard to identify a UK government agency that carries out similar activities. Even for older methods of interacting with citizens and business (such as the design of government forms) hardly any agencies have ever carried out focus group research [35]. In contrast, Canada's position as the world leader in e-government in many international rankings (see for example [1–4]) has been ascribed, at least in the part, to the fact that Canada makes more effort to survey citizens than any other country; in 2002–2003 more than 10,000 Canadians participated in e-government surveys and focus groups.

4. Risks from information technology outsourcing

The ways in which government information systems are now developed introduce distinctive risks. In the early days of IT, governments like the US and the UK developed their own IT systems, but by 2003 governments across the world varied enormously in the extent to which they used private sector providers to develop and maintain their information technology. In the US, around half to three-quarters of federal government IT is outsourced while in Canada, this proportion is much lower. Likewise, the markets of computer services providers to government vary greatly: in the Netherlands and Japan, these markets are dominated by domestic companies while in Australia and the UK the markets are dominated by global corporations, particularly the giant Electronic Data Systems (EDS). Radical outsourcing of IT by the UK government in particular means that virtually no UK departments or agencies manage their own information systems and EDS manages over 65 per cent of central government IT spend. So UK government information systems are developed and maintained through a range of long-term large-scale contracts introducing specific risks relating to relationship management.

The risks relating to outsourcing have been analysed in a general sense (i.e. for organisations of all kinds, not just government) by various specialists in information technology and business management. Lacity and Willcocks [26] identify the following 'risk factors' in IT outsourcing:

- Treating IT as an undifferentiated commodity to be outsourced;
- Incomplete contracting;
- Lack of active management of the supplier on contract and relationship dimensions;
- Failure to build and retain requisite in-house capabilities and skills;
- Power asymmetries developing in favour of the vendor;
- Difficulties in constructing and adapting deals in the face of rapid business/technical change;
- Lack of maturity and experience of contracting for and managing 'total' outsourcing arrangements;
- Outsourcing for short-term financial restructuring or cash injection rather than to levering IT assets for business advantage;
- Unrealistic expectations with multiple objectives for outsourcing;
- Poor sourcing and contracting for development and new technologies.

Source: [26, p. 205].

Research into outsourcing in general suggests that "an important distinction must be made between the risks that arise from the contracting process – the separation of the purchaser from the provider – and the risks that are inherent to the activity being contracted" [9, p. 123]. Therefore, while these newer risks enter government, those inherent in development of IT systems remain. The UK government has experimented with ways of transferring these inherent IT-based risks to private sector vendors (see below), but that does not mean that they disappear: recent UK experience has shown these companies grappling with just the type of problems experienced by government agencies in the past.

The shape of government contracts means that these general risks of outsourcing are distinctive when applied to government in general and to the UK in particular. Extensive research into IT outsourcing specifically suggests that *"long-term, large-scale, single-supplier deals have been particularly risky"* and that *"even proponents of this approach point out that it can be a high risk strategy"* [26, p. 203]. Therefore, the UK pattern of very large IT contracts with very large companies (see [13,29]) seems likely to be particularly prone to risk. An important factor in making the UK's contracting regime distinctive in terms of long-term and large-scale contracts has been the Treasury's Private Finance Initiative (PFI), an arrangement for procurement whereby the public sector contracts to purchase services on a long-term basis so as to *"take advantage of private sector management skills incentivized by having private sector finance at risk*" and now accounting for around 11 per cent of public service investment, around £4.6 billion in 2003 [19, p. 3]. Indeed, as this definition suggests, the transfer of risk away from the public sector was at the heart of the idea of PFI: use of PFI was intended "to introduce third-party finance into IT projects to effect risk transfer, impose further commercial discipline and ensure risk mitigation in the delivery of IT contracts" [19, p. 54]. The idea is that the public sector retains some of the risk of a conventionally procured project, such as:

- the need for the facility on the date given and the adequacy of its overall size to meet public service needs,
- the possibility of a change in public sector requirements in the future,
- whether the standards of delivery set by the public sector sufficiently meet public needs,
- the extent to which the facility is used or not over the contracts life and
- general inflation risk.

The risks that are transferred are:

- meeting required standards of delivery;
- cost overrun risk during development;
- timely completion of the facility; underlying costs to the operator of service delivery and the future costs associated with the asset;
- risk of industrial action or physical damage to the asset;
- certain market risks [19, p. 36].

However, the distinctive features of risk engendered by information technology as opposed to other types of activity funded through PFI, such as construction, were eventually recognised by the Treasury itself, whose 2003 review of PFI [19] outlined the differences between IT procurement and other types of contracting. In particular it noted the following as reasons why risk transfer in IT projects was not successful through PFI [19, p. 56]:

- Difficulty of specifying requirements, due to the close links between IT infrastructure and organisational operational needs combined with the rapid pace of technological change;
- Difficulty of substituting suppliers;
- Lack of third-party finance, "removing a powerful driver ensuring appropriate and effective risk allocation in a project" [19, p. 87];
- Nature of capital investment, where project assets often account for less than a third of the present value of projects;
- Duration and phasing of investment, typically shorter than that of PFI projects in other sectors.

For these reasons, and in particular "the difficulties with achieving appropriate risk transfer in IT PFI", the Treasury abandoned PFI for IT projects and return to conventional procurement methods. However, the legacy is there in a number of long-term high-value partnerships between UK government departments and their suppliers. PFI fuelled the existing trends for UK government IT contracts to increase in size, and for the distinctive shape of the UK contracting market, meaning that the risks associated with large-scale long-term contracts will be a feature of UK government IT contracting for decades to come. Additional risks may be introduced where the outsourced activity is actually carried out abroad, as in the US where public sector IT has been outsourced to India and other offshore locations, amid heated political debate.

5. Tackling risks from contracting: Relationship management and reshaping government contracting regimes

As with information technology development itself, *"nowhere does the outsourcing of IT emerge as anywhere near a low risk enterprise"* [26, p. 204]. Although the same authors bemoan the fact that *"practitioners have not been aided by the surprisingly scant systematic attention given to risk issues"*, some research has identified risk mitigation techniques and frameworks (see [25,26,41]), which endeavour to minimise the risk factors inherent in IT outsourcing noted above. Two key risks that have received less attention in terms of mitigation are the retention of in-house capabilities and the formation, development and sustaining of client/vendor relationships. Both these have proved particular problems for government agencies in general and for government organisations in the UK in particular. But examples from overseas governments and from the private sector provide some examples of more successful risk mitigation strategies.

With respect to risks associated with failing to retain in-house capability and total dependence on computer services providers, many of the partnerships entered into by UK government agencies come into the category of 'total outsourcing', that is with over 80 per cent of the IT budget under third party management of a single or multiple suppliers. Clearly, in such arrangements the likelihood of retaining sufficient in-house expertise to mitigate against risk is reduced. Governments in other countries have evolved highly distinctive 'contracting regimes' [13,14] where more capabilities are retained within government. In Canada and most European countries, levels of outsourcing are extremely low and government agencies retain far more expertise in-house. The Canada Customs and Revenue Agency for example, contracts out around 1 per cent of its IT budget. Canada's reputation as a world leader in e-government suggests that this strategy has to some extent been successful. In the Netherlands, companies looking for contracts need to "work their way up from the work floor" and work with smaller contracts than they might in other countries, as Cap Gemini claims to have done. Thus while Cap Gemini in the UK goes for big outsourcing deals, Cap Gemini in the Netherlands has started with small IT assignments tendered by personnel faced with specific problems. Other governments also provide examples of more diffuse markets of computer services providers, with less risk of dependence on a few huge suppliers. In the US, for example, federal regulations geared at preserving competition in contracting and carving out a role for small companies appear to have been successful in maintaining a far less oligopolistic market than the UK. While in the UK the top five companies held about 90 per cent of the IT contracting market in 2001, in the US this figure was only 20 per cent.

UK practice in terms of the percentage of IT activity that is outsourced is increasingly out of line with private sector practice. Extensive research on outsourcing in the private sector has found that although *"One could be forgiven for believing this type of total outsourcing to be the dominant trend . . . globally, this is the reverse of the case"* [40, p. 18]. In fact, total outsourcing is a minority pursuit (8 per cent of organizations in the US and 2 per cent in the UK) and by far the dominant mode is 'selective sourcing', especially in the USA (82 per cent of organizations) and the UK (75 per cent). These type of arrangements generally see around 15–25 per cent of the IT budget under third party management, with other IT needs met through buying in resources under in-house management and internal IT staffing. Many organizations (10 per cent in the USA and 23 per cent in the UK) have no significant IT outsourcing contracts. An early example of a company to move back this way was the US corporation Sears, who in contrast to the trend within many government agencies, cut back its use of IT contracts from 40 per cent to 16 per cent in the late 1990s and employs a unit of staff dedicated to recruiting information technology staff. Overall the company aims to achieve a 92 per cent to 8 per cent staff-contractors ratio (*Computer Weekly,* 17th December 1998).

All this evidence points to a strong argument for smaller scale, shorter-term contract arrangements. It seems likely that, in the UK, the withdrawal of PFI for IT procurement will help in moving towards such type of arrangements. But many PFI deals for IT projects are destined to be in operation for many years to come. Furthermore, the concentrated nature of the IT outsourcing market in the UK noted above makes it difficult to move away from the particularly risky sole-supplier arrangements. In contrast to the UK, in the Netherlands, government ministries deliberately avoid the risk of becoming too reliant on one supplier. The market is dominated by a neo-corporatist arrangement of domestic players building up personal networks with government agencies. There is some change in the market – as companies leading the field in the US, UK and Australasia try to penetrate the European market – but the most aggressive of these companies, unwilling to go through the painful process of gaining experience of the Dutch culture, find it hard to gain a foothold.

Another way of mitigating against risk factors must be through tackling questions of relationship management noted above. In the private sector, 'relational contracting' emphasises the relationship aspect, rather than the rules and regulations associated with the contract. Research from private sector outsourcing experience indicates that relationship management is a crucial factor in the overall success or failure of an outsourcing arrangement ([16, p. 223]; [26,41]). Governmental organisations have always found this type of contracting difficult, with fear of allegations of 'sleaze' and 'capture' driving officials to operate a rule-based model which restricts private sector profits (see [27]). The style of contracting in the UK typifies this characteristic of government contracting, with even the largest of contracts characterised by their low-trust, adversarial nature which many IT vendors suggest do not come into the category of partnership. These arrangements, as in the US, Australia and New Zealand typify an 'Anglo-Saxon' model of contracting. Asymmetries of expertise evoke insecurity in government officials who respond with 'control tendency' characteristics [29]. Under this model, contracts are adversarily managed, with all efforts geared towards price reductions. Tenders are tightly negotiated and as one observer noted after the disastrous Pathway project, a contract between the Benefits Agency, the Post Office and ICL, the *"Post Office has a history of over defining requirements"*. The UK government's obsessional 'control tendency' approach to contract management works against the development of relationships – although always called partnerships, the emphasis is always on the contract rather than the relationship. As the head of UK contracts for one firm put it in an interview with the author, *"there is far more emphasis on culture and relationships ... in the private sector than there is in the public and that I think is fundamentally the problem of why government contracts don't work"* (Interview, 4th September 2002).

For relationship management, there could well be lessons for the UK from across Europe and in particular from the Netherlands, where another contracting model is observable – the Rhineland model. The Rhineland model is the contracting equivalent of the 'Rhineland' economic model where a regulated market economy relies heavily on consultation between government, employers' organisations and labour unions – where stakeholders or interested parties try to achieve harmony, a balance between market forces and social and environmental responsibility. In the "polder" model, developed to overcome some of the inefficiencies of the Rhineland model, labour market flexibility in terms of an increase in part-time work, decentralisation of wage bargaining and reforms to the benefit system play a key role – although some commentators have cast doubts on Dutch success or ascribed it to moves towards the Anglo Saxon model rather than a re-emphasising of characteristics of the Rhineland model.[1] In contracting terms, participants view the Rhineland model as one based on consensus between parties, with the minimal possible confrontation and conflict. It is characterised as typical of Germany, Scandinavia,

[1] Speech by EU commissioner Fritz Bolkestein, Brussels, 5th December 2000.

the Netherlands and France although in the Netherlands, such an extreme version is visible that some officials described it as the 'polder model' – Dutch exceptionalism. While in the Anglo Saxon model financial control is more important than a good relationship, the Rhineland model involves consensus, discussion and mutual support (what could be labelled a relational model). The emphasis is on developing relationships between client and vendor; as one CEO of a Dutch computer services provider put it, in this environment "client knowledge is as important as professional knowledge".

6. Integration of technology, business processes and policy innovation

A third way in which new risks are entering public administration through use of information technology is the increasing dependence of policy innovation on technological innovation. Indeed, some commentators have observed a new tendency for technological innovation to drive policy innovation, rather than the other way round [33]. Some authors have pointed to the capability of new technologies to solve problems that otherwise appear to be market failures, thereby suggesting that "technological advancement tends to enhance the case for free-enterprise policy" [15, p. 1]. The congestion charge policy introduced in London in 2003, whereby all motorists must pay a charge before or immediately after entering the central zone, could not have worked without complex information systems and an Internet payment facility which the majority of payers are using (*Guardian*, 4 September 2003). Emerging issues such as cyber-terrorism, cyber-crime, e-commerce require technological policy solutions to deal with them. Once new forms of information storage and manipulation such as stem cell research, DNA databases and genetic modification become possible, new policies also become possible and new forms of regulation become essential to deal with the creation and control of new data forms. For example, once police organisations have developed a database of DNA samples taken from crime suspects, as they have in the UK, the database by its very existence makes new kinds of policing possible through data management and proactive search capabilities.

This increasing integration of technology into business processes of all kinds means that it is increasingly difficult to separate out the risks due to information systems from more generalised business risk. Up until the 1990s, information systems were more likely to exist as discrete applications for financial management, purchasing, stock control etc. But since then, for organisations of all kinds, almost all processes have become more dependent on some kind of technology. For private sector organisations, this drives IT to the heart of all operations: as the CEO of a major US corporation put it *"Information technology risks are becoming increasingly entangled with business risks ... technology has become integrated with almost every aspect of the business"* (*Harvard Business Review*, September–October, 1995). For government, it becomes more difficult than ever before to separate policy from administration. Hood and Rothstein break down the notion of risk management into two types, those applied to policy, and 'business risks' [23, p. 21], which incorporate more generic risks and ways of dealing with them imported from the private sector. But the increasing entanglement of policy and technologically aided administration means that this separation becomes less sustainable.

7. Tackling risks from integration of technology into business processes: Leadership and information technology

The increasing embeddedness of technological tasks in the business processes of government, and the increasing likelihood that policy innovations have been in some way driven by technological innovation, means that government agencies really have to re-evaluate their roles with respect to technology. Many government agencies tend to be risk-adverse in their approach to technology-based projects, possibly because of a troubled history of such projects within government or a general view that technology is something that government is not 'good at', in contrast to bureaucracy [27]. But if, for example, some government organisations are to 'become' their web sites (as one official in the Australian Tax Office put it in 1999, see [10]) – then development of those web sites and linkages to the systems that support them will become the most important task of those agencies. Agencies have to accept therefore that some aspects of technological development are an inevitable aspect of what they do, for example by following recent Public Accounts Committee recommendations and guidance on how to develop and maintain active web sites [10,11].

If technological issues have become inextricably tangled with general governmental processes, then clearly the way to mitigate against risk is to ensure that organisational arrangements for dealing with them are fully integrated into the rest of the organisation and dealt with at the highest level. It was for a long time a cliché in the private sector that information technology 'must' be dealt with at Board level – but never was. However, the pace of technological change in the last decade and the crucial nature of technology to so many aspects of competitive advantage seem to have provoked a business response. The first step was the rise of the Chief Information Officer (CIO) during the 1990s. But by 1994 the *Harvard Business Review* (72, No. 5 1994) was arguing that *"The CEO of 1995 must incorporate the capabilities of IT into his theory of business"*. In 1995 another article in the *Harvard Business Review* entitled 'The End of Delegation? Information Technology and the CEO' (1995, September–October) showed clearly how the Chief Executives of several major US corporations from a range of sectors were paying attention to such advice, with six experts clearly arguing for strategic understanding of IT as a clear part of the CEO's role. For example, as the CEO of the publishing operation Simon & Schuster put it *"I need to understand how information technology is changing our business and I must ensure that our organization uses technology effectively. Consequently I spend a lot of my time trying to understand the implications of new technologies, such as the electronic distribution of information products or software programs bundled with books ... At Simon & Schuster, information technology is not a back-office operation. It is not systems. It is not telecommunications. It is a valuable source of business solutions, touching virtually every aspect of our company"*.

In the UK government, there was a mild attempt to introduce Chief Information Officers (long a feature of the US federal government) into core departments at the end of the 1990s. But this move, in which designated officials were optimistically titled "Information Champions" and were given CIO-type roles on top of existing responsibilities, reeked of 'too little too late' and there is great scope for far more integration of IT management into the operation of government. The creation of the 'e-Envoy' with a substantial annual budget of £52 million and an associated office of around 250 staff (at its peak) as part of the Cabinet Office in 1999 reflected a welcome prioritisation of issues surrounding e-government from political leadership. But the creation of a separate (both administratively and geographically) office, located in a newly acquired privately rented building in central London, the fact that the e-Envoy's contract ended in 2004 (the year before the achievement or otherwise of 100 per cent electronic availability of all government services promised by Tony Blair) and the generally loose and temporary feel of his office, dislocated from both the rest of the Cabinet Office as well as the departments and agencies, always made it unlikely that the structure would really integrate into the rest of UK government. Organ [36, p. 33] in a study of the history of IT co-ordination in UK government concluded that *"The focus and channels for coordination have varied considerably and ineffectiveness is a constant feature"*. The Guardian newspaper in an article otherwise positive about the future of digital government observed on

5th September 2003 that *"The office of the e-envoy has failed both to exert influence across Whitehall and to demonstrate sufficient public value added through the application of digital technology. It has also been focused too much on online service delivery and not enough on the wider aim of demonstrating positive impact on service experiences and outcomes through subtle and innovative uses of technology"* and heralded the departure of Andrew Pinder, the current e-Envoy as a chance to do something about it. In the same year, many regulatory operations evolving to deal with new forms of e-based crime or new issues arising from the storage of electronic information (such as freedom of information) remained separate from the government bodies in which they were based. And the national programme for IT in the NHS (NPfIT), a £2.3 billion procurement designed to provide more effective, efficient and seamless services, was widely criticised for not doing enough to *"win the hearts and minds of the frontline health workers who will need to embrace the system"* (*Guardian*, 5th September 2003).

In the autumn of 2004, the UK government appeared to heed advice of the type quoted above and the Office of the e-Envoy was replaced with a new eGovernment unit, headed up by a new Head of e-government (initially Ian Watmore, formerly of Accenture). The role has been defined as analogous to that of a group chief information officer (CIO) in a conglomerate or large enterprise and will cover the full breadth of government IT, including the big transaction-processing systems at the heart of government, such as benefit payments, tax collection and internal governmental systems dealing with human resources and finance. The eGovernment Unit is also to develop the government's internal IT and programme management skills, set architectural standards, encourage departments and agencies to 'join up', and help improve the success rate of major IT programmes – a formidable task in view of the afore mentioned weaknesses of UK government agencies in this respect. The eGovernment Unit is to rely on the "powers of persuasion rather than authority or major budget": at the time of writing it remains to be seen whether it will be persuasive enough and whether this new approach will be successful in mitigating the risks identified in UK e-government. Watmore's first move was to set up networks of CIOs across government agencies, with regular meetings and a 'fostering of professional culture' and he planned to prioritise the setting up a single identifier for citizens, claiming *"If ever a topic is screaming to the top of the agenda, it is the whole identification issue"*.

8. Conclusion: Re-evaluating the core competency of government

All three of the trends identified above mean that some types of risk more commonly associated with private sector organisations are taken on by the public sector, exacerbating a trend noted by Margetts and Willcocks [31, p. 17] for "governmental organizations to become less distinctive" and implying that techniques for risk management and mitigation might usefully be borrowed from the private sector. This paper has suggested some ways in which private sector experience, as well as that of overseas governments, might be used to manage and minimise these types of risk in the UK.

The new risks associated with technological innovation, and the tentative suggestions as to how to manage and minimize them presented here, point to government agencies re-evaluating their core tasks. During the 1980s and 1990s in the UK government in particular developed the idea that information technology was not something that government 'did', it was something that government 'bought'. When William Waldergrave, then Minister for the Civil Service, declared in 1994 that "information technology was an area from which it was best for the government to withdraw" [39, p. xvii], he appears to have had a vision of separate and discrete information systems purchased and maintained from expert companies in a hands-off fashion. But experience of government computing highlights the problems with that vision. Rather than transferring out of government the risks inherent in developing information systems, the type of contract arrangements operated by the UK government have introduced new risks, distinctive to the UK which UK agencies must work hard to mitigate. Just as many private sector companies have come to acknowledge that IT touches every aspect of their business, many government agencies must also realise that they are in the same position.

The three risks discussed here would need to be incorporated into any risk management strategy developed for government. They do not fall easily, however, into the distinction between 'policy-domain-specific risk' (the way risk management has been tackled traditionally in the public sector) and more generic 'business risk' identified by Hood et al. [22]. All three risk factors – keeping apace with technological change, building contract relationships and accepting the entanglement of systems issues with business operations – have the potential to derail government activity and should be built into the business risk management approach developed by Hood and Rothstein and others. In particular, contract relationship management is a vital business risk that will need to be given the highest priority in the post-PFI world of information systems, with attention to research into IT outsourcing in the private sector and the risk factors identified by Lacity and Willcocks ([26], listed above). But in addition, the discussion here has suggested that some risk factors associated with information systems come into the category of policy risk as well, given the reliance of policy innovation on technological innovation and the moving target of a 'smart' citizenry and business world with whom government needs to transact. Such a risk is not domain specific in that it involves people at the highest levels of all government organisations factoring in technological issues, in the same way that private sector CEOs have started to do, to incorporate the capabilities of IT into a 'theory of government'.

Acknowledgements

This essay is based on a paper presented to Risk, Regulation and Good Governance Joint Workshop organised by the Institute of Governance, QUB and the ESRC Centre for Analysis of Risk and Regulation, LSE 10th September 2003. It draws on research carried out for the ESRC-funded project, Public-private Partnerships and Policy Transfer in Central Government ICT Systems, Award number: L216252030, Award holders: Helen Margetts (UCL) and Patrick Dunleavy (LSE), Research fellows: Simon Bastow (UCL, LSE) and Jane Tinkler (UCL).

References

[1] Accenture, *Rhetoric vs. Reality – Closing the Gap,* Government Executive Series, 2001, available at www.accenture.com.
[2] Accenture, *eGovernment Leadership – Realizing the Vision,* Government Executive Series, 2002, available at www.accenture.com.
[3] Accenture, *eGovernment Leadership – Engaging the Customer,* Government Executive Series, 2003, available at www.accenture.com.
[4] Accenture, *eGovernment Leadership – High Performance, Maximum Value,* Government Executive Series, 2004, available at www.accenture.com.
[5] CCTA, *Privatisation. IS Planning Subject Guides,* London: HMSO, 1992.
[6] J. Crabtree, M. Nathan and R. Reeves, *Reality IT: Technology and Everyday Life,* London: Work Foundation iSociety Programme, 2002.
[7] N. Curthoys and J. Crabtree, *SmartGov: Renewing Electronic Government for Improved Service Delivery,* London: The Work Foundation, 2003.
[8] R. Dewan, B. Jing and A. Seidmann, *Adoption of Internet-based Product Customization and Pricing Strategies,* Proceedings of the 33rd Hawaii International Conference on System Sciences, 2000.
[9] S. Domberger, *The Contracting Organization: A Strategic Guide to Outsourcing,* Oxford University Press, 1998.

[10] P. Dunleavy and H. Margetts, *Government on the Web,* London: National Audit Office, HC 87, 1999.

[11] P. Dunleavy and H. Margetts, *Government on the Web II,* London: National Audit Office, HC 764, 2002, for both reports see www.governmentontheweb.org.

[12] P. Dunleavy, H. Margetts, S. Bastow and J. Tinkler, *E-government and Policy Innovation in Seven Liberal Democracies,* Paper for the Political Studies Association's Annual Conference 2003, 15–17 April, Leicester University, 2003, www.governmentontheweb.org.

[13] P. Dunleavy, H. Margetts, S. Bastow and J. Tinkler, *Government IT Performance and the Power of the IT Industry: A Cross-National Analysis,* paper to annual meeting of American Political Science Association, Chicago, 1st–5th September 2004, Panel 25-2 'Digital Policy Issues: Inequality, E-government', 4th Sep. 2004.

[14] P. Dunleavy, H. Margetts, S. Bastow and J. Tinkler, *Government, Contracts and IT Corporations: How Bureaucrats and Business Drive Global Public Policy Change,* unpublished book manuscript, forthcoming.

[15] F. Foldvary and D. Klein, eds, *The Half-Life of Policy Rationales: How new technology affects old policy issues,* New York University Press, Cato Institute, 2003.

[16] T. Goles and W. Chin, Relational Exchange Theory and IS Outsourcing: Developing a Scale to Measure Relationship Factors, in: *Information Systems Outsourcing,* R. Hirschheim, A. Heinzl and J. Dibbern, eds, Berlin: Springer, 2002.

[17] J.B. Heywood, *The Outsourcing Dilemma: the Search for Competitiveness,* Financial Times Prentice Hall, 2001.

[18] H.M. Treasury, *Management of Risk: A Strategic Overview,* London: HM Treasury, Orange Book, 2000.

[19] H.M. Treasury, *PFI: Meeting the Investment Challenge,* London: HMSO, July 2003.

[20] D. Holmes, *e.gov: e-business strategies for government,* Nicholas Brealey: London, 2001.

[21] C. Hood, *The Tools of Government,* London: Macmillan, 1983.

[22] C. Hood, H. Rothstein and R. Baldwin, *The Government of Risk: Understanding Risk Regulation Regimes,* Oxford University Press, 2001.

[23] C. Hood and H. Rothstein, *Business Risk in Management in Government: Pitfalls and Possibilities,* Annex 2 to NAO, 2000.

[24] K. Loudon and J. Loudon, *Management Information Systems: A Contemporary Perspective,* Macmillan: New York, 1991.

[25] M. Lacity and L. Willocks, A Ruvry of IT Outsourcing Experiences in USA and UK, *Journal of Global Information Management* **8**(2) (April–June 2000).

[26] M. Lacity and L. Willcocks, *Global Information Technology Outsourcing: In Search of Business Advantage,* Chichester: Wiley, 2001.

[27] H. Margetts, The Automated State, in: *British Public Management: Achievements, Problems and Prospects,* P. Dunleavy and A. Massey, eds, *Special issue of Public Policy and Administration* **10**(2) (1995).

[28] H. Margetts, Political Participation and Protest, in: *Developments in British Politics 6,* P. Dunleavy, A. Gamble, I. Holliday and G. Peele, eds, London: Macmillan, 2000, pp. 185–202.

[29] H. Margetts, *Electronic Government: Method or Madness?* Inaugural lecture, University College London, 13th February 2003.

[30] H. Margetts, P. Dunleavy, S. Bastow and J. Tinkler, *Leaders and Followers: E-government, Policy Innovation and Policy Transfer in the European Union,* paper to the European Union Studies Association (EUSA) conference, Nashville, Tennessee, USA, 27th March 2003.

[31] H. Margetts and L. Willcocks, Informatization in the Public Sector: Distinctive or Common Risks? *Informatization in the Public Sector* **3**(1) (1994), 1–20.

[32] H. Margetts and L. Willcocks, Information technology in public services: disaster faster? *Public Money and Management* **13**(2) (April–June 1993).

[33] H. Margetts and H. Yared, *Incentivization of e-government,* Academic Report published by the National Audit Office, 20th November 2003 to accompany *Transforming the performance of HM Customs and Excise through Electronic Service Delivery,* 2002–2003, HC1267, 2003.

[34] National Audit Office (NAO), *Supporting Innovation: Managing Risk in Government Departments,* London: The Stationary Office, HC 664, 2000.

[35] National Audit Office (NAO), *Difficult Forms,* London: The Stationary Office, 2003.

[36] J. Organ, The Coordination of e-Government in Historical Context, *Public Policy and Administration* **18**(2) (Summer 2003).

[37] M. Parker, R. Benson and E. Trainor, *Information Economics: Linking Business Performance to Information Technology,* New Jersey: Prentice Hall, 1998.

[38] Taylor Nelson Sofres, *Government Online: An International Perspective 2003,* Global Summary, 2003, available at www.tnsofres.com/21451_global_27nov03.

[39] Treasury and Civil Service Select Committee, *The Role of the Civil Service: Fifth Report,* (Vol. 1), London: HMSO, 1994.

[40] L. Willcocks, Outsourcing IT and e-business, in: *IT Make or Break issues in IT Management,* D. Remenyi and A. Brown, eds, Oxford: Butterworth-Heinemann, 2002.
[41] L. Willcocks, M. Lacity and T. Kern, Risk in IT Outsourcing Strategy Revisited: Longitudinal Case Research at LISA, *Journal of Strategic Information Systems* (April 2000).

Information Polity 10 (2005) 95–104
IOS Press

Just how risky is online voting?

Stephen Coleman
Oxford University, Oxford, UK
E-mail: stephen.coleman@oii.ox.ac.uk

Abstract. The UK Government is committed to experimentation with online voting and has promoted Internet voting in local elections in 2002 and 2003. This article examines the risks of online voting and suggests that political risks should not be conceived in terms of an elusive scientific objectivity, but should be understood as arising from reflexive contestations involving a range of actors and contexts. After examining the risk of online voting from several perspectives, the article concludes by arguing for a more politicised and nuanced conception of risk which takes into account non-functional aspects of voting, such as the symbolic.

1. An ongoing debate

The debate about the risks of online voting evokes passionate and polarised expressions of certainty. Those who see Internet voting as inherently dangerous argue that there is a high systemic risk of virtual ballot boxes being hacked into, infected by viruses and rigged by unscrupulous interests. Critics of e-voting claim that it is impossible to authenticate the identity of voters, ensure the privacy of remote voting or make e-voting accessible to the digitally excluded.

"Given the current state of insecurity of hosts and the vulnerability of the Internet to manipulation and denial of service attacks, there is no way that a public election of any significance involving remote electronic voting could be carried out securely" [17].

"The shining lure of these "hype-tech" voting schemes is only technological fool's gold that will create new problems far more intractable than those they claim to solve" [14].

"We do not believe it can ever be possible for a voter to "receive assurance that their vote was recorded as it was intended" in an unsupervised location without opening the way to coercion and vote-buying" [9].

"At this time, it would not be legally, practically or fiscally feasible to develop a comprehensive remote Internet voting system that would completely replace the current paper process used for voter registration, voting, and the collection of initiative, referendum and recall petition signatures" [3].

Proponents of online voting claim that the risks have been exaggerated and that such panics follow most technological innovations. Advocates argue that Internet ballots will enable people to vote remotely, at their own convenience; that online voting will be especially attractive to younger voters who are currently the most likely to abstain and that online voting will bring major cost reductions to the conduct of public elections.

"Whether or not e-voting increased turnout, it would still be worthwhile in its own right if it made voting more convenient for the citizen. There is no law of democracy which insists that voting must be inconvenient or that votes are any more worthwhile if they require a trip to the local Primary School rather than a vote from the comfort of your home or the convenience of your local supermarket" [4].

1570-1255/05/$17.00

"... we now feel that Internet voting – implemented responsibly and judiciously – can dramatically increase voter access and reinvigorate voter participation in the political process around the world ... As the Internet continues to revolutionize communications, commerce, and recreation worldwide, equally dramatic changes are promised for the mechanisms of democracy worldwide. Given that the defining characteristics of this technology revolution include cost savings, improved efficiency, and consumer empowerment, the benefits of applying these advances to the democratic process are equally apparent" [13].

What are we to make of these radically opposed assessments of risk? Is it the case that opponents of online voting understand the risks, while proponents are turning a blind eye? Or are the opponents twenty-first-century luddites, failing to take a balanced view of necessary risks? The aim of this paper is to support neither of these conclusions, but to explore the multidimensional nature of risk.

Risk cannot be measured on a single register. The probability of a policy or project ending in disaster depends upon how one conceives of success. For example, in the 2004 all-postal voting in the UK local and European elections, the Opposition took the view that the process was *"open to fraud"*, presented *"a dangerous backward step for democracy"* and was *"at every turn open to fiddles"*, whereas the Government argued that *"Millions more people found postal voting more convenient"* and that *"returning officers ... have not reported any greater incidence of fraud or malpractice than that which typically occurs in every election campaign."* The Electoral Commission, as an independent watchdog charged with scrutinising the fairness of voting methods, observed that *"one of the biggest concerns of electors is that they do not feel that the current arrangements for postal voting facilitate the casting of a ballot in secret"* and arrived at the conclusion that *"all-postal voting should not be pursued for use at UK statutory elections."* Clearly, there was more than one definition of risk in play in these analyses.

Attempts to evaluate hazards on the basis of scientifically demonstrable objectivity fail to grasp the reflexive and contested nature of risk. Instead, the appropriate research questions are Risk for whom? What sort of democratic outcomes are at risk? Are risks purely technological or are there other processes at stake? In which spatial sphere is risk greatest? The risks of online voting will be theorised and evaluated in this article in response to these questions.

2. What is online voting?

Before outlining the risks, what exactly is online voting and why is it being introduced?

Democracy entails rule by the people. But the public is unable to rule itself directly because it lacks the time, inclination and (sometimes) cognition or competence to arrive at judgements about the vast array of complex policy issues involved in governance. Furthermore, the public is *a collective principal*, i.e. it comprises a range of diverse, often inconsistent, interests, preferences and values which must be represented as if there were a single public interest. So, representatives are elected to speak for the public. The agent-principal relationship inherent to representative democracy is complicated by three factors. Firstly, because the public comprises multiple preferences, often arrived at on the basis of imperfect information, representatives adopt an aggretatory notion of public interests and preferences. Aggregation is crude and has the effect of leaving many citizens feeling like part of an amorphous mass, unheard and powerless. Secondly, there is the problem of what Downs [7, p. 259] called "rational ignorance":

"In general, it is irrational to be politically well informed because the low returns from data simply do not justify their cost in time and other scarce resources. Therefore many voters do not bother to discover

their true views before voting, and most citizens are not well enough informed to influence directly the formulation of those policies that affect them".

Thirdly, because aggregation is crude, it sometimes lacks sensitivity to the salience or intensity of public concerns. In order to aggregate preferences, voters support packages of policy proposals, but it is not infrequently the case that, in order to vote for a package of moderately supported policies one must sacrifice a vote for a strongly supported policy offered as part of another package, or not on offer at all. So, while voting in elections is a fundamental feature of democracy, it is a blunt instrument for sensing, reflecting and responding to public interests, preferences and values. Consequently, many citizens regard voting as being a waste of time or a democratic opportunity of such limited value that they choose not to use it.

With only a few exceptions, most advanced democracies are experiencing a significant fall in voter turnout. In the 2001 UK election turnout fell for the first time to under 60%; before then it had never fallen below 70%. These trends are accompanied by a long-term problem of unequal representation of key demographic groups: the young, ethnic minorities and the less educated are all under-represented amongst active voters.

Online voting experiments have arisen as part of a drive by the Government to find ways to increase turnout and broaden the representative characteristics of voters. As the UK Government's [19] policy paper, *In the Service of Democracy,* puts it,

"Modernising the voting process through the use of ICT may broaden participation in elections. It may, for example, make voting more attractive to those young people who are competent in ICT but who find traditional methods of voting unattractive or inconvenient."

The idea of using technology to make democracy more accessible is not new. Ever since the emergence of interactive communication technologies, the prospect of televoting or electronic polling has been a subject of speculation. For example, in their 1970 book, *The Computerized Society,* Martin and Norman [12, p. 298] observed that:

"Voting from home is a technical possibility, and perhaps will be implemented in some countries before the end of the century. Continuous computerized referendums on all matters of public importance may appear to be the logical extension of Western democracy . . . "

Unlike the broader term, e-voting, which describes a range of uses of electronic applications in the voting and counting process, online voting refers to the use of digital communication networks, such as the Internet, to cast votes in an election. Online voting can be conducted via regulated computers in conventional polling stations, but its most ambitious use is as a means of remote voting, allowing voters to participate in elections wherever they have access to an Internet connection.

In the US election primaries of 2000 remote voting via the Internet was an option in two states: in Alaska fewer than 50 (out of 3,500) eligible Republicans used the option to vote online; in Arizona approximately 5% of eligible Democrats (41% of those who voted) cast their votes online. But these were not public elections, conducted in line with the rigours of electoral law.

The British Government was the first to experiment with remote online voting in legally binding public elections. These pilots have provided an opportunity to evaluate the use of the Internet and other digital technologies in the context of a state-administered election. In May 2002 Internet voting was available in five English electoral areas and text-message (sms) voting in two electoral areas, following which the Government decided to fund three more years of experimentation with new voting methods, including online voting. In May 2003 17 e-voting pilots were conducted, again in English local elections. These pilots are part of a preparatory process for the UK Government's declared aim of running what it calls an e-enabled general election by 2006, i.e. an election in which some form of online voting will be a universal option for voters.

Since the passage of the 2000 Political Parties, Elections and Referendums Act, the newly-established Electoral Commission has had responsibility for evaluating experimentation with innovative electoral methods. The Commission sponsored studies on online voting before and after the 2002 and 2003 pilots; and has published evaluations of each pilot, as well as a comprehensive study of the use of new voting methods. The Electoral Commission is also responsible for establishing clear security standards which are consistent with the requirements of electoral law. CESG (the UK's National Technical Authority for Information Assurance) has set out some standards to which local authorities and online voting technology suppliers are expected to adhere.

What are the criteria of success upon which online voting should be judged? It is in the pluralistic responses to this key question that contestation emerges, for different definitions of success – and failure – give rise to a range of ways of evaluating the value and risk of voting via the Internet. In the following sections competing conceptions of risk are identified.

3. Actor interests: Politicians and the public

As legislators, politicians are called upon to make the final judgement about the risks of new voting methods, but they generally lack the technical knowledge needed to debate the intricacies of system security. So politicians are dependent upon the advice of experts and the translation techniques which make such advice accessible and politically meaningful. The translation of technical discourses is never a neutral process. Expertise can appeal to conservative fear of change or be couched in the seductive language of utopian innovation. Above all, discourses of technical expertise rely upon claims to scientific knowledge that is above the fray of competing interests – although such discourses only acquire political value if they can be attached to such interests.

The main concern of political actors (parties, candidates, senior civil servants) is that any method of voting preserves and strengthens the legitimacy of political authorisation. Political actors need the relationship between voting and political legitimacy to be transparent and trusted. For politicians, online voting gives rise to three main risks:

- Firstly, that election campaigns could be disrupted by new methods of voting. Election campaigns are highly ordered and rhythmic processes, culminating in a single vote on a single day. The effect upon voting behaviour when remote ballots are spread over several days is a matter of uncertainty. After the 2004 all-postal pilots, in which the voting period was extended, the Opposition spokesperson complained that "One of the problems of all-postal voting is that it destroys the process of any genuine election campaign and puts an end to polling day as judgement day in our British democracy."
- Secondly, political actors, who live in 'the real world' of naked competition for power, are sensitive to the potential danger of organised vote rigging. Unlikely as it may be for such attempts to occur or succeed, within a centralised system of e-voting (or e-counting) such manipulation could have an impact upon tens of thousands of votes, rather than one ballot box or polling station.
- Thirdly, political actors have concerns about the right of candidates to demand a recount of votes in cases of highly marginal results. Recounts are key symbolic guarantors of trust in the reliability of election results. In an e-election, if a candidate or his agent demands a recount, the only recourse available to them will be to press the same buttons on the computer that produced the original result. If this replicates the first result (as it should), they will be dissatisfied, but will have no way of proving the inaccuracy of the count; if the result is different, they will quite reasonably question the validity of the computer program.

Members of the public, as eligible voters, have a different set of requirements of the electoral system, and therefore quite different perceptions of risk. As trusting users of the electoral process, voters are not particularly interested in its detailed operation, but are very concerned about perceptions of fairness. The public want elections not only to be fair, secure and accurate, but also to be seen to be so. The symbolic significance of rituals of voting secrecy and counting transparency are crucial to this sense of public trust. For the public, there are three key risks to be considered:

- Firstly, voters must be sure that their votes remain secret and that information about their vote is protected with as great or greater force than any other personal data. The common fear that all online activity leaves tracks and that anyone who is clever enough can find out how one has behaved online must be allayed before online voting can win public trust. Allied to this is the fear of being overseen during the act of voting in an unregulated space. (This is discussed below.)
- Secondly, the instructions given to online voters might complicate the election process and serve as a disincentive for some people to vote. The simplicity of online voting, like many other online transactions, is easier for technologists to design than for busy lay people to use. There are risks of potential voters becoming confused by the voting instructions, as reportedly happened to some people in the 2004 all-postal voting pilots. The technical process of logging on, finding the right website and clicking in the appropriate places could be seen as more bothersome than the simple act of putting a cross on a piece of paper.
- Thirdly, citizens who do not have – or want – Internet access might regard online voting as an act of discrimination, especially if there is a policy of cutting the number of polling stations as more people vote at home.

4. Democratic conflicts: Turnout and representativeness

Making elections more democratic can be interpreted in two broad ways. It could mean ensuring that more people vote, so that if 80% rather than 60% of eligible voters participate in an election it is therefore a more democratic reflection of the public's will. Alternatively, democratising elections could be understood in terms of the extent to which those voting reflect the socio-demographic composition of the eligible electorate. In this sense, an increase in turnout from 60% to 80%, based on greater convenience for richer or more educated voters to participate, could weaken further position of under-represented, disadvantaged strata of the electorate.

If the cost of voting is spread in an equal demographic fashion across gender, ethnicity, age and socio-economic class, this could result in an overall benefit for democracy. But if, as is currently the case, those with easy access to and familiarity with the Internet are unrepresentative of the rest of the population, this could further marginalise and disadvantage certain groups. The Arizona Democratic party, which offered Internet voting as one option in its 2000 primary, claimed great success in boosting turnout and reaching traditionally excluded voters. Detailed research by Alvarez and Nagle [2] on voters in that election suggests that three groups were disproportionately under-represented amongst e-voters: non-whites, the unemployed and people from rural areas. These are precisely the same groups that have low home Internet access. In the light of Pratchett et al.'s [16] claim that young UK citizens are less likely than their elders to use the Internet to vote, e-voting could even exaggerate the current age skew in voting.

There is strong evidence that enabling people to vote remotely by post has had a positive effect on turnout. But there is also evidence to suggest that increased turnout adds to the representative skew by boosting the proportion of middle-class citizens able to vote from home. In their studies of all-postal elections in Oregon, Karp and Banducci [10] found that "reforms designed to make voting easier may not make the electorate more demographically representative and may even further bias the electorate in favour of the better off." In the Swindon local election pilot in 2002, where Internet voting was an available option, half (50.3%) of Internet voters were from professional or managerial/technical occupations, compared with 20.7% of phone voters and 32.2% of voters at polling stations. This accords with findings from public opinion research conducted as part of a Government-sponsored study which concluded that

"Among those who have access to the technology, middle-aged and older people are more likely to use internet voting than younger people, and social grades AB are, similarly, more likely to do so than grades C2DE. This finding suggests that even if access to the internet was universal, fewer people from lower socio-economic grades would use the technology for voting than older, more middle-class people".

Pratchett et al. [16]. Such a finding has important implications for the criteria by which implementation might be evaluated. Turnout through electronic means is likely to mirror conventional voting patterns rather than greatly alter them.

5. Modus operandi: Technologies and procedures

The debate about online voting risks has tended to over-emphasise the importance of hard technologies and has concentrated excessively on questions about which computer scientists believe they monopolise knowledge. In fact, technologies are always cultural products, embedded in social relationships which are themselves technically constructed and politically contested. Voting software is designed for the conduct of generic elections, but not all elections have the same rules and culture. Established election procedures, which are codified by law and reinforced by custom and habit, are often more complex than technologists realise. For software designers the question might be, How do we enable remote electors to cast a vote at a time and place that suits them? Election administrators and lawyers are more likely to ask questions about the procedures ensuring the probity, accuracy and security of the ballot.

For technologists, there are three key risks at stake:

- Firstly, they are concerned about the possibility of system attack or breakdown. Computer scientists have expressed deep anxieties about the vulnerability of Internet-based voting.
- Secondly, there is the problem of voter authentication. Democratic elections in mass societies require means of ensuring that voters are who they say they are. Without ubiquitous electronic signatures or biometric identification, it is technically difficult to authenticate the identity of a disembodied, remote voter.
- Thirdly, as Lessig [11] and others have argued, all software programmes reflects certain relationships of power. The only way to ensure the transparency of these underlying relations is to have open code or open source e-voting software. Alexander [1] argues that *"One way to build public confidence in computerized voting is to require voting software code be made public"* and that *"there is consensus in the security industry that public source code leads to more secure computer systems than closed source."* The concern of software vendors to preserve the value of their products and protect their source codes conflicts with a public interest in having transparent access to the voting process.

Independent of these technological perceptions of risk, there are rigorous technical-procedural requirements of election law which concern election administrators and lawyers:

- Firstly, precisely because election officials are not likely to be technicians or software specialists, they face the risk of losing control over scrutiny of key areas of the electoral process, forcing them to be dependent upon vendors who have an interest in protecting their systems from public criticism.
- Secondly, and related to the above risk, there is the problem of vote audits. The paradoxical legal requirement, which exists in the electoral law of some countries (such as the UK), that votes must be both secret and traceable, has not caused much public unease in the past, but implementing both secrecy and audit of the vote electronically is a far more complicated process. Where votes are encrypted, can election officials be sure that they would be able to satisfy a judge that Voter A voted online for Candidate X?
- Thirdly, there is the challenging problem of how election officials are to deal with the risk of duplicate voting. If a voter arrives at a polling station claiming not to have voted online, even though the marked register indicates that she has, would she be refused a vote (in which case she will be disenfranchised if she had tried to vote online, but failed) or allowed to vote (with the obvious possibility that she has voted twice?) There would only need to be a few examples of this happening to undermine public trust in the fairness of the election.

6. Spatial contexts: Regulated and remote

Risk is related to spatial context. For example, in the case of drug abuse, there is a huge difference between the risks faced by addicts who survive on the streets and those who can afford to indulge their habit in the insulated comfort of an affluent home. Over-technologised conceptions of e-voting assume that the security of technical systems is the key to managing risk, whereas a broader view might regard the unregulated nature of remote voting spaces as a greater risk.

Since the introduction of the secret ballot in 1872, a principle of all voting in the UK (and beyond) has been the right to cast a vote privately, without fear of influence or intimidation by others. A key characteristic of e-voting (like postal voting) is that it takes place outside the highly regulated environment of a polling station. Indeed, the capacity to vote anywhere is its most publicised advantage. Domestic and workplace voting is incompatible with the requirement that all votes shall be cast in secret and by the voter only, with no coercion or interference from anybody. In some family units one member (often the father) will insist upon the right to influence or control important decisions made by their wives and children. The same might apply to some workplaces where the presence of superiors or peers could influence voting. Given the reality of authoritarian relationships in such private spaces, how can the individual privacy of remote e-voting be assured? It is difficult to measure the extent of such interference or intimidation, because private spaces are by definition unobservable – and the kind of people prepared to submit to authoritarian pressure are the least likely to report this to the authorities.

After the UK's 2004 all-postal voting pilots, which saw the most extensive use of remote voting in any British election, there was reference in the subsequent parliamentary debate to "fairly widespread reports of household intimidation." Watt [20] has argued that a range of international laws and protocols are designed to guarantee the right to vote in secret without undue influence. Domestic and workplace voting could jeopardise such a right and Watt concludes that "If there were a section of the population who were able to show that household influences prevented them from voting in accordance with their own conscience, there is likely to be a significant [legal] challenge." Such a challenge has yet to be made, but even the risk of public perceptions that voter privacy is being undermined should be regarded as a threat to the legitimacy of democracy.

7. Democratising the debate about democracy

Ironically, most discussions about how to improve democracy take place at an elite level, with little consideration given to involving the demos itself. Even consultations about constitutional issues tend to be conducted as if the only likely respondents will be experts. A democratic language of democracy has yet to evolve. Added to this tendency for debates about elections to be conducted in the remote discourses of lawyers and bureaucrats, the debate about e-voting is obscured further by the expert discourses of technologists which tend to be opaque, exclusive and surrounded by mystique. Consequently, although voting via the internet is proposed as a way of making elections more accessible and participatory, the policy discussion about online voting has been quite the opposite.

What would characterise a more democratic debate about the risks of online voting? Firstly, there is a need to link conceptions of risk to more candid recognition of the interests at stake. Secondly, risk needs to be conceived in a more nuanced fashion, taking into account possibilities for trade-offs. Thirdly, conceptions of risk should embrace symbolic concerns that do not fit neatly into rationalist accounts of risk.

7.1. Politicising risk

By presenting risk as an objectively measurable concept, the tensions and contestations outlined in this article are compressed into a pseudo-scientific conglomerate called risk. In reality, risk is messier and politically disputed. Before there can be a meaningful public discussion about online voting, competing interests need to be disentangled and stated for what they are. For example, much of the drive for online voting in the UK came from that section of Government charged with promoting e-government. They see online voting as a way of being seen to extend transactions between citizens and the state. In turn, the government's objective was supported by corporate vendors of voting software for whom online voting offers a potentially lucrative market. The objectives of civil servants promoting e-government and vendors selling new uses of the Internet should not be conflated with the public-interest debate about how to modernise elections or increase turnout. The public might be more willing to accept risks for normative democratic than instrumental government ends.

Even the objective of raising turnout is far from being non-political. Lower turnout in particular constituencies benefits some parties more than others. In the UK's 2004 all-voting pilots the Labour Party accused the Conservatives and Liberal Democrats of not caring about low turnout, while the Opposition parties accused the Government of seeking to boost turnout in traditional Labour areas regardless of risks to the fairness of the election.

As discussed above, elections confer legitimacy upon politicians, but citizens are less interested in their rulers' claims to legitimacy than the quality of representation. For citizens, the use of the Internet to improve communication between representatives and represented, *in between elections,* might be regarded as more valuable than the mechanical use of digital technology to cast and count votes. The UK Government's policy document on e-democracy, *In The Service of Democracy,* proposed that "e-democracy policy should be based on two separate but interdependent tracks: electronic participation (e-participation) and electronic voting (e-voting)." The Government's rationale was that: "Implementing ICT in voting is mainly a question of offering a package of electronic services, such as online voting and online registration, although there are important questions of building voters' confidence in the robustness and security of the technology. Using ICT to open new channels of participation between elections, on the other hand, is much more complex. It requires the creation of new relationships between government, citizens and representatives." [19].

Given that resources are not unlimited, choices between promoting online voting and Internet-enabled participation (essentially, elections and in between elections) should be a matter for public debate. In fact, the debate about online voting has rarely made connections with the wider possibilities of e-democracy and has certainly not addressed the question of which policy 'track' deserves most public funding.

7.2. Beyond black and white conceptions of risk

In the polarised debate about online voting, risk tends to be presented as if online elections will either be ruinous to, or panaceas for, existing problems of democracy. In reality, most successful processes operate on the basis of low risk rather than no risk. Managing risks is more achievable than seeking to eliminate them.

Opponents of online voting sometimes depict existing electoral practices as being risk-free. In fact, fraudulence has always existed to some extent in paper-ballot elections; in Northern Ireland it has been widespread. The major problems in the US 2000 election were caused by voting machines and counting methods that had been used for over thirty years.

As with other areas in which risks need to be explained to or discussed with the public, communication should be characterised by openness and credibility. Innovatory techniques of risk communication, developed in recent years, can help to frame public debate in more meaningful terms [6,15]. In the case of online voting, this entails recognition of the fact that some risks are greater and more intractable than others and that, because all activity is potentially hazardous, it is necessary to think in terms of trade-offs rather than risk-free ends. Instead of a polarised debate between technophiles and luddites, perhaps online voting requires a more mature public debate about the level of risk that is acceptable in modernising elections.

7.3. Recognising the symbolic

Intangible losses of community also constitute risk, even though it may not be quantifiable. Sclove argues that "An overwired world would be one in which virtual life and online activities increasingly crowd out traditional forms of social engagement, leisure activities or time spent in the natural world, thus creating a pathological self-reinforcing dynamic" [18]. Some voters prefer to go to the polling station than stay at home and regard online voting as a slippery slope to the privatisation of a symbolically important public activity.

In research that I have been conducting in collaboration with the Design Council, it has become clear that many citizens appreciate the ritualistic nature of elections. Some express frustration at having too little part to play in elections; for them, voting as a remote, atomised activity might only reinforce the ethereality of the democratic process [5]. Recognising such symbolic concerns and incorporating them into a rationalist discourse about risk would serve to democratise a debate which often seems to ignore or belittle the value of the experiential.

8. The risk of inertia

Finally, there is the risk entailed by failing to modernise obsolete practices. Demonstrating the consequences of inertia is methodologically problematic, for inaction is an amorphous variable. Nonetheless, in a dynamic social and technological environment inaction can have negative consequences. If cultures of shopping, banking, playing games and socialising are increasingly moving online, the failure of the political sphere to move in tandem risks confining it to eccentric marginality. This might be the strongest argument for voting online: the symbolic message is delivered that democracy is consistent with contemporary culture. The risk of such symbolism for the political elite – and a democratic opportunity for citizens – is that online voting will stimulate a public appetite for a more interactive system of representation before and after elections. The movement towards more direct representation presents a formidable challenge to remote representatives, but, as I have argued elsewhere, may be one of the most hopeful options for the future of democracy.

References

[1] K. Alexander, *Ten Things I Want People To Know About Voting Technology,* 2001, downloaded from http://www.calvoter.org/issues/votingtech/pub/0101KAtenthings.html.

[2] R.M. Alvarez and J. Nagler, The Likely Consequences of Internet Voting for Political Representation, *Loyola Law Review* **34** (2001), 1115–1153.

[3] California Internet Voting Task Force, *A Report on the Feasibility of Internet Voting,* Sacramento, California, 2001, downloaded from http://www.cs.jhu.edu/~rubin/courses/sp03/papers/california.report.pdf.

[4] R. Cook, Speech to YouGov Conference, Reviving Democracy, QEII Centre, London, 10th April 2002.

[5] Design Council, *Touching the State: What does it mean to be a citizen in the 21st Century?* London, 2004.

[6] B.-M. Drottz-Sjoberg, Risk perception and definition of risk, *Working paper,* European Institute for Advanced Studies in Management, Brussels, 2003.

[7] A. Downs, *An Economic Theory of Democracy,* NY, 1957, p. 259.

[8] Electoral Commission, *Delivering democracy? The future of postal voting,* Electoral Commission, London, 2004.

[9] N.B. Fairweather, Response of the Centre for Computing and Social Responsibility, De Montfort University to the CESG report on eVoting Security, 2002, downloaded from http://www.edemocracy.gov.uk/feedback/responses/centre_for_computing_and_social_responsibility_cesg.doc.

[10] J. Karp and S. Banducci, *Political Efficacy and Participation in Eighteen Democracies: How Electoral Rules Shape Political Behavior,* paper presented at the XVIII World Congress of the International Political Science Association, Quebec City, Canada, 2000.

[11] L. Lessig, *Code and Other Laws of Cyberspace,* Nbasic Books, NY, 1999.

[12] J. Martin and A. Norman, *The Computerized Society: An Appraisal of the Impact of Computers on Society over the Next Fifteen Years,* Prentice-Hall, NJ, 1970, p. 298.

[13] J. Mohen and J. Glidden, The Case for Internet Voting, *Communications of the ACM* **44**(1) (2001), 72.

[14] P. Neumann, R. Mercuri and L. Weinstein, *Perspectives on Electronic Processes,* 2000, http://www.ejfi.org/Voting/Voting-15.htm.

[15] S.A. Nohrstedt and A. Tassew, *Communication and crisis. An inventory of current research,* Psykologiskt försvar rapport nr 163:1, Stockholm, 1993.

[16] L. Pratchett, S. Birch, S. Candy, N.B. Fairweather, S. Rogerson, V. Stone, B. Watt and M. Wingfield, *The Implementation of Electronic Voting in the UK,* LGA, 2002, p. 33.

[17] Rubin, Security Considerations for Remote Electronic Voting over the Internet, *Communications of the ACM,* December 2002.

[18] Sclove, The Democratic Uses of Technology, 2002, downloaded at http://www.nea.org/he/heta98/s98pg9.pdf.

[19] UK Government, *In The Service of Democracy,* HMSO, London, 2002.

[20] B. Watt, *Implementing Electronic Voting: A Report Addressing the Legal Issues Raised by the Implementation of Electronic Voting,* unpublished paper, 2002.

Information Polity 10 (2005) 105–113
IOS Press

Risk maps on the Internet: Transparency and the management of risks

Albert Jacob Meijer
Utrecht School of Governance, Utrecht, The Netherlands
E-mail: a.meijer@usg.uu.nl

Abstract. In this essay the consequences of the transparency of physical risks through the Internet are explored by posing three questions: do citizens in the Netherlands use risk maps to find out what risks there are in their neighbourhoods, does this enhance their involvement in the management of risks, and, do risk maps on the Internet and citizen involvement improve the quality of risk management? It is argued that transparency does not lead to a better informed citizenry since few citizens look at the risk maps on the Internet and, as a consequence, citizens are not more involved in the management of physical risks. In spite of the lack of citizen involvement, transparency does improve the quality of risk management. Transparency puts pressure on governments and companies and stimulates them into performing better. In addition to this optimistic conclusion, the essay also points at a dark side to openness: terrorists may use the information about physical risks to plan attacks.

1. Does transparency improve the quality of risk management?

In 2000 a fireworks factory exploded in a densely populated neighborhood in Enschede (the Netherlands). Twenty two people were killed and more than 900 people were injured. 4100 people became homeless after the explosion. Over 400 houses and more than 100 businesses were totally destroyed, 1500 houses and 280 businesses were damaged. The total damage amounted to 550 million euro.

An important complaint of citizens in Enschede was that many of them did not even know there was a fireworks factory in their neighborhood. Since then, Dutch local and national governments have paid more attention to risk management and communication of risks. The Internet plays an important role in the communication of risks: there are several risk maps on the Internet that citizens can use to look up risks in their vicinity. The question is whether this increased transparency has a positive effect on the management of risks.

In this essay I will explore the consequences of the transparency of physical risks through the Internet. The first set of questions concerns the use of risk maps by citizens to find out what risks there are in their neighborhood. Does the use of risk maps lead to a better informed citizenry? Are citizens more aware of the risks that are present in their immediate environment? Citizens have a chance to look at risk maps. But do they?

The second set of questions relates to the use of the information for influencing risk management and political action. Does the availability of risk maps lead to more citizen involvement in the management of risks? Do citizens protest against risks in their neighborhoods? If citizens are better informed, their participation in risk management could increase. But does that actually happen?

A third set of questions relates to the effects of risk maps on actions of government agencies and private companies. If citizens know what they are doing and take political action, government agencies and private companies might be pressured to take additional measures. Do they take more appropriate measures to manage risks? Does transparency improve the quality of risk management?

In this essay I will argue that transparency does not lead to a better informed citizenry. In fact, few citizens bother to look at the risk maps on the Internet. These citizens do not use the risk maps to pressure governments and private companies into improving risk management. They mainly ask informative questions. However, this does not mean that public risk maps do not influence risk management. Transparency directly influences the behavior of governments and companies. [1] However, there is also a dark side to openness: terrorists may use the information to plan attacks. Governments will need to find ways to use risk maps for improving safety without diminishing security.

2. Management of physical risks: A key function of government

In modern societies, governments have to deal with all kinds of risks. The focus in this essay is on physical risks: risks that have a direct impact on human beings and other living creatures but also on houses, buildings, roads, railways, and so forth. Citizens expect from their governments that they set rules, develop legislation and implement policies to protect their physical environments. Governments cannot guarantee the safety of physical environments but they can limit risks and develop adequate plans for dealing with threats.

Risks to the physical environment can be of various natures. A first type of risk concerns natural events like floods, earth quakes, heavy storms, tornados, and volcanic eruptions. Of course, governments can't prevent these natural events but they can take measures to manage the risk of these events. These measures include, among others, spatial planning to prevent people from building houses in dangerous areas, setting rules for building houses and building in these locations, providing adequate information to citizens in the case of upcoming danger, and developing plans for evacuating areas. In the Netherlands floods have always been a major threat to humans and their property. In fact, managing the risk of floods can be regarded as the reason for creating the first democratic government bodies – the Water Boards – as early as the thirteenth century.

Risks to the physical environments can also be created by humans. Buildings can be constructed inadequately and therefore cause catastrophes. Recently, in the Netherlands the balcony of a building in Maastricht collapsed killing two people. Citizens expect from their governments that they prevent these disasters from happening by setting guidelines for constructing buildings and inspecting whether these guidelines are being followed. Another type of risk created by humans concerns the transport, production and storage of hazardous materials. These materials are needed for the production of goods and energy but create risks to their environments. Private companies need to take measures for preventing these risks but governments need to control whether they are doing that adequately.

A third type of risk is also man made and concerns the risk of people that intentionally want to create disasters. Since 9/11 there has been much more attention for this type of risk. How can governments prevent terrorist attacks? And how can they minimize the effects of these attacks? This type of risk has been considered in the case of high risk locations such as nuclear plants. The attack on the Twin Towers has changed this perception. Many more locations are now considered to be at risk and governments have developed – and are developing – plans to deal with attacks on a wide variety of locations.

[1] The findings are based on empirical research I have conducted in the Netherlands. The method of research and the full findings are presented in Meijer [4].

The policy domain of physical risk management is complicated and concerns the involvement of many government agencies. Ministries of spatial planning, water works, physical infrastructures and national safety are involved, but also local governments and police, fire and health departments play a role in risk management. These government bodies all play a role in identifying, preventing and dealing with a broad variety of risks. Management of physical risks can be regarded as one of the key functions of government.

3. Crisis forces increase in transparency

In the Netherlands, governments were not used to open communication about risks. Before the fireworks factory exploded in the year 2000, many local governments argued that it was better to not actively inform citizens about risks in their direct environment since this could lead to irrational fear in their communities. The general opinion was that governments should take appropriate measures and develop plans to protect citizens against risks, but citizens did not have to know about these risks. The general attitude was a paternalistic one.

The explosion of the fireworks factory in Enschede changed all this. Why did many citizens not know that there was a fireworks factory in their neighborhood? A paternalistic attitude of government was no longer accepted. The general opinion changed quickly: citizens had the right to be informed about risks. The crisis forced an increase in transparency about risks. Through the Internet, risks maps were made available to the general public.

Originally, the risk maps were not created for risk communication. At the start, these maps were created by Dutch provinces – first Friesland, later Limburg, Utrecht and others – to facilitate cooperation between the various organizations that are involved in risk management. After the disaster in Enschede, all these provinces decided to make the information public through their websites. Since 2004, provision of public risk maps is a legal obligation for Dutch provinces.

Their risk maps display sources of risks (factories, airports, gas pipes, storages) and targets (schools, hospitals, shopping centers). Risk map visitors can view maps and zoom in on areas they are interested in. They can click on symbols and get additional information on the nature of risks. The risk map does not provide information about risk management. Citizens can contact their local government for information on emergency plans.

City governments also publish risk maps on the Internet. An interesting case is Eindhoven. The risk map of this city does not only display sources and targets of risks but also shows the results of inspections of hazardous facilities. The risk map indicates what the results of the inspection are – for example: additional safety facilities need to be created – and what the company has done in response to the inspection – for example: safety facilities have been created.

4. Citizens do not become more politically active

Risk maps increase the transparency of risk and thus enable political participation by citizens. Citizens can look at the maps and find out what risks there are in their neighborhoods. They can find out whether they live near a fireworks factory and see whether there are fuel pipelines and storage of hazardous material nearby. On the basis of this information they could pressure government agencies and private companies to improve risk management.

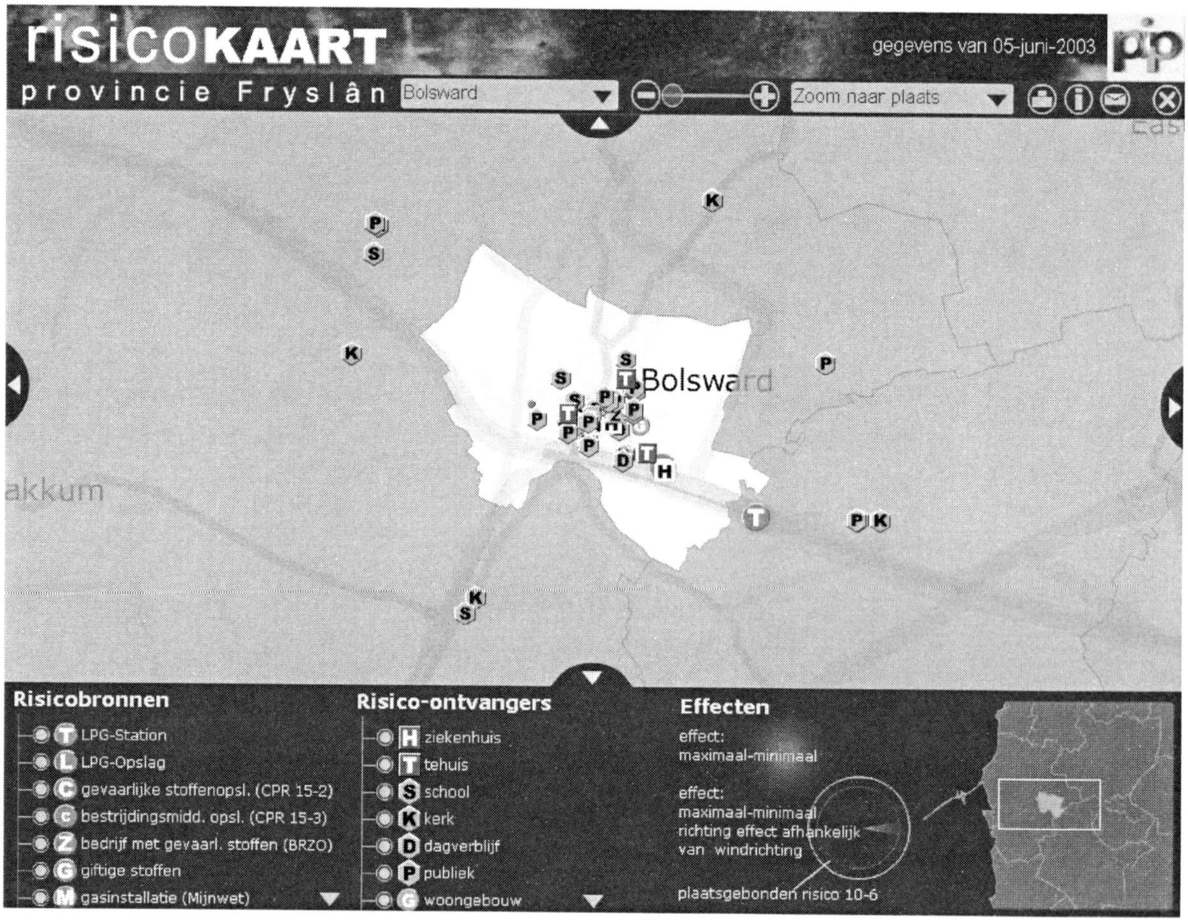

Fig. 1. Risk map of the province of Friesland.

These ideas about citizen participation fit with within Barber's [1] conception of a 'strong democracy'. Citizens should not only vote for representatives but also become actively involved in public affairs. Public affairs should not only be discussed in formalized institutions: direct citizen participation could increase the legitimacy of government and the effectiveness of policies.

The idea of direct participation puts high demands on citizens: they need to spend time and energy on public affairs. A perspective on citizenship that takes these limitations into account is the idea of the 'monitorial citizen' [5]: these citizens should be informed enough to identify danger to their personal good and danger to the public good. According to Schudson, monitorial citizens will protest against decision or actions when these directly influence their own situation or when these actions or decisions have an important impact on matters that are important to them (e.g. environmental issue or animal rights).

Theoretically, transparency could lead to a better informed citizenry and hence more citizen involvement in risk management. 'Monitorial citizens' could pressure government agencies and private companies into improving their risk management. Does it work like that? On the basis of exploratory empirical research I will test this argument. First I will evaluate whether risk maps on the Internet do actually lead to a better informed citizenry.

5. Just a small group of citizens is better informed

To find out whether citizens are better informed about risks in their immediate environments, I have looked at the number of hits on websites. The risk map of the province of Friesland (population: 640,000) receives approximately 1500 hits per month. The province has put a short questionnaire on the website to find out who the visitors are. This questionnaire indicated that approximately halve of the visitors are citizens, the other halve concerns people that have a professional interest in risk maps such as real estate agents and civil servants responsible for spatial planning.

The province of Utrecht also has a risk map on its website which is fairly similar to the risk map in Friesland. Utrecht has more inhabitants than the province of Friesland – population: 1,160,000 – but receives less hits on its website: between 300 and 1000 visitors per month. A large portion of these visitors again concerns people with a professional interest.

The city of Eindhoven (population: 200,000) has a risk map on its website that also show the results of inspection. This risk map received many hits when the website was just made public – 5500 hits in six weeks – but later the number of hits went down to 700 to 1000 hits per month. The city has not investigated who the visitors to the website are.

On the basis of this research, I conclude that the number of citizens that have looked at risk maps is limited. Furthermore, there is been little media attention for the risk maps. Even local newspapers do not write about these risk maps on the Internet. Thus, we cannot expect that the risk maps have indirectly increased the knowledge of citizens about risks.

Risk maps do not seem to be an appropriate medium to inform large groups of citizens about risks in their neighborhoods. Nevertheless, one could still argue that a small group is better informed and can use this information for political action. Do the citizens who look at the risk maps, use this information to pressure government agencies and private companies into improving their risk management?

6. Risks maps do not lead to citizen involvement

To evaluate whether the transparency of risks in their neighborhoods leads to more citizen involvement, I have investigated whether citizens reacted to the information on websites. The research indicated that the province of Friesland has received few reactions: only five comments per e-mail and one comment per telephone. These reactions mostly concerned comments on the (mis)location of factories and storages on the map. People also mentioned missing risks.

The province of Utrecht receives approximately three reactions per month concerning the risk map. These reactions mostly concern missing risks. Often these were deliberately not put on the map since they are risks of a relatively limited nature. The citizens then receive an answer to inform them about the character of the risk map on the Internet.

Occasionally, the city of Eindhoven receives questions from citizens concerning the nature of the risks. Generally, these questions can be answered easily. Citizens ask for more information, the city has not received reactions that pressured them into other forms of risk management.

Apart from these reactions, citizens might use the information in other ways to influence risk management. They could for example pressure private companies into limiting the storage of hazardous waste or moving the production of fireworks to another location. Or citizens could pressure their local governments into improving their plans for risk management. Do citizens use the information for this type of political action?

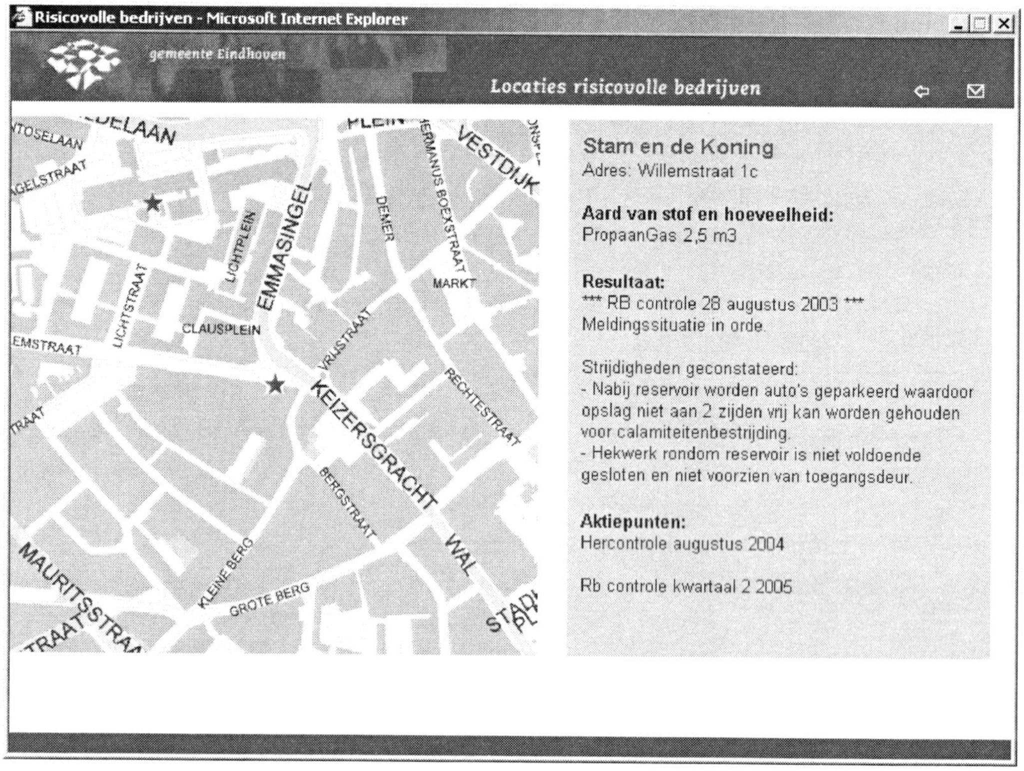

Fig. 2. Risk map of the city of Eindhoven.

None of these government organizations has investigated what the risk maps are used for. The dominant view is that citizens want to know about the risks in their neighborhood but do no use this information to act. As far as the respondents knew, the risk maps on the Internet do not lead to public protest, letters in newspapers, complaints to governments or to private companies. There was one exception. In Bilthoven (province of Utrecht) the risk map on the Internet was used by citizens in their protests against a factory.

The conclusion is that a small group of citizens does look at the risk maps on the Internet but this group does not use the information for putting pressure on governments and private companies. Does this mean that the transparency of risks has no influence on the management of risks? Maybe not. There are other relations between transparency of risks and risk management. Transparency may not lead to pressure from citizens but can directly put pressure on governments and private companies to improve their management of risks. To understand this relation, I will use the classical idea of anticipating accountability [3].

7. Transparency puts pressure on governments and private companies

Accountability arrangements often work through anticipation: governments and companies are not actually called to account, but still act as if they will be called to account. In his classical work on accountability, Friedrich [3, p. 203] calls this the 'rule of anticipated reactions'. The fiction of accountability – which can become reality – influences their behavior. In risk management, anticipating public accountability is an important mechanism that affects both private companies and local governments.

A first effect of the publication of risk maps on the Internet is that companies re-evaluate their permits. Before openness was created, many companies would ask a permit to store large amounts of chemicals and use this permit to store only a limited amount. For governments this meant that they had to be prepared for large risks whereas actually the risks were only of a limited nature. Now, the risk maps indicates the risks associated with the maximum amount allowed for by the permit. In reaction to the risk maps, many companies have changed their permits because they feared reactions from citizens. Citizens do not actually hold companies accountable but companies still anticipate accountability.

A second, more interesting effect, was that the publication of risk maps in the city of Eindhoven led to better risk management. In Eindhoven the compliance of companies to recommendations made by inspectors has increased significantly from 11% of the companies before the risk map was published to 85% now. Respondents have indicated that companies fear media attention and damage to their image. Anticipating media attention, they comply with recommendations concerning the prevention of disasters.

In the future, risk maps on the Internet may lead to a third effect. The province of Utrecht has indicated that they will indicate whether local governments have developed plans for risk management. At this moment, not all local governments have developed such plans. Publication on the Internet can stimulate local governments to develop plans for risk management. If a local government is one of the few local governments that has not developed plans for risk management, this could damage its reputation and lead to public pressure. Anticipating public and media attention, local governments will be stimulated to make plans for risk management.

In three different ways the transparency of risks influences – or may influence – the behavior of governments and private companies. They do not wait for citizens to protest but anticipate protests and take measures. Although the changes may not only be attributed to the public risk maps on the Internet, transparency creates an extra incentive to take measures. These measures could indeed improve the quality of risk management and enhance safety. But do risk maps also enhance security?

8. Do risk maps facilitate terrorist attacks?

Recently, Members of Parliament in the Netherlands have asked the minister of Internal Affairs whether risk maps facilitate terrorist attacks.[2] The maps indicate specifically where hazardous materials are stored or transported and could thus be used to plan an attack. The MP's wondered whether the citizens' right to know did not create security hazards.

The minister of Internal Affairs indicated that the national governments has considered security issues in implementing risk maps. The National Information Agency has been involved in decision making about providing information to the public and this has led to certain limitation. The national government has decided not to put information on the estimated amount of casualties and the area that would be affected by a disaster.

Security issues have played a role in deciding which information concerning risks and risk management could be made available to the public. For every hazardous location, companies in close cooperation with fire departments develop contingency plans. These plans indicate specifically what routes are to be used for evacuation and also for rescue services entering the location. These plans contain highly specific information concerning the hazardous location and therefore could be used breaking entry by criminals. Even under the Freedom of Information Act, these plans are not available to the public.

---

[2]The liberal MP's De Krom & Wilders sent their written question to the Minister of Internal Affairs Remkes on 29 March 2004. This question was answered by the minister April 29th 2004.

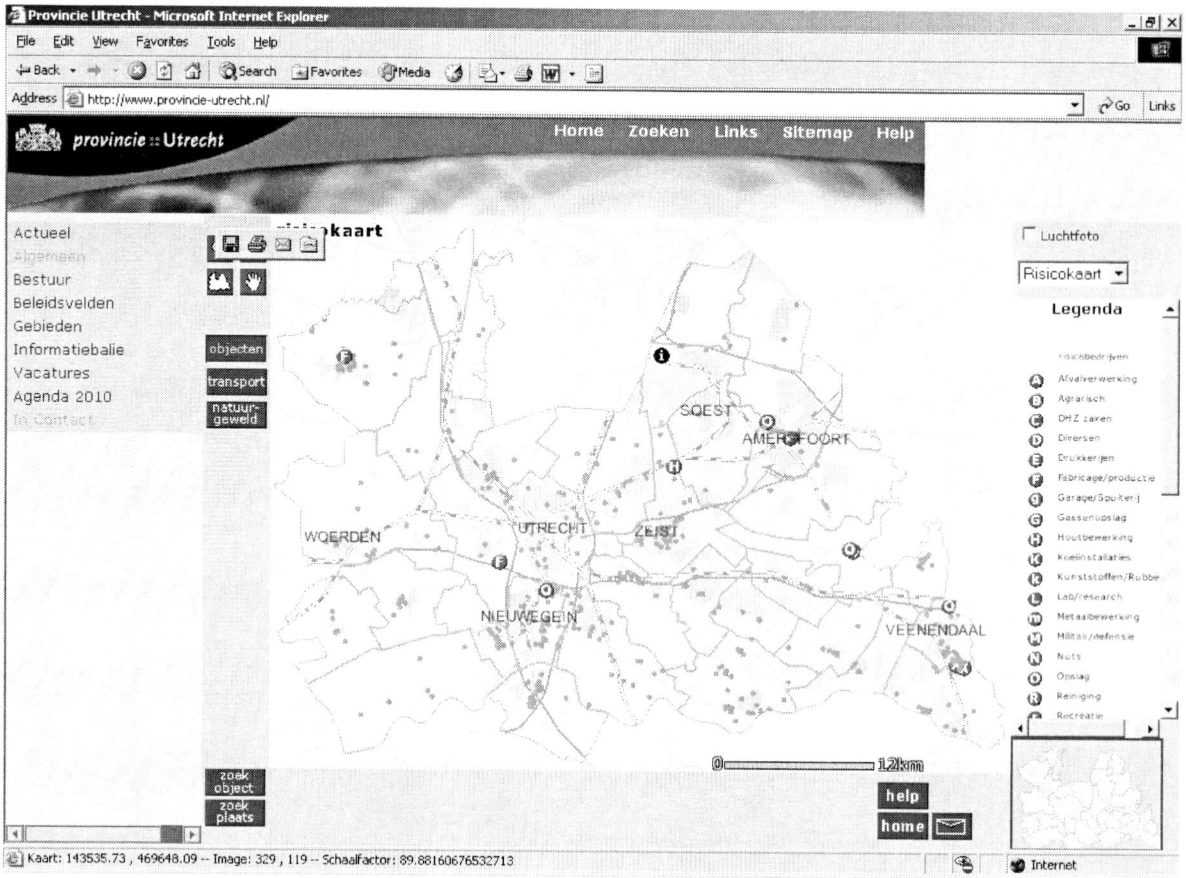

Fig. 3. Risk map of the province of Utrecht.

The terrorist threat, however, adds a new dimension to the debate between freedom of information and security. In the Netherlands, security issues have played a limited role in policies concerning risk maps. Since the disaster with the fireworks factory, governments have focused on safety issues and the general opinion is that safety is served by openness. In the near future the debate may shift and openness may be considered to be a threat to security.

9. Public information improves safety but may threaten security

I have shown that Dutch citizens make little use of the risk maps on the Internet. Few citizens access the maps and the risk maps are not used to pressure companies and governments into reducing risks and improving safety. The information on provincial and city websites enables accountability to citizens but these opportunities are not – or hardly – used.

Proponents of public accountability stress that a better informed citizenry holds for a strong democracy [1]. Risk maps, however, do little to make democracy stronger since there are few citizens that access risk maps on the Internet. The Internet does not seem to be a suitable medium for actively informing citizens on risks since it is not a mass medium. Monitorial citizens [5] can find information on risk maps but – with one exception – this has not led to protests against governments or companies.

However, this does not mean that transparency through public risk maps on the Internet has no effects. Government organizations and private companies fear negative media attention. The prime driver for change in risk management is reputation management. Organizations anticipate media attention and try to avoid negative publications.

Proponents of transparency argue that citizens can detect failures and, therefore, improve the effectiveness of government [2]. In the case of risk maps, failures are mostly detected by private companies themselves. They see that their permits are not in accordance with the actual situation and therefore ask for a more limited permit. This leads to a more adequate mapping of risks and thus better risk management.

A more significant effect concerns the increased compliance of companies with the recommendations of environmental inspectors. The risk map on the Internet grants the environmental inspection a public nature. Private companies fear negative media attention and, therefore, comply with the recommendations. The effectiveness of environmental inspections is thus increased.

Lately, the benefits of risk maps have been challenged by those emphasizing that risk maps may create security risks. The maps could be used by terrorist planning an attack aimed at causing as many casualties as possible. So far, this argument has not played a crucial role in the development of risk maps in the public sector. In the near future, however, this argument may become more important and this could lead to a decline in transparency concerning physical risks.

I conclude that transparency through the Internet improves risk management. Governments and companies feel that they are 'being' watched and take measures to avoid damage to their reputation. These measures may help to prevent future disasters like the explosion of the fireworks factory in Enschede. These benefits of transparency, however, are threatened because openness can also be used for terrorist attacks. A challenge for the future is to create intelligent, open systems for risk management that improve the safety of citizens and do no threaten their security.

References

[1] B.R. Barber, *Strong Democracy*, University of California Press, Berkeley, 1984.
[2] D. Brin, *The Transparent Society*, Perseus, Reading, 1998.
[3] C.J. Friedrich, *Man and His Government. An Empirical Theory of Politics*, McGraw-Hill Book Company, New York, 1963.
[4] A. Meijer, *Vreemde ogen dwingen. De betekenis van internet voor maatschappelijke controle in de publieke sector*, Boom Juridische Uitgevers, The Hague, 2002.
[5] M. Schudson, *The Good Citizen. A History of American Civic Life*, The Free Press, New York, 1998.

Risks to Internet Governance

Information Polity 10 (2005) 117–128
IOS Press

Who regulates and manages the Internet infrastructure? Democratic and legal risks in shadow global governance

Miriam Lips* and Bert-Jaap Koops
Tilburg Institute for Law, Technology, and Society (TILT), Tilburg University, P.O. Box 90153, 5000 LE Tilburg, The Netherlands

Abstract. This essay explores the democratic and legal risks related to the emerging situation of global Internet governance. This situation can be considered as an outcome of the 1997 US Federal Government's policy aims towards privatisation and self-regulation of the technical management of the increasingly global Internet at that time. Thus far there is little empirical knowledge available about the nature and functioning of the various relatively unknown international organisations that are involved in the technical development and management of the Internet. Attention in this respect seems to be exclusively focused on only one of these organisations, the Internet Corporation for Assigned Names and Numbers (ICANN), which continues to have a unique relationship with the US Federal Government's Department of Commerce. The empirical question of who actually regulates and manages the Internet infrastructure further rises in importance if we consider that the technical development of the Internet might not be a 'neutral' development but could involve the building in of regulatory norms into the technology.

1. Introduction

In the 1990s, during the Clinton-Gore Administration, the following anecdote could be learned from civil servants of the United States Federal Government. Immediately after their meeting with President Clinton, internationally distinguished political leaders were taken by Vice President Gore to the vaults of the White House. There, the Vice President, who liked to present himself as a visionary regarding the Internet, showed these prominent guests a scale model of the public Internet of the future with the message:

> *"This is the Internet. This is also the way in which you should develop the Internet in your own country."*

This anecdote is interesting for several reasons. It suggests that the Internet can be captured in a physical model, an architecture, something you could see and control. It also indicates that Gore was convinced about the position and power of the United States to determine the future of the Internet. If we look at the Internet's history this conviction of Al Gore is not surprising: after all, the Internet originates from the US and mainly has been shaped by the US Federal government.

Gradually, however, the Internet has become a global medium. The US Federal Government observed this development, and in 1997, decided to initiate the privatisation and self-regulation of the technical

*Corresponding author. Tel.: +31 13 4668345; Fax: +31 13 4663750; E-mail: A.M.B.Lips@uvt.nl.

management of the Internet [30]. But what does privatisation and self-regulation of the technical management of an increasingly global medium such as the Internet actually imply? Before the Internet became a public medium in the mid 1990s, responsibility for its technical management was more or less clear in the sense that it was mainly related to the US government and it at least could be located within the borders of the United States (see for instance [1]). Since then however, it seems to be unclear which organisations are actually determining the technical development of the Internet. Is the US Federal Government still a dominant player in this, or do other governments perhaps have a voice in the development and maintenance of the Internet architecture also? Or, are NGOs or private companies perhaps deciding upon the technical management and development of the Internet?

These questions on the implications of the development towards privatisation and self-regulation are currently highly important for several reasons. First, with the acknowledgement of the Internet as a public and increasingly global medium it is important to know more about the democratic implications of this development. Who has decision-making powers over the development of the Internet infrastructure now, and to what extent are these decision makers representing the global public? At the same time, the legal implications of this development are important so as to find out about the extent to which the parties involved are in the position to make binding decisions. Who has prescriptive jurisdiction over the Internet at present? Also, to what extent is it actually possible to make legitimate decisions in an increasingly global environment? Moreover, these questions rise in importance even further if we consider that the technical development of the Internet might not be a 'neutral' development.

Thus far however, there is little empirical knowledge available about the nature and functioning of the various organisations that are involved in the technical development and management of the Internet. Attention in this respect seems to be exclusively focused on the Internet Corporation for Assigned Names and Numbers (ICANN), the main policy maker for Internet domain names and numbers, and its unique relationship with the US Federal Government's Department of Commerce (e.g. [9,19]). For this latter reason in particular and because of the pending reorganisation of the Internet's Domain Name System, several 'ICANN Watch'-organisations have been created[1] to follow developments closely over the question 'who is ruling the roots' (see for instance [20]).

The worldwide importance of who regulates and manages the Internet infrastructure is illustrated by the fact that this issue has been put on the agenda for the forthcoming United Nation's World Summit on the Information Society (WSIS) in November 2005. However, with the strong focus on ICANN, we may forget that there are at least nine other organisations that make decisions about global Internet management and development. In this essay, therefore, we would like to set out more about the nature and functioning of these organisations and the way in which they influence the technical management and development of the global Internet infrastructure. In doing so, we will focus on the 'lower' layers of the Internet: the network and transport layers enabling the transportation of data. We will leave aside the applications layer and the divergent management and development issues it raises, therefore (for a discussion of regulatory and management implications for the 'higher' content level see the contribution of Hoff and Bjerke in this issue). In particular, we explore the potential democratic and legal risks related to the emerging situation of global Internet governance. Firstly, however we would like to explain further why in our view these risks might be even more important for consideration than might initially have been expected.

[1] See for instance www.icannwatch.org.

2. The Internet is not technology neutral

The public medium of the Internet has not reached its definitive shape: rather it can be considered as a medium in continuous development. Characteristics of the Internet, such as its open, decentralised, networked and digital character, support various possibilities for further expansion. Both established and emerging media can be easily connected to the Internet, for example, and more and more huge multimedia files can be exchanged between an increasing number of locations around the world. However, this expanding, almost all-embracing 'network of networks' in our view cannot be considered to be technology neutral. More and more we may observe that norms are being built into the technology of the Internet. With 'norms' we do not intend so much to refer to technological standards, but even more so towards legal or ethical standards. This development of building in regulatory norms into the technology is often referred to as 'code as code' [16,17]: the software code has been designed and therefore regulates analogously to a principle of law, a legal Code [17,23].[2] For instance, the present architecture of the Internet has not only much to do with the possibility, but also the *desirability*, of filtering of information, the distribution of spam and the tapping of email messages, for example. The design and further development of the Internet does not only have technical implications, but also legal, economical and societal consequences, therefore. For instance the allocation of domain names, or the creation of new, generic domains like '.aero' or '.sex' may have a profound impact on market developments or social perceptions of online activities. More importantly, the Internet infrastructure increasingly seems to allow for building-in 'switches and valves' that enable states to re-territorialize the Internet. Contrary to the tendency of earlier Internet development, states can more and more block and filter information regionally, because the infrastructure enables them to do so [24,25].[3]

This situation makes it highly relevant to explore further the relatively unknown international organisations that have tasks and responsibilities in respect of the technical management of the Internet. In both their activities and their views on Internet policy these Internet organisations seem to determine Internet technology, the Internet architecture and 'code'. For example, one of the main guiding principles of the Internet Society (ISOC) is to achieve open, unencumbered, beneficial use of the Internet.[4] Moreover, according to ISOC, online free expression should not be restricted by other indirect means such as excessively restrictive governmental or private controls over computer hardware or software, telecommunications infrastructure, or other essential components of the Internet. The World Wide Web Consortium (W3C) has similar objectives in achieving universal access to the Internet, a semantic web and a 'web of trust' in which the technology takes into account the legal, social and commercial environment. W3C has much influence on the technical development of the Internet by means of its publications of technical specifications as so-called 'W3C Recommendations', which can be compared to standards published by other organisations.[5] A last but not unimportant example for the technical development of the Internet is the so-called RFC Editor, the publisher of 'Requests for Comment' (RFCs) and responsible for the final editing of these documents, which, after publication, can be considered as Internet standards. Every

---

[2] See for an extensive discussion of the normative role of technology, with more detailed analyses in the areas of intellectual property, freedom of speech, and privacy: [2].

[3] The power of the Internet infrastructure to regulate behaviour in this way is comparable to the power of, for instance, Microsoft to influence the behaviour of computer and Internet users through its software design. Since our essay is concerned with the infrastructure of the Internet, that is, the physical and logical layers that enable the transport of data, we shall not go into the issue of the legitimacy of the applications, such as browsers and operating systems.

[4] <http://www.isoc.org/isoc/mission/principles>.

[5] <http://www.w3.org/TR/>.

individual can submit a proposal for a RFC but in practice most RFCs are generated by the Internet Engineering Task Force (IETF).

So far however there has been little public attention to the development and functioning of these various Internet organisations, as an outcome of the US Federal Government's policy aims towards privatisation and self-regulation. Neither in academic publications[6] nor in professional journal articles do we have the power of these organisations in respect of Internet development explained. This situation is unlike national or supranational organisations familiar to us, such as the United States Federal Government or the European Union, which clearly have an influential position on international public decision-making and regulation of important topics for further technological development of the Internet, like interconnection obligations or communications tapping requirements.

3. Democratic risks in global governance: Who decides upon the public Internet?

What do we actually know in general about outcomes of privatisation and self-regulation efforts at an international level of governance, as aimed at by the US Federal Government for instance?

Privatisation in a broad sense can be defined in the following way: *"the involvement of the private sector in activities currently the responsibility of the public sector involving the transfer of risk to the private sector"* (Allen, 2001).[7] According to this definition risk transfer does not need to be completely targeted on the removal of tasks and responsibilities from the public sector, but activities can be done in partnership between the two sectors. To make a certain choice for the organisation of public activities, as we could consider to be the case for Internet infrastructure management and development, a key question always seems to be how to organise public services more efficiently and effectively, the latter implying how to restore authority for these public services to citizens for which these services are meant [18]. In privatisation efforts, the protection of public interests requires an assessment based on specific public norms and values, such as democratic legitimacy, legal certainty, equality for the law, effectiveness and efficiency [21, p. 31]. Interestingly, research on conditions for successful self-regulation initiatives points in the same direction, in stressing the importance of collective interests, representing all parties involved, guaranteeing legal security and legal protection, and protecting the autonomy of all parties involved [28, pp. 21–22].

If we look at the current situation of the technical management of the Internet it is far from clear which sector(s) and actor(s) have authority in these respects and therefore are deciding upon the Internet infrastructure. In the case of ICANN this 'shadowy situation' is publicly known and an important reason in itself for many to watch this organisation, with its far-reaching powers of Internet regulation, closely. Created as an international non-profit corporation in which many companies, governments, technical organisations, scientific organisations and user organisations are involved in a public-private partnership, ICANN remains subject to a 1998 Memorandum of Understanding (MoU) with the US Department of Commerce in which a test period has been settled for the transition of the domain name system. Originally targeted for a two-year period, this test period has been renewed several times since 2000.

[6]An exception in this area is the academic contribution of Sassen 1998, pp. 557–558.

[7]*Issues in Privatisation. Critical success factors,* text of a presentation made by Nick Allen at a one-day seminar jointly organised by the Bureau of Public Enterprises (BPE) and PricewaterhouseCoopers for Ministers, top Government officials and other senior stakeholders at Nicon-Hilton Hotel, Abuja on 26 March 2001. Presentation available at http://www.bpeng.org/CGI-BIN/publications/Presentations/Nick%20Allen%20-%20Issues%20In%20Privatization-%20Critical%20Success%20Factors.doc.

Consequently the US Federal Government retains final authority with regard to ICANN's activities for the time being.

Not only ICANN's situation is unclear regarding the transparency of authority and related decision-making powers. Other Internet organisations also have organisational structures and arrangements which make it difficult to grasp where responsibility and accountability lie. The World Wide Web Consortium (W3C) for instance is an international consortium with more than 360 members mainly coming from a variety of private sector organisations and academia, but also from the public sector (e.g. the United States Defence Information Systems Agency, the London Metropolitan Police, the BBC, the InfoComm Development Authority of Singapore and the Government of India's Department of Information Technology), standardisation organisations (e.g. the US National Institute of Standards and Technology) and even some civil liberty organisations (e.g. Center for Democracy and Technology). Tim Berners-Lee, the inventor of the World Wide Web, has been Director of W3C since its creation in 1994. Formally, W3C's Director is appointed by MIT, where part of the W3C staff (about 60 researchers) is located. The two other W3C staff locations, ERCIM (in France) and Keio University (in Japan), are responsible for appointing W3C's Vice Directors. The appointments of the W3C chairman and the Chief Operating Officer are an internal procedure within MIT. MIT, ERCIM and Keio University together constitute the legal entity of W3C.

Another example is the international non-profit organisation Internet Society (ISOC), which consists of more than 100 organisations and 20,000 individual members, with national, regional, and local organisations ('chapters') in over 180 countries.[8] ISOC uses differentiated organisational memberships based on different yearly financial contribution levels: the more a member would like to pay the more influence on ISOC it can have. At the highest, 'Platina', contribution level is the possibility of having two representatives on the ISOC Advisory Council, involvement in the election of 6 ISOC Board of Trustee Members, and participation in the development of ISOC's public policy positions. At present, ISOC's 'Platina' sponsors are three Regional Internet Registry organisations, namely the Asia Pacific Network Information Centre (APNIC), the American Registry for Internet Numbers (ARIN) and RIPE Network Coordination Centre (RIPE NCC); Afilias (a global domain name registry service company), Microsoft and The Swedish International Development Agency (SIDA).

All of these Internet organisations appear to have some involvement from the private, public and not-for profit sector. A clear choice between the public or private sector to manage and develop the Internet infrastructure has not been made so far, therefore, and the unique global character of the Internet makes it questionable whether this choice could or even should be made. Consequently, risk transfer seems to be happening from one dominant actor in the public domain (the US Federal Government) to a variety of actors with roots in the public, private and non-profit domains and with members scattered over the globe. However, the collective interest of the public Internet would at least require an assessment of Internet management and development activities along certain public norms and values, such as described above. A major problem for global Internet infrastructure management though is how to assess privatisation and self-regulation efforts at an *international* level. Held points out that *"global interconnectedness contests the traditional national resolutions of the central questions of democratic theory and practice ... the very process of governance seems to be 'escaping the categories' of the nation-state"* [11, p. 338]. Throughout the twentieth century an almost taken-for-granted conception of sovereignty existed at the level of the nation-state, leading to a situation in which issues of governance and jurisdiction were mainly focused at the national level [11, pp. 335–336]. As a result, national territorial boundaries usually

[8]<http://www.isoc.org/isoc/>.

delineate the basis on which individuals are included and excluded from democratic decision-making and public participation.

In the last decades however a general development in practice can be observed from national to international arenas in which decisions about public activities are being taken (e.g. [5]). This development takes place both in a vertical and horizontal way. Vertically, national governments are losing decision making power to intergovernmental institutions and regimes (e.g. WTO, WIPO), which are hardly subject to any forms of democratic control; a horizontal displacement can be observed in the strong increase of influence and decision making powers of NGOs and big transnational companies. Consequently, an accumulation of democratic risks may be observed for these emerging international arenas. Where the traditional setting for public decision making in the democratic nation-state offers clarity about the functioning and meaning of representation, the nature of the constituency, the form and scope of political participation, and the regulations in place to guarantee rights and duties of national subjects in international arenas, in many cases there seems to be a situation of disproportionate and unbalanced representation of interests, administrators that are not elected, no parliamentary control, limited publicity and a lack of public accountability [5]. As these Internet organisations have decision-making powers over increasingly global Internet regulatory and governance issues, the question for these international organisations raises in importance on how to establish global democratic legitimacy. For instance, how are the interests of various individual Internet users represented and guaranteed, particularly if we consider the fact that the Internet generally has been acknowledged as a public medium which should be accessible for all (e.g. UN WSIS 2003)?

4. Legal risks in global governance: Who rules the Internet?

Given the view that Internet technology is not only technical but can also be normative in practice, the standardising and architectural development activities of Internet organisations may raise questions not only of legitimacy in terms of democracy, but also in terms of legal jurisdiction. After all, the rule of law traditionally presupposes that prescriptive jurisdiction – i.e. jurisdiction to prescribe legally effective norms that bind people – is restricted to national governments. The fact that international rule-making has become increasingly important over the past decades, does not alter this fact: it is national governments that have the legitimacy to enact rules, be it by themselves or within supranational or international bodies and agreements. How then does the management and development of the global Internet architecture fit within this picture? How can the Internet be regulated in a more horizontal and international way in relation to the existing vertical authority of nation states over their territory? Who has, or should have, prescriptive jurisdiction over the Internet: sovereign states, supra- or international organisations, multinationals, Internet organisations, everybody, or no one (cf. [20])?

The traditional notion of jurisdiction closely relates to territoriality and sovereignty. At first sight however, this notion does not seem to fit with the emerging Internet world. Many Internet scholars for instance claim that the Internet does not comply with territoriality and state sovereignty is becoming irrelevant therefore. This belief has even led to anarchistic declarations of independence, such as the declaration of J.P. Barlow [3], and also to considerable doom-mongering. But is the Internet really that independent of territory?

There are two lines of argument in this respect. On the one hand, there are those who view the Internet as an independent space, remote from the 'traditional' world. Johnson and Post [12] for instance speak of the application of one simple principle: conceiving of cyberspace as a distinct "place" for purposes of legal analysis and recognising a legally significant border between cyberspace and the "real world".

Advocates of this line of argument stress the software, the bits and bytes, the virtual *personae* and the multiple (pseudo-) identities the technical 'Internauts' assume to do virtual things; in short, the intangible, elusive part of the Internet. On the other hand, the observation can be made that the spatial metaphor of 'cyberspace' is used actually to view the Internet as part of traditional territory (see [10]): 'Instead of concluding that cyberspace is outside of the physical world, courts are increasingly using the metaphor of cyberspace as a "place" to justify application of traditional laws governing real property to this new medium [15].' Proponents of this line of argument stress the cables and satellites, the real persons who use the Internet for real, daily-life things; that is, the tangible, 'bricks-and-mortar' parts of the Internet.

Whichever approach one follows, the question of jurisdiction is equally relevant in both cases: as a primarily territorial unit the Internet does raise the question of 'who rules' in this territory. The 'virtualists' will answer sooner by pointing at the Internet community itself, the 'realists' will rather relate to sovereign states. We could continue this theoretical debate to decide upon this issue but we could also have a closer look at who actually is deciding upon Internet territory and the borders of cyberspace – the topic of the following section.

5. Who is regulating the Internet?

To provide some answers to questions about risk transfer in global Internet regulation and management and related potential democratic and legal risks, we explored ten international organisations that currently influence the development of the Internet; not as much by legislative activities as through technological management and attempts towards standardisation (see [14][9]). We focused on those organisations that are influencing the various 'technical layers' of the Internet, namely the technical infrastructure, network architecture and communication and application protocols, which may include the creation of norms built into the technology as we explained earlier. As a consequence we left out of consideration the 'content layer' of the Internet, as this particular area entails a different regulatory involvement for organisations.

The ten organisations we looked at can be briefly described, as follows:

- The World Wide Web Consortium (W3C) can be considered to influence the development of Internet technology in the most general and often indirect way compared to other Internet organisations.
- Less focused on technology development and more on the technical management of the Internet is the Internet Society (ISOC).
- Technical Internet standards are to a large extent determined by the Internet Engineering Task Force (IETF), the Internet Engineering Steering Group (IESG) and the Internet Architecture Board (IAB).
- The Internet Research Task Force (IRTF), in particular, supports the long-term development of the Internet.
- The main documents to arrive at Internet proposals, standards and protocols are the so-called 'Requests for Comments' (RFCs). Internet standards are published by an assigned functionary, the so-called 'RFC Editor'.
- One of the most important conditions for effective, flexible Internet communications and for finding Internet users is the organisation and management of Internet domain names and numbers. As set

[9]The analysis of the ten organisations is available in our Dutch essay for the IT & Law Programme of the Dutch Council for Scientific Research (NWO): B.J. Koops and A.M.B. Lips [14], 'Wie reguleert het Internet? Horizontalisering en rechtsmacht bij de technische regulering van het Internet', in: H. Franken et al., *Zeven essays over informatietechnologie en recht*, The Hague: Sdu 2003, pp. 261–315.

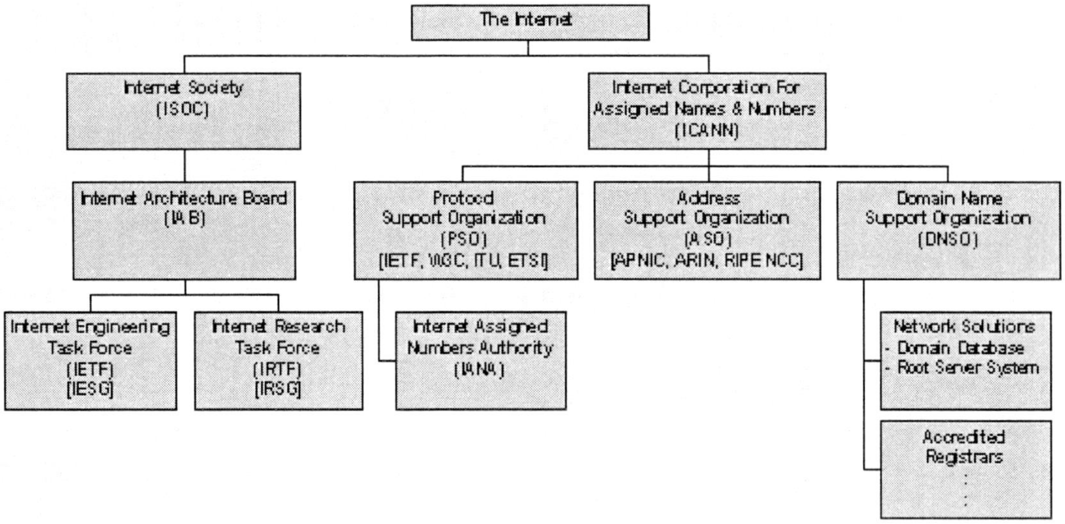

Fig. 1.

out in the introductory section of this essay ICANN is the main policy maker in this particular area. More operationally active in this respect however are the Internet Assigned Numbers Authority (IANA, actually part of ICANN) and regional registries such as RIPE NCC. Figure 1 presents an overview of the interrelationships of these organisations.[10]

For each of these organisations we focused our research on three main areas. First, the nature of the organisation and its specific tasks and responsibilities through which it influences the development and management of the Internet. Secondly, the extent to which the US federal government's aim of 'horizontalisation' has been achieved: the relation between the organisation and the worldwide Internet community, or even society in general; moreover its representativeness at an international level as well as its democratic functioning. Thirdly, we look at the jurisdictional basis on which the organisation can exert its influence on the global Internet.

These main areas have been further explored by looking at the aims, tasks and responsibilities of each Internet organisation; its constitution and membership; its administrative procedures; and its resource basis. On the basis of our empirical findings we observe the following general characteristics of Internet organisations at present:

– The *international not-for-profit* character of Internet organisations. As a rule members of these organisations cannot act as representative for a specific organisation in the day-to-day world, but are appointed as individuals. This procedure points towards a situation in which Internet organisations do not strive for commercial interests or activities. Additionally most organisations aim at a worldwide representation, for instance through the organisation of regionally distributed physical meetings (e.g. IAB, IETF), the use of email to coordinate work within the organisation (e.g. IETF mailing lists; W3C decision making), regular telco's (e.g. IESG) and the use of email to organise (public) elections (e.g. IETF, Regional Internet Registries). Nevertheless, US participation in these organisations still remains considerable compared to other countries and continents. Regions such as South America, Africa, and Oceania hardly are represented or even not at all.

[10]<http://livinginternet.com/i/iw_mgmt.htm>.

- Most Internet organisations are *independent from government* (national or supranational), at least from a formal organisational, financial and jurisdictional point of view. For example, all IESG members (all technical experts) come from the private sector. Moreover Internet organisations have loosened their ties with academic institutions: where academics used to hold most functions within these organisations, nowadays internal functions are taken mainly by people from the private sector. An interesting mixture of individuals coming from the private, public and non-profit sector is elected to occupy the chairs of these organisations' management boards. Financing from a variety of organisation members is often used to support the organisation's secretariat or annual physical public meetings for example. Some of these Internet organisations also finance others; such as ISOC financially supports IETF, and IAB, IETF and ISOC finance IRTF activities.
  Another example of government independency is the fact that not government but ISOC has legal authority to globally defend the free use of the term 'Internet' in ensuring that this generic term is not used as a trademark and is not appropriated by companies or individuals.
  We therefore may conclude that the US federal government's policy aim towards privatisation of the technical management of the Internet has been carried out successfully, at least to some extent.
- The principle of *self-regulation.* Most Internet organisations draft their own charter or statutes, which guide the organisation's management and activities. In some cases, notably the IRTF and IETF, there is not even a formal charter but rather a collection of meetings with their own guidelines and procedures. In the case of IETF the majority of work is done by means of mailing lists. Even for ICANN, where influence of the US federal government is still considerable, self-regulation continues to be a guiding principle in changing ICANN's functioning and structure. Moreover within the 'network' of Internet organisations (see also the organisational diagram) 'internal checks and balances' have been organised like IESG supervising the results of different IETF working groups, IAB being both an IETF committee as well as an advisory board to ISOC, and the RFC editor under general responsibility of IAB and 100% funded by ISOC.
- In line with the former characteristic we can observe that activities are occurring *bottom-up*: in terms of both actual work and financing, most organisations thrive on professional users and companies that develop Internet technologies, and therefore in particular on the technical part of the Internet community. Similarly in many of these organisations consensus is a key word in the sense that agreement among Internet users and developers is necessary according to various decision-making procedures.
- The mutual *interrelatedness* of Internet organisations: many of these organisations have a member, advisor, or observer with one or more other organisations, or they have a liaison officer at least (see also the organisational diagram). Moreover several of these organisations have the same private companies and public institutions as their member. Hence, there seems to be a true, but perhaps restricted web of organisations that steer the development of the Internet.
- The contribution of the *'Internet community'*: activities are mostly performed by technical people, who often have been involved from the early days of the Internet on. At present, we may observe active participation of a broader and more professional Internet community compared to the past of the public Internet. In contrast however Internet users in the individual or private sphere, such as consumers, youngsters, and citizens, seem to be underrepresented in these Internet organisations. In addition, interest groups like consumer associations and citizen-rights groups only to a limited extent take part in standardisation processes (see also [23][11]). Hence, the Internet is being shaped mainly by professional, technical Internauts but not by the entire Internet community.

[11] Reidenberg has noticed the same in traditional standard-setting bodies such as ANSI [23, p. 97].

- The development of Internet technology takes place largely through *public standardisation procedures*: mailing lists and frequent physical meetings open to the public enable all individuals, in principle, to take part in developing Internet standards. Moreover, the public availability of RFCs through which standards and standardisation procedures are published, combined with the fact that anyone can submit a proposal for an RFC, point to the public character of the development of Internet technology. Nevertheless, it should be noted that most organisations and their procedures are not known to the general public, which implies that, in practice, input is largely restricted to technically interested professionals.

All in all, the common metaphor of the Internet as a 'network of networks' appears to apply equally well to the collection of organisations that perform tasks and activities for the technical management and development of the Internet. The functioning of these organisations seem to link up perfectly with the image of modern governance [13, pp. 24–25], showing us characteristics like deploying a pluricentric rather than a unicentric approach; an important role for networks organising relations between relatively autonomous but interdependent actors, with limited importance or even absence of hierarchy or monocratic leadership; government as merely one actor among many others; and an emphasis on processes of governing as opposed to structures of government, which concern negotiation, accommodation, concertation, co-operation and alliance-formation rather than the traditional processes in government of coercion, command and control. However, the empirical outcomes of this image of modern, but especially *global* governance, have been struggling with the displacement of democracy (who is representing), politics (who is deciding) and regulation (who is ruling); all functions traditionally embedded in national public institutions and therefore shaped to more or less 'controllable' geographic areas. This therefore leaves us with an accumulation of democratic and legal risks at the global level at which these Internet organisations are forced to operate and the important question of how to tackle these risks.

6. Conclusion: How to remove shadows from global Internet governance

The influence of Internet organisations on the management and development of the global Internet infrastructure, not only in a technological sense but also regarding its policy and normative development, has become substantial. Moreover, if we consider developments through time, involvement of these Internet organisations with Internet policy and normative issues appears to have grown rapidly. At the same time, through their usually open constitution, varying members and (financial) contributors, it is often unclear as to what kind of parties actually have or will have the power to decide upon these important public issues. Moreover, at this stage, the international decision making arena regarding Internet governance is predominantly occupied by a professional community with a technical background – i.e. not by the general Internet public.

Generally, scholars who reflect upon the problems of Internet regulation related to horizontalisation, democratic legitimacy, and prescriptive jurisdiction, come to the conclusion that traditional territory-bound notions of democratic representation and jurisdiction are in need of revision. We need to find a new paradigm for governance (e.g. [7,23]), to rethink the roles of the nation state and international relations (e.g. [22,27]), and to reconceptualise the notions of democracy (e.g. [3,8,11]), sovereignty (e.g. [12,29]) and jurisdiction (e.g. [4]).

With this situation in mind should we then come to award prescriptive jurisdiction and democratic accountability structures to these Internet organisations? These measures are primarily envisioned by proponents of the 'virtual' Internet. 'Network borders replace national borders. (...) [N]etwork communities also develop distinct sovereign powers. Infrastructure organizations acquire attributes of traditional territorial sovereigns' [23, p. 88]; also [12]). Place is still important, but place now refers to the "owned" territory "out there" of the Internet. Within the sovereign Internet space, jurisdiction exists because it is preferred by the Internet community. Rather than being bound to national states, Internauts choose their own "citizenship" and decide themselves how they envision and implement democracy – in the direction of 'government by consent' or an 'Internet republic'.

This idea of sovereignty over Internet territory and therefore legitimacy of complete Internet self-governance is, we believe, mainly supported by two observations: a) it seems to happen, and b) it seems to function to some extent. These observations are buttressed by arguments that justify legitimacy also in a more democratic sense, such as the fact that Internet organisations have expert knowledge, democratic decision-making procedures, and effective forms of self-enforcement. But it should be questioned whether this situation is sufficient. It is noteworthy that most pleas for independent Internet sovereignty still take as an example the Internet community of roughly the mid-1990s. Since then, the Internet architecture has been changing (cf. [2,24]), and, more importantly, the function of the Internet and the composition of the Internet community have expanded rapidly, in a dramatic way perhaps. Internet is no longer a space of its own "out there", but a space that – just like the street, the pub, and the television – is part of the "physical", public space in which we live. A space therefore with a huge variety of individual and organisational inhabitants, different levels of inclusions and exclusions, desired and undesired activities, huge differences in expertise and knowledge, and varying means of influence. A space, also, that is in continuous development.

The idea of a fully sovereign Internet space outside of the physical world seems to us outdated, and that is why we consider granting Internet organisations exclusive jurisdiction to prescribe norms for Internet architecture is not – or no longer can be – a satisfying answer to the questions of democratic and legal legitimacy currently raised by developments in the infrastructure of the Internet.

References

[1] J. Abbate, *Inventing the Internet,* The MIT Press, Cambridge MA, USA/London, England, 1st paperback edition, 2000.

[2] L.F. Asscher, (ed.), *Coding Regulation. Essays on the normative role of information technology,* IT & Law Series, T.M.C. Asser Press, The Hague, 2005.

[3] J.P. Barlow, *A Declaration of the Independence of Cyberspace,* 8 February 1996. Available at: http://www.eff.org/~barlow/Declaration-Final.html.

[4] P.S. Berman, The Globalization of Jurisdiction, in: *University of Pennsylvania Law Review,* (Vol. 151), SSRN Library, 2002, pp. 311–343, http://ssrn.com/abstract=361861.

[5] M.A.P. Bovens, *De verplaatsing van de democratie* (*the displacement of democracy*), public lecture at the Netherlands Scientific Council for Government Policy, 14 September 2004. Available at: http://wcms.wrr.nl/bestandupload/WCMS_wrr/Bovens.htm.

[6] B. Carpenter, *What Does the IAB Do, Anyway?* 1996. Available at: www.iab.org.

[7] M. Castells, *The Rise of the Network Society,* Volume I in The Information Age: Economy, Society and Culture, Blackwell Publishers, Cambridge, MA, 1996.

[8] P.H.A. Frissen, *De Anarchistische Republiek. Representatie in de Informatiesamenleving,* Machiavelli-lezing 2000, Stichting Machiavelli, 2000.

[9] A.M. Froomkin, Wrong Turn in Cyberspace: Using ICANN to Route Around the APA and the Constitution, in: *50 Duke Law Journal 17,* 2000. Available at: http://personal.law.miami.edu/~froomkin/articles/icann-main.htm.

[10] J.L. Goldsmith, The Internet and the Abiding Significance of Territorial Sovereignty, *Indiana Journal of Global Legal Studies* **5** (1998), 475–491.

[11] D. Held, *Models of Democracy,* (2nd ed.), Polity Press, Cambridge, UK, 1996.

[12] D.R. Johnson and D.G. Post, Law And Borders – The Rise of Law in Cyberspace, *Stanford Law Review* **48** (1996), 1367–1402.

[13] K. van Kersbergen and F. van Waarden, *Shifts in Governance: Problems of Legitimacy and Accountability*, the Netherlands Organisation for Scientific Research, The Hague, 2001.

[14] E.J. Koops and A.M.B. Lips, Wie reguleert het Internet? Horizontalisering en rechtsmacht bij de technische regulering van het Internet, in: *Zeven Essays over Informatietechnologie en Recht*, H. Franken et al., eds, SDU, The Hague, 2003, pp. 261–315.

[15] M.A. Lemley, Place and Cyberspace, *California Law Review*, **91** (2003), 521–542. Available at SSRN Library: http://papers.ssrn.com/abstract_id=349760.

[16] L. Lessig, The Zones of Cyberspace, *Stanford Law Review* **48** (1996), 1403–1411.

[17] L. Lessig, *Code, and Other Laws of Cyberspace*, Basic Books, New York, 1999.

[18] J.G.A. Van Mierlo, Over de verhouding tussen overheid, marktwerking en privatisering. Een economische meta-analyse, *Bestuurswetenschappen* **55**(5) (2001), 368–385.

[19] M.L. Mueller, ICANN and Internet Governance. Sorting through the debris of 'self-regulation', *Info* **1**(6) (December 1999), Camford Publishing Ltd. Available at http://www.icannwatch.org/archive/muell.pdf.

[20] M.L. Mueller, *Ruling the Root: Internet Governance and the Taming of Cyberspace*, (1st ed.), The MIT Press, Cambridge MA, USA, 2002.

[21] Netherlands Scientific Council for Government Policy, *Safeguarding the Public Interest*, Report 56, The Hague, 2000.

[22] H.H. Jr. Perrit, The Internet as a Threat to Sovereignty? Thoughts on the Internet's Role in Strengthening National and Global Governance, *Indiana Journal of Global Legal Studies* **5** (1998), 423–442.

[23] J.R. Reidenberg, Governing Networks and Rule-Making in Cyberspace, in: *Borders in Cyberspace: Information Policy and the Global Information Infrastructure*, B. Kahin and C. Nesson, eds, The MIT Press, Cambridge, UK, 1996.

[24] J.R. Reidenberg, States and Internet Enforcement, in: *University of Ottawa Law & Technology Journal*, Vol. 1, 2004, http://ssrn.com/abstract=487965.

[25] J.R. Reidenberg, Technology and Internet Jurisdiction, in: *University of Pennsylvania Law Review*, Vol. 153, 2005, http://ssrn.com/abstract=691501.

[26] RFC 3160, *The Tao of IETF – A Novice's Guide to the IETF*, 2001. Available at: http://rfc.sunsite.dk/rfc/rfc3160.html.

[27] S. Sassen, On the Internet and Sovereignty, *Indiana Journal of Global Legal Studies* **5** (1998), 545–559.

[28] N.F. Sitompoel, F. Tonkens, N. Van Eijk and E. Dommering, *(Zelf)regulering van nummers en domeinnamen*, ITeR no. 46, Sdu, The Hague, 2001.

[29] J.P. Trachtman, Cyberspace, Sovereignty, Jurisdiction, and Modernism, *Indiana Journal of Global Legal Studies* **5** (1998), 561–581.

[30] US Federal Government's Policy Memorandum, *A Framework for Global Electronic Commerce*, 1 July 1997. Available at: http://www.technology.gov/digeconomy/framewrk.htm.

Information Polity 10 (2005) 129–139
IOS Press

Fighting untrustworthy Internet content: In search of regulatory scenarios[1]

J.E.J. Prins and M.H.M. Schellekens
Tilburg Institute for Law, Technology and Society (TILT), Tilburg, The Netherlands
E-mail: {j.e.j.prins, m.h.m.schellekens}@uvt.nl

Abstract. The question of liability for the consequences of misleading information on the Internet is deeply problematic. The information chain can be long and pass through several jurisdictions *en route* from information supplier to information consumer. Organisations along the chain, such as ISPs, which attempt to provide quality or reliability checks, are inhibited from so doing by potential liabilites if they make public statements about their filtering policy. Self regulation would seem to offer one possible solution, but here too there are difficulties in both enforcement and with bodies which are outside the self regulatory environment. These problems are discussed and some proposals are put forward as to how self regulation could be made more effective and provide a greater degree of assurance to the consumer of online information.

1. Introduction

On September 13, 2004, *Internet Law News* reported that the US financial intermediary PayPal was going to levy a 'fine' of up to $500 on customers who violate its use policies – i.e. on those customers who use PayPal to pay for gaming, pornography ('adult content') and pharmaceuticals from unregistered pharmacies [2]. The new policy, which took effect almost two weeks later and applies to both buyers and sellers, marked the first time PayPal imposed fines for violations of its use policy. Although *Internet Law News* speculates that PayPal had been pressed by regulators to take this kind of step, the company denied it.[2] Given this initiative, a highly interesting question would of course be: will the PayPal scenario become the politics of every intermediaries in these days of enforcement actions against anyone the regulators or any other interested party (e.g. copyright holders) can find? Whatever the answer to this question may be, the PayPal initiative is indeed a clear sign of the growing pressure on Internet intermediaries to introduce enforcement policies against bad and/or untrustworthy Internet content. And this in turn raises the interesting question of what exactly 'bad' or 'untrustworthy' Internet content is. Simple scenarios are, of course, related to content containing child pornography or clear violations of copyright. However, imagine a scenario where a consumer orders some medically necessary drug online and his financial intermediary docks his credit card for $500 because the pharmacy he ordered from happened not to have the right kind of license.

---

[1]This article was written as part of research project on the quality of health information on the Internet, subsidized by the Netherlands Organisation for Scientific Research (NWO).

[2]Given that PayPal was sued in the past for processing payments related to Internet gaming (charges laid under the Patriot Act), this initiative could have been a measure to forestall other actions.

1570-1255/05/$17.00

In a world of information overload, it is often extremely difficult to get a grip on the correctness, completeness, and legitimacy of the information and material available on the Internet. Often a clear statement regarding the source of the information is lacking as well as the name, address and credentials of the information provider. Furthermore, providers fail to update their site on a regular basis and websites usually lack a statement describing what procedure and criteria were used for selection of the content. But even when these indicators are available, it still appears to be difficult for users (consumers, citizens or patients) to cope with the torrent of information on the Internet and distil out that which is most appropriate. When considering Internet content, clear differences arise between off- and online worlds. Litman [3] argues that: "*Some of this derived from the magic of digital technology. [...]. The ability to interact with the content you're reading changes your relationship with the content and that, eventually, changes both the way the content is written and displayed and what the content means.* In the offline world, distribution of information is structured through well-established channels. This allows for some form of 'filtering' of the information as well as focus on the specific audience for which it is intended. In contrast, the online world offers any individual the potential to distribute and consume any information that they wish. Health-related information is a good illustration of this. On the Internet, one can find professional medical or health-related information, commercial information on medical products and information based on individual experiences of patients as well as quacks. The characteristics of the online information chain are a clear example of the new opportunities that Internet offers to consumers in reinforcing their positions.[3] In the offline world, producers usually act as the first link in the information chain. Consumers are positioned at the end of the chain and can do nothing more than accept the information on products. In the online world, individual citizens and consumers can take the initiative and create the chain ('chain reversal'). 'Looking and (automatically) comparing' has become considerably easier on the Internet, especially when using (intelligent) search agents such as Google and MySimon. Dissatisfied patients or concerned lobbyists can use the Internet to make their dissatisfaction, interest or other feelings and ambitions known to a worldwide audience. Features such as self-organisation, self-help, self-publishing, worldwide distribution by pushing a single button and electronic social interaction appear to be key instruments in creating a whole new information environment. In other words, in addition to a rise in the quantity of information, the electronic environment also offers important new publication as well as medical services opportunities and thus whole new sources of information and service distribution.

This contribution does not aim to discuss criteria for evaluating the reliability or trustworthiness of content in an electronic world [8]. Instead, we focus on an issue that is related to the quality criteria debate. For in the realm of the debate on bad and untrustworthy Internet content and the search for reliability criteria, lies the question: what is, or could be the role of regulatory initiatives in addressing content that is bad and/or unreliable and, what is the legal status of the various efforts (guidelines, trustmarks and other quality schemes) that try to limit the risks involved in bad and unreliable content? Further on in this chapter, we want to make a contribution to the quality criteria debate from the legal perspective, and thus analyse the potential of instruments of self-regulation in addressing content-related risks in an online environment. In doing so, we will not deal with the obvious examples of 'bad' Internet content, such as child pornography and software or film piracy. Instead, we will focus on the more troublesome area of (un)reliable information. The key questions that we will be dealing with below are:

---

[3]Some of the key words describing this new position are 'consumer sovereignty', 'mass individualism' and 'demand-based supply' [5].

- What structures of self-regulatory control and private rulemaking could be used as instruments in enhancing the quality and trustworthiness of information? And
- What legal implications could arise when private initiatives regarding quality measures are taken?

Addressing the latter question appears to be of particular importance when looking at developments in the area of Internet Service Provider (ISP) liability. Court rulings in the US show that an ISP that explicitly markets itself as a provider which, as part of its value-added services, controls the distributed information and prevents the publication of inappropriate messages, can be held liable if he fails to do so.[4] The unfortunate result of these rulings is that an ISP – from a liability perspective – should do as little as possible to monitor and edit the content of the information it distributes. We will discuss the implications of this 'principle' in light of the development of measures to enhance the reliability of information, and propose an alternative way to deal with this issue. Finally, this article aims to provide some indications on what type of quality criteria and what enforcement mechanisms appear to be relevant when addressing unreliable information through regulatory measures. As will become clear, information is so flexible and diverse that it seems to resist attempts to regulate its quality. But first we will start of with a brief introduction to trust, online information and regulatory dimensions.

2. Trust, regulatory challenges and online information

Trust deals with belief, or the willingness to believe, that one can rely on the goodness, strength, and ability of somebody whether they are the seller or the buyer or in something, for example, certain online information. Of course, trust is highly subjective. It is the expectation that arises within a community where regular, honest, and cooperative behavior is the norm, and is based on commonly shared standards. Some of the trustworthiness that is a matter of fact in conventional communication of certain information no longer exists in electronic information delivery. For instance: an http address (URL) is not as reliable as a physical address; verification of an identity by means of a passport or a driver's license is not possible virtually; changes in a paper document are more easily detected than in a digital document; confidentiality of information is more easily guaranteed in a physical encounter (e.g. in a dialogue with a consultant or other professional) than in a virtual encounter. These securities, however, are of essential importance for the success of electronic information distribution and use. In addition to the trustworthiness of the information channel and the electronic communication itself, attention should be given to the trustworthiness of the information that is distributed and used, as well as the procedure followed.

Do we need new forms of trust in an electronic environment? How, otherwise, can parties know, whether certain information is of the required quality or whether the individual claiming to be a professional is indeed this person? Thus, the challenge lies in the perceived trustworthiness of the potential partners in the information chain. Of course, reputation, previous experience, and the size of the company that distributes the information may influence the perceived trustworthiness but the law may also play a role. For trust between parties can be enhanced by legislation (e.g. consumer protection), self-regulatory mechanisms (trustmarks, codes of conduct) and agreements (e.g. general terms and conditions, privacy agreements). A formalization of certain quality protocols could, for example, lead to more trustworthy ways of distributing and using information. On the technical side, trust in online information can also

[4]See: *Stratton Oakmont Inc v. Prodigy Services*, 1995 NY Misc., 23 *Media L. Rep.* 1794. Compare to *Cubby v. CompuServe*, 766 F. Supp 135 (SD NY 1991).

be enhanced by using technologies such as cryptographic applications; digital certificates to ensure both the authenticity of information and that of the persons behind this information; digital signatures and time-stamps to secure the authenticity of information and documents; encryption to protect information. However, these technological means for building trust do not always fit seamlessly into the legal system. Consequently, the legal system is currently finding a way to deal with the shifts in the basis of both instruments in online information and in trust. One of these areas is the legal status of self-regulatory instruments used to enhance trust in online information.

3. The challenge for self-regulatory mechanisms

A brief glance at the Internet shows that self-regulatory instruments[5] appear to have an increasingly substantial role with regard to the regulation of social and economic relationships. The rise of self-regulatory mechanisms is due to characteristics such as direct relationships between providers and users, simplicity, interactivity and flexibility. Moreover, the Internet transcends geographic frontiers. Thus, parties may wish to use codes of conduct and contracts to eliminate the differences between the various legal systems around the world. As a result, the cross-border dimension of Internet provides an excellent basis for experiments with private agreements between parties. Finally, the argument has been put forward that only the actors themselves are capable of perceiving the risks involved in particular types of electronic communication, business or use of services. Thus, the adoption of a code of conduct or some other self-regulatory instrument would assure a set of norms and sanctions tailored to the specifics of the situation.

The key challenge for all self-regulatory initiatives appears to be their enforcement. Although many responsible organisations try to ensure the adherence to the norms, either by sanctions and or by means of labelling and rating mechanisms, the characteristics of the online world make it difficult to effectively apply sanctions when parties fail to respect the set norms. Ensuring that the initiative passes from letter to action appears, in particular, to be difficult in light of the borderless environment in an online world. Furthermore, given that self-regulatory sources are often localized only in a certain territory, or that the initiatives are often limited to a group of actors that share a certain attitude towards professional behaviour, one may question the overall effect of self-regulatory initiatives. For if an organisation lacks the means, power and authority to enforce its norms, then their value remains symbolic instead of real. If a site owner is not a member of the regulatory scheme, the owner is, of course, under no obligation to abide by the rules set by the self-regulatory body. In principle, self-regulatory mechanisms do not establish law. Legal rules are binding to all citizens in a certain country; regulatory rules are not for the simple reason that self-regulatory mechanisms are not created by democratic means such as control by an elected parliament. Thus, a third party that is not a member of the self-regulatory scheme is not obliged to follow any suggestions that the body might make. In fact, the party may do nothing. This appears to be a rather disappointing outcome of the instrument of self-regulation. However, a self-regulatory instrument will have a positive effect on the quality of the information made available by those organisations that adhere to the self-regulatory instrument.

Self-regulatory schemes often work with a code of conduct, stating what is considered to be 'reliable' information under the code and what actions are expected of those adhering to the code to ensure that

[5]The phenomenon of self-regulation, sometimes called 'soft' law, refers to norms that are voluntarily developed, accepted and administered by members and authorities of a certain community.

only reliable information is placed on the Internet. Those providing the information to the public often state publicly that they adhere to the code by, for example, attaching the applicable seal of the trustmark to their website. Such a public commitment raises the expectations of the general public as well as of specific information consumers. Such expectations cannot be waived when a dispute arises about damage as a result of harmful or misleading information. Thus, commitment to a code prevents a debate on the applicable norms.[6] The fact that norms, definitions and responsibilities have been made clear, makes it generally easier to win a possible liability case. Let us therefore look at the relation between liability and self-regulatory mechanisms.

4. Liability for self-regulatory mechanisms

To a certain extent, the instigation of liability proceedings is a risky undertaking. Costs are definitely going to be incurred while it is uncertain whether either successful results can be booked or a conviction can be secured. It may also prove impossible to execute a conviction. Therefore the risk of failure seems to be reasonably high in the liability cases. Moreover, in Europe the issue of liability for unreliable mass information is virtually *terra incognita*, making it difficult to predict the outcome of a possible court proceeding. Things become even more complicated if the parties involved reside in different countries, which is not uncommon in conflicts arising on the Internet. Paradoxically, the (high) risk of failure for the instigator of proceedings does not necessarily mean that certifiers of information face little or no risks. Certifiers have to contend with the fact that their issued trustmarks are accessible in every country in the world. This makes it difficult – given differences in culture and levels of education – to predict how a trustmark and the information it relates to will be interpreted by those seeking the relevant information. Apart from the risks of misunderstanding or misinterpretation, there are cultural and legal differences in how to deal with damage as a result of unreliable information: the propensity to sue will inevitably vary from country to country as will the law of liability.

When looking at the instrument of liability in relation to unreliable information, it is clear that with the assumption of liability of mass information providers, such as publishers, concerning the provision of unreliable information to the general public the law is generally reticent. There is hardly any case law in Europe strictly regarding the liability for mass provision of unreliable information.[7] In literature, it is assumed that reticence with respect to such liability is necessary.[8] There is more case law in the US, but the courts are no less reticent.[9] One of the situations in which liability is more likely than elsewhere is where a (certification) provider attaches a seal or certification to a product, service or information, thereby (implicitly) representing that it has taken reasonable steps to make an independent examination of the product, service or information endorsed and that it found this satisfactory.[10] If this knowledge about liability law is applied to the provision of information on the Internet, it is clear that the certifier of

[6]Where we have hitherto simply talked about the provider of the information it must be noted that in case of a self-regulatory scheme many parties are involved in the provision of information: the provider of the information, the information-intermediary, a trustmark licensee, a custodian of a trustmark and a medical expert who reviews the information that is to be published.

[7]See e.g. BGH 7 Juli 1970 Neue Juristische Wochenschrift 1970, p. 1963 (Carter-Robbin-Test) and TGI Paris 28 Mai 1986 Revue trimestrielle de droit civil 1986 (3) juill.-sept., p. 552 (Fruits et plants comestibles). In the first mentioned case the editor was not found liable, in the second he was.

[8]Druey ([1, p. 135]) states: 'Die Freiheit der Information bringt mit sich, dass es grundsatzlich weder im öffentlichen Recht noch im Privatrecht einen allgemeinen Schutz gegen schlechte Information [. . .] gibt'.

[9]For an overview, see [7].

[10]See Hanberry v Hearst Corp. 81 Cal. Rptr. 519 (Cal. App. Dist. 1969).

certain types of information on the Internet is the link in the information distribution chain that is most exposed to liability risks.[11]

Liability for self-regulation, thus, may have a two-sided effect. On the one hand, it may spur the providers of information to take even greater care with the quality of the information. However, on the other hand, it may make information providers spurn self-regulatory schemes. They may fear that their efforts to enhance the reliability and quality of their information will turn against them. They fear that even a small mistake may be mercilessly exploited to bring a liability claim to a successful conclusion. Here, an interesting implication may arise from attempts to enhance the reliability of information because, following the reasoning of the Prodigy case decided in the United States, providers of reliability services that profile themselves as such, could be held liable for their added-value services. Prodigy was found liable for publishing illegal material.[12] The provider had explicitly marketed itself as an ISP (Internet Service Provider) and, as such, it would control and prevent the publication of inappropriate messages. Such an active approach led the Court to conclude that Prodigy was liable for not adequately checking the material it published. If this ruling is applied to reliability-conferring organisations, the Prodigy principle could imply that organisations taking an active role in checking and, where necessary removing Internet content, run the risk of being held liable, whereas those who do nothing avoid liability. The chilling-effect of the liability regime on measures to enhance the reliability and quality is however, neither a strange nor a new phenomenon. The effect is a well-known feature under liability law. Any organisation profiling itself as a trustworthy organisation that guards over the quality of its services raises a certain expectation with the public. Such an expectation may very well be enough to base liability upon.[13]

Nevertheless, there may be situations in which the chilling-effect is considered undesirable in light of certain interests or objectives. The US Congress (USC), for example, has recognized the negative side effect of the liability regime for ISPs and provided for protection for Good Samaritan blocking and screening of offensive material: 'No provider or user of an interactive computer service shall be treated as the publisher or speaker of any information provided by another information content provider.' (Art. 47 USC 230). Hence, in the US an Internet Service Provider is given legal leeway to screen and block offensive material: screening and blocking does not make an organisation a speaker or publisher. The question thus arises whether the interests in enhancing the quality of certain types of information, e.g. health-related information, may also justify an exemption under liability law. At first sight, one could argue that such interests indeed apply. The initiatives aim to enhance the quality of a highly 'sensitive' type of information, i.e. information that focuses on the health and well being of people. Unreliable health-related information may involve particular risks and there is a clear societal interest in stimulating measures to screen and block unreliable information. The above-described chilling-effect may have unwanted implications.

A closer look reveals that a liability exemption for certain types of information may have negative consequences. First, what should be done with providers of quality mechanisms (such as trustmarks) that fail to apply the expected level of care? Second, the afore-mentioned US approach has not been followed in other parts of the world. The European Union Directive on E-Commerce does not provide

[11] Apart from the implicit representation other factors have to be considered as well, e.g. whether the provider of the seal acted commercially or whether the seal constitutes an inducement to buy or use the product, service or information to which the seal is attached. Dependent on the case at hand, these factors may or may not make liability of a trustmark provider more likely.

[12] *Stratton Oakmont Inc v. Prodigy Services*, 1995 NY Misc., 23 *Media L. Rep.* 1794.

[13] Compare in this respect the liability of banks for unreliable prospectuses when issuing stock.

for such far-reaching protection.[14] In applying the European regime to trustmarks, we note that an organisation managing a trustmark scheme for reliable 'third party' information is not covered by the exemptions in the Directive since what the organisation does is more than merely transmitting or storing information. The organisation arranges for information to be evaluated, and allows a trustmark to be attached if the information complies with certain reliability criteria. If and under what conditions such an activity gives rise to liability is to be determined under the national laws of liability of the Member States of the European Union. Often, no clear-cut answer is available under the different national laws. As the US exemption approach under Article 47 USC 230 is not followed in other countries around the world, we are then confronted with the question as to which of the legal regimes applies, given that the online world is a world without borders. Are there other options available to address the unfortunate effect of liability for organisations that take an active role in Internet control? Are mechanisms available that mitigate liability without directly establishing immunity for liability? We think there are, and we would like to propose an alternative approach.

5. An alternative approach

The very essence of a trustmark scheme is that it presents itself as a trustworthy party; it claims implicitly or explicitly that users can depend on the information that is cleared by its scheme. As we concluded above, such a 'presentation' tends to enhance the standard by which the conduct of the trustmark manager scheme is measured. One could say that this standard tends to be measured by the end-result. If the cleared information appeared to be unreliable, the trustmark has failed to act according to expectations and is thus liable. To improve the liability position of trustmarks, we propose not to focus on the result, i.e. did the trustmark make sure that only reliable information was 'awarded' an authenticated graphic mark? Instead, we suggest determining liability on the basis of an established set of minimum measures to be taken by trustmark manager. Within this approach the liability standard will (with the understanding that not everything is foreseeable) concentrate on the specific implementation measures required to make the trustmark scheme reliable and less on the result.

Of course, this alternative approach would mean that careful consideration should be given to what exactly can and must be expected from trustmarks to ensure the reliability of information. For example, what requirements must the information meet? What measures must be taken to ensure that the information meets these requirements? What measures must be taken to ensure that the logo is not used without authorization? How can the persons providing the information be identified? Clearly, establishing such criteria (to be laid down in, for example, a code of conduct) is a challenge in itself. Also, the suggested approach has its downsides. The regime would be less flexible and it would hinder anonymous information distribution.[15] However, the benefits are clear. First, contrary to a liability exemption as established under the previously discussed US regime, the manager of a trustmark must

[14]As is apparent from recital 42: 'The exemptions from liability established in this Directive cover only cases where the activity of the information society service provider is limited to the technical process of operating and giving access to a communication network over which information made available by third parties is transmitted or temporarily stored, for the sole purpose of making the transmission more efficient; this activity is of a mere technical, automatic and passive nature, which implies that the information society service provider has neither knowledge of nor control over the information which is transmitted or stored.' Directive 2000/31/EC of the European Parliament and of the Council of 8 June 2000 on certain legal aspects of information society services, in particular electronic commerce, OJ L 178, 17 July 2000.

[15]See Nicoll and Prins [4] on the issue of anonymity.

take certain efforts to guarantee the reliability of information (i.e. make sure that the scheme conforms to rules of the code of conduct). Second, a trustmark manager who does not conform to the code can still be held liable for possible damages. Third, the person who suffers damages can always hold a person or organisation liable for these damages. Finally, the regime will give trustmarks managers some feeling of a safe harbor in establishing that they are exempt from liability if they acted according to the code of conduct.

In the meantime, how do private initiatives deal with possible liability situations resulting from trustmarks and other reliability enhancing mechanisms? A search through various websites that use reliability enhancing instruments reveals that many use disclaimers.[16] By using disclaimers they waive their liability. It may be no surprise that in the context of quality instruments, disclaimers appear to be a bit out of place. As mentioned earlier, there is in itself nothing wrong if an organisation implements certain measures to downplay the liability risks it may face. However, the organisations on which we have focussed in this particular case are those dealing in trust and enhancing quality. A disclaimer appears to be a bit of an odd instrument here. The consumer's trust in the quality of information will not be enhanced if those who provide the information or check its quality walk away from each and every liability. A brief glance at the terms and conditions of some of the organisations providing reliability instruments shows however that disclaimers are widely used. Two illustrative examples:

- "Although we carefully review our content, X cannot guarantee nor take responsibility for the medical accuracy of documents, we publish, nor can X assume any liability for the content of websites linked to our site."
- "... X et Y, ne sauraient etre rendues responsables de tout préjudice, direct ou indirect, de quelque nature que ce soit, résultant de l'utilisation, même partielle, des information de ce site".

It would reinforce consumer trust if the persons providing or checking the information would at least to some extent carry the burden if damages were suffered as a consequence of the consumer's reliance on this data. We believe that such an approach is not too far-fetched. Disclaimers are not all homogeneous. They exist in various forms and lengths and can thus be tailored to the needs within the specific context they are used. So, if for example, little money can be made from making information available on the Internet, a disclaimer could reflect this by maximising the amount of compensation payable to a user. If insurance coverage of the cost of liability is available, then the maximum cover and/or the maximum insurance compensation for damages payable could be stated. These and other aspects can be reflected in a disclaimer. If the efforts to heighten the quality of health-related information are to protect the health of individual persons, then a disclaimer could state that purely economic loss is not grounds for compensation. In other words, liability for information provided should be well considered. Neither denying the existence of liability, nor exaggerating it will lead to satisfactory results. Liability calls for an active approach, whereby the real issues are discerned, so that liability can fulfil a useful role in enforcement of self-regulatory schemes without 'overdoing it'.

6. In search of legally relevant quality criteria

In discussing enforcement scenarios for self-regulatory mechanisms one final interesting question arises. Do self-regulatory initiatives have an external effect, i.e. can a code of conduct adopted by

[16]It should be noted that disclaimers on websites may or may not, and under certain conditions, be valid in all jurisdictions.

representatives of certain actors, influence or even determine the required behaviour of actors who are not a party to the code of conduct? Although the recognition of such an effect would not guarantee an optimal sanctioning and enforcement of violations of the private norms, it may certainly contribute to the efficacy of such norms. A step further is a situation in which the adopted norms, such as quality standards for information, may become a professional standard whereby contravention automatically constitutes a fault. This would create a situation in which self-regulation becomes a key source of law complementary to the rules issued by the government, and could perhaps even replace the latter. Is it realistic in that the quality criteria for electronic information become more than just the professional standard, but also a *de jure* standard? An answer to this question requires a discussion on the legal status of self-regulatory initiatives versus third parties.

We already mentioned in the previous section that self-regulatory mechanisms do not establish law in the meaning of legal rules that are binding to all citizens in a certain country for the reason that the self-regulatory mechanisms were not created, discussed and adopted by democratic means such as control by an elected parliament. In addition, scholars of private law have been either reluctant to debate the status of self-regulatory mechanisms under private law or even completely ignored such a discussion. Given, the prominent role expected of self-regulatory mechanisms, at least in an online environment, it appears high time that such a debate is put on the agenda.

But even if self-regulatory mechanisms were to gain importance under private law, many other important questions arise. What criteria should decide upon the 'quality' of certain types of information? What about the status of possible contesting criteria? Who will be responsible for drawing up the criteria and what about meaningful participation of all those affected by the adopted criteria? All of these questions bring us to the legitimacy of the process and the criteria needed to define when a self-regulatory mechanism can claim legitimacy. Below, we will try to distil legal duties from reliability criteria and thus make a contribution to the scientific discussion, from a legal perspective, on 'categorizing' quality criteria. We thus intend to explore, what could be gained by establishing 'new' rules to deal with the reliability of information and, what difficulties have to be overcome. This will be followed by a tentative sketch of such an approach.

Approaching the regulatory dimension of the reliability of information from a liability perspective – which is the traditional approach – introduces a certain bias in the duties that rest upon those who provide and (ought to) check information. The duties focus on avoiding anything that could be a link in the causal chain leading up to damage though reliance on the information. A typical example is a duty stating that information must be accurate. Inaccurate information can lead to damage, if somebody relies on it. A new approach to regulation would be to try to distil duties from criteria for reliability. To a certain extent this leads to other duties. One of these duties could be, for example, the duty to mention the name and quality, e.g. profession, of the author or a certain type of information, e.g. medical or financial. From the traditional liability perspective, not mentioning a name or quality could hardly be relevant because the omission of such information could seldom be the cause of the damage somebody suffered because they relied on the information given. However, when one considers the perspective of reliability duties, mentioning a name and quality appear to be very important. Put differently, where the focus of liability law and ensuing duties is on avoidance and causation of damage, the focus of reliability criteria and ensuing duties is more on user empowerment and making the reliability of information verifiable.

If the reliability duty approach were to be taken, use of the liability law regime would only be useful to a limited extent; the new approach would require the development of criteria and rules that may hardly be relevant in the context of liability. These rules would need to be established outside and independent of the regime of liability law. The 'diverging' rules could be formulated as a code in the context of a self-regulatory initiative or as statutory law. The former may, for the time being, be preferable. The development of new rules will have to gain acceptance and, self-regulation can act as basis to build up such rules. Competing self-regulatory schemes may exhibit different rules and thus create a pool of rules from which to choose. By fostering the online presence of established credibility-conferring institutions, indications will appear on what criteria and rules function best. In the long run, such rules could (perhaps) be upgraded to *de jure* norms.

The course proposed here should however not be thought of lightly. Translation of reliability criteria into duties is far from a straightforward job. To illustrate the challenges, we shall sketch just a few of the 'problem areas':

- Experts generally know in how much detail they have to explain certain issues to their colleagues. However, when certain specialized information is available freely on the Internet it is also used by non-experts. What should then be the scope of the ensuing 'duties' in providing and checking the information? Should these important duties be ignored if they state that the information is only for experts?
- Consistency, coherence and accuracy appear to be important criteria, just like interpretability and accessibility. For an author, this implies that he or she has to make the information consistent, coherent, accurate etc. However, when trying to translate these criteria into legal norms, one comes across the problem that these qualities are difficult to measure. In general, legal norms should be sufficiently clear so that those, to whom the duties are directed, clearly understand what is expected of them. How can these duties be enforced? For example, what level of inconsistency is sufficient to take enforcement measures (in the absence of damage)?
- Information should conform with observations and consensus. The user of information can be helped by references to such observations or consensus. But, forcing an author of information to refer to sources puts a burden on their shoulders because it is not clear exactly how much research into observations and consensus is required.
- Finally, key criteria to determine reliability are authority, trustworthiness and credibility of the persons or organisations behind the information. These criteria may, perhaps, be translated into a duty to identify the persons and organisations behind the information. It is however, not clear how this relates to the 'good' intentions an individual may have to want to remain anonymous or act under pseudonym? Do we follow the approach taken under the European Union e-Commerce Directive and require that providers of information society services provide certain information (among which information on their identity)? How would this relate to citizens, consumers or patients who wish to communicate about their situation or condition in an anonymous way?

7. Conclusion

The distribution and presence of unreliable information on the Internet appears to be a problem of growing importance. Clearly, risks arise as a result of this information. Considering the possible negative consequences, it appears desirable that the law plays its part in addressing this problem. Traditionally, the law approaches the unreliability of information as a liability problem. This approach appears however to be insufficient [6]. As has happened in many other areas where a new normative solution to 'online' problems have been sought, self-regulatory mechanisms appear to be an interesting option. In many areas of online regulation, self-regulation has proven to provide a sound basis to develop new rules. Based on the earlier experiences, we have discussed possible new rules that may help enhance the reliability of information on the Internet. These rules need to address those that provide and check information and guide them towards more reliable information. Besides the organisational measures such as user education and by making the reliability of information more transparent and thus verifiable, a regulatory approach enhancing reliability seems to be the establishment of criteria for the quality of information. Based on this view, we have proposed a different approach to regulating the reliability of information in an online environment. The discussion also showed that the step from reliability criteria to enforceable norms that regulate the behavior of the providers of information appears far from trivial. The very characteristic of information is that it is so flexible and diverse that it seems to resist every attempt to regulate it. Nevertheless, we feel that in addressing the reliability of information on the Internet one must look beyond the borders of the traditional regulatory mechanisms (e.g. liability law) and look for possible new approaches. We hope in this contribution to have made some tentative steps towards another approach.

References

[1] J.N. Druey, *Information als Gegenstand des Rechts, Entwurf einer Grundlegung*, Zurich: Schulthess Polygraphischer Verlag, 1995.

[2] Internet Law News, *PayPal to levy fines for gambling, porn*, available at: http://news.com.com/2100-1026_3-5362576.html, 2004.

[3] J. Litman, Electronic Commerce and Free Speech, in: *The Commodification of Information*, N. Elkin-Koren and N. Weinstock Netanel, eds, The Hague, London, New York: Kluwer Law International, 2002, p. 26.

[4] C. Nicoll and J.E.J. Prins, Anonymity: Challenges for Politics and Law, in: *Digital Anonymity and the Law. Tensions and Dimensions*, C. Nicoll, J.E.J. Prins and M. van Dellen, eds, The Hague: T.M.C. Asser Press, 2003, pp. 287–297.

[5] J.E.J. Prins, Consumers, Liability, and the Online World, *Information & Communications Technology Law* **12**(2) (2003), 143–164.

[6] J.E.J. Prins and M.H.M. Schellekens, The Chilling-Effect of Liability Law on Initiatives to Enhance the Reliability of On-Line Health-Related Information, *European Journal of Health Law* **11** (2004), 201–207.

[7] J. Rothstein Wolfson, Electronic mass information providers and section 552 of the restatement (second) of torts: the first amendment casts a long shadow, *Rutgers Law Journal*, **29**(1) (2001).

[8] A. Vedder and R. Wachbroit, Reliability of Information: Some Distinctions, *Ethics & Information Technology* **6**(1) (2004).

Information Polity 10 (2005) 141–151
IOS Press

Fences and gates in cyberspace: Is the Internet becoming a threat to democracy?

Jens Hoff and Flemming Bjerke
Department of Political Science & Danish Political Science Research School, University of Copenhagen, Rosenborggade 15, DK-1130 Copenhagen K., Denmark
E-mail: jh@ifs.ku.dk; bjerke@polforsk.dk

Abstract. Departing from the concept of media citizenship, a concept implying certain personal informational rights such as the rights to seek, receive and impart information and ideas through any medium without interference and regardless of frontiers (cf. WSIS (UN World Summit on Information Society) declaration on the Information Society), and seeing such rights as a fundamental dimension of democratic citizenship on equal footing with fundamental civil, political and social rights, this essay analyses the extent to which ICT/the Internet in its current form contributes to the realisation of such media citizenship. Through an analysis of recent developments within the copyright protection area and the software patent area, it is demonstrated that these developments constitute a serious undermining of the freedom to seek, receive and impart information on and through the Internet, and thus significantly confines and restricts media citizenship. Furthermore, these developments delegate significant legislative, executive and judicial power to a few international companies and industry organisations, and work to set up especially Microsoft as a decisive political authority in the information society.

1. Introduction

Two trends are of particular importance when discussing the relationship between the Internet and democracy. The first is the *mediatization of politics*; the fact that to an increasing degree communication between politicians/the political system and citizens takes place through the media [1–3]. The second is the 'explosion' or *the multiplication of the public sphere*; a development initiated by cable TV, and radically stepped up by the development of the Internet. Thus, today it seems more than ever appropriate to talk about a multitude of functionally and thematically specialised public spheres, rather than a united and coherent public sphere [4,5].

In the post-war period Habermas was one of the first to deal seriously with the possible democratic problems of the mediatization of politics [6]. In his account, a 'refeudalization' of the public took place, based on the dominance of TV in the communication between citizens and the political system, and, we may add, based also on the character of the medium as an instrument of one-way communication and the *de facto* privileged access of politicians to the broadcast networks.

The Internet contained a promise to change this. The high hopes for a reinvigoration of democracy held by a wide range of citizens, politicians, researchers, etc. – at least for a while – connected with the rise and spread of the internet was based on five properties [7,8]:

– *Increased interaction between participants*
  Compared to traditional mass media (newspapers, TV or radio) ICT contains the possibility of interactivity between sender and receiver of a message. Rather than the "one-to-all" principle of traditional media the Internet creates an "all-to-all" communication environment. Typical examples are debate fora and chats.

- *The declining importance of time and space*
  With the Internet it is possible to access for example the homepages of political organisations or to participate in virtual political debates around-the-clock. Also, territorial boundaries become less important as it is possible to access information and engage in dialogue on a global scale.
- *Easier and more equal access to the public sphere*
  Compared to traditional mass media the possibilities for 'ordinary people' to reach a large audience has been significantly enlarged with Internet technology. It is relatively easy and cheap to create a homepage, and in this way share ones ideas with other people without the censorship of (state owned or commercial) TV, radio and newspapers. Also, virtual communication is more egalitarian than face-to-face communication as participants do not have to reveal for example their gender, age, ethnicity or social position.
- *Easier access to and control over large amounts of information*
  Compared to paper based information, ICT makes it much easier to find, store and organise huge amounts of information, thus potentially giving the user of such information greater knowledge and oversight capacity than before.
- *Decentralisation of control with information*
  In contrast to traditional mass media where the control of information is in the hands of state owned or commercial TV-companies or multinational media networks, ICT gives the individual citizen and all types of organisations the possibility of becoming their own editor and publisher, potentially able to reach a global audience.

Thus, the new ICTs, especially the Internet, seemed to create a new political opportunity structure ("communicative affordance" [9]) shifting power away from governments and media monopolies towards citizens and social movements, and at the same time laying a foundation for a more transparent and participatory polity. This impression was underpinned by the virtual presence of a steeply increasing number of organisations of all kinds, some of them especially concerned with democracy and the Internet (e.g. Minnesota E-democracy, the WELL, UK citizens online), and associated or free-standing debate fora. Also, the democratic character of the Internet was stressed by the accounts of how the Net had successfully been used by suppressed groups like the Zapatistas [1] in Mexico to inform about and create global support for their cause, and accounts of how the Net had been used to circumvent state controlled media in for example China in relation to the events on the Tiananmen Square, or in Russia in relation to Yeltsin's coming to power. Furthermore the democratic potential of ICT was stressed in national ICT plans in both Europe and the USA during the 1990s. Together, these developments served to cement a myth about the inherent democratic character of ICT. Thus, the more the possibilities of the technology could be unfolded, and the more PC's and Internet could be spread to all corners of society, the more democracy would prevail.

These observations accentuate the fact that in the era of mediated politics, it becomes of crucial importance for the type of democracy we are likely to see developing not only who controls information, and who has access to what types of information (this has arguably been the case for maintaining control in all societies), but also what the character of communication and representation [2] is like, and how the public sphere(s), through which such communication and representation takes place, functions.

---

[1] Castells [10:68ff] even call the Zapatistas the "First Informational Guerilla Movement".

[2] Representation is a crucial, but also difficult concept in democratic theory. In the era of mediated politics representation to a very high degree takes place through public debate in different media. Thus, the quality of democracy very much depends on how succesful such representation is; i.e. how well the – in reality absent – public or citizens, and their diverse interests are represented. See also [11].

This is clearly recognised by WSIS (UN World Summit on Information Society), which in 2003 declared that:

> It is ... "an essential foundation of the Information Society, and as outlined in Article 19 of the Universal Declaration of Human Rights, that everyone has the right to freedom of opinion and expression; that this right includes freedom to hold opinions without interference and *to seek, receive and impart information and ideas through any media* and regardless of frontiers. Communication is a fundamental social process, a basic human need and the foundation of all social organisation. It is central to the Information Society." [12].

The centrality of information and communication in the era of mediatized politics has led some to advocate for the institutionalisation of a media citizenship. Such media citizenship should entail "... overlapping rights to information, rights to receive and register opinions, and rights to fair and diverse representation." [11:75]. It should function as a democratic norm alongside and in addition to the form of citizenship we normally associate with the fundamental rights in Western welfare democracies, i.e. civil, political and social rights. To these we might now add informational rights, and as with the dimensions of 'traditional' citizenship, we might ask what the preconditions are for the realisation of a 'full media citizenship' [13,14].

Thus, what we want to do in this contribution is to discuss whether ICT/the internet in its current form contributes to such full media citizenship, or whether it can rather be seen to confine and limit media citizenship.

As we shall see below, a discussion of this issue is very much a discussion about the extent and form of regulation and control with ICT in general, and with the Internet in particular. Ronald Deibert [15] discusses these issues using the terms 'state' and 'commercial censorship'. In this contribution we will focus on 'commercial censorship', even though the area of 'state censorship' is surely also of great relevance for democracy, and in need of thorough studies [15]. Another limitation of the analysis done here is that it does not deal extensively with the questions of privacy. However, as this issue has already been given some attention in the scholarly literature [16–18], we will give more emphasis to the problems of access to and dissemination of information.

2. Dimensions of regulation

ICT has the basic property that it can perform symbolic activities that would otherwise have required human thinking. ICT 'thinks' for us, and does so extremely quickly and in incredible amounts. When computers are used to control and facilitate material and social processes, they perform practices that would otherwise have involved human thinking. Computers are integrated with human practices because they can perform some part of these practices. Sorting and distributing mail is a good example.

So, by thinking for us, ICT takes over, mingles with or establishes discourses and practices of social life. Thus, concerning politics and democracy, ICT is important in two ways: 1) the massive dissemination of hardware and software in society (the ICT infrastructure) and the steeply increased access to this infrastructure by government, politicians, organisations, companies and individuals has created new possibilities and new preconditions for the exercise of politics (homepages, mailing lists, debate fora, weblogs, etc.), 2) computers perform a still larger part of the reproduction, dissemination, storing, presentation, formatting, organising, filtering and control of the discourses relevant for politics. Thus, even though computers do not understand the meaning of the information, they are extremely important for the availability and exchange of politically relevant information and discourses.

As ICT changes the basis for politics and democracy a set of political issues concerning access, privacy, copyright, supervision, standards, etc. come to the fore. None of these issues are entirely new, but they take on new meanings and a new importance in the information society, and the outcomes of political struggles concerning these issues again have important repercussions for democracy. An example is the current changes of copyright legislation, which has a very direct impact on access to (political) information.

As programs have taken over much of the reproduction, dissemination, storing, presentation, formatting, organising, filtering and control of political relevant discourse, the control over programs becomes decisive for the availability of information. Hence, how software and its development is controlled, is decisive for democracy. As Lessig writes: 'Code is law and code is made' [19:60]. In a later work [20] Lessig, inspired by Benkler [21], has expanded and made more sophisticated his idea about control to other spheres relevant for the use of ICT, namely the physical layer (the hardware: computers, wires, hubs, etc.) and the content layer (what is said or transmitted across the wires [20,23]). Thus, Lessig now operates with a model where the physical layer is at the bottom, the code layer on top of this layer and the content layer at the very top. Each of these layers is subject to different types of control, and each are of course human constructs, and thus subject to changes and modifications.

In a recent work [22] we have developed a four-layer model, which has some similarities to Lessig's model, but which has two further advantages: 1) it illustrates more clearly how hardware and software conditions the practices of which ICT is a part, and how these practices constitute the foundation for (political) discourses on the use of ICT. Thus, the model is an illustration of how changes in, for example, the regulation of hardware and software will have important repercussions for the practices of which such hardware and software form a part, and therefore for the discourses around the very same practices, 2) it does away with the inherent technological determinism in Lessig's model, as our model might be read both from the top as well as from the bottom. At a given time it should probably be read from the bottom, but over time there is no doubt that strong discourses (hegemonies) can change the developmental path of both hardware and software.

Thus, we understand ICT as interplay between four levels: hardware, software, practices and discourses. The arrows pointing upwards should be read as 'constitutes the basis for'. Thus, hardware constitutes the basis for software; software constitutes the basis for the practical usefulness of ICT, etc. The arrows pointing downwards should be read as 'affects' or 'put demands on'. Thus, discourses in the form of hegemonies put demands on the practices, practices put demands on the software, etc.

With the concept 'commercial censorship', Deibert [15] denotes the different ways in which commercial actors try to influence and dominate the Internet; especially the two bottom layers of our model. However, Deibert [23] is very conscious of the fact that the model also works from the top down; that for example the different types of security discourses, which he sees as struggling for hegemony, will put demands on and have clear consequences for both hardware and software development and regulation, and thereby for politics and authority in the 21st century. The 'commercial censorship' which Deibert describes, takes effect through a number of existing and especially emerging practices that have properties, which impinge on issues like access (in the broadest sense), privacy, diversity and openness in a negative way, thereby undermining important aspects of media citizenship.

Concretely, 'commercial censorship' (in our interpretation) takes place through at least five strategies concerning digital rights that commercial actors use in trying to maximise their profits when dealing with ICT, in particular the Internet: 1) to become market leaders (set *de facto* standards; examples are Microsoft (Office, Internet Explorer), Oracle (databases) and Adobe (PDF-files), 2) work in international

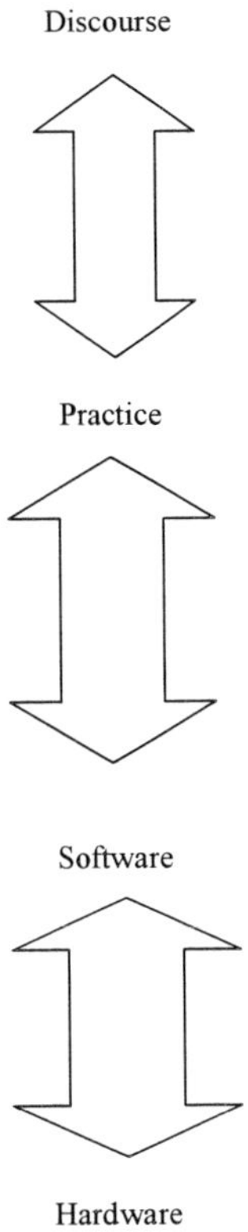

Fig. 1. The interplay between hardware, software, practice and discourse.

standards organisations to set de jure standards (CEN, ETSI, IEC, TCG, etc.[3] 3) to take out patents (on hardware or software), 4) to register copyright on their products, and 5) to ensure copyright protection by developing digital rights management systems.

Here we deal only with recent developments within the copyright and copyright protection area, and the software patent area, because these developments are of particular democratic concern.

3. Copyright protection

Concerning copyright we know that with the digitalisation of a wide range of consumer products, including movies, music and books, duplication and distribution is regarded as a problem by information providers. Companies in the affected industries such as the recording industry and the motion picture industry have claimed large losses in potential sales, though determining exact figures is very difficult. It is therefore not surprising that the involved companies and their associations such as IFPI (International Federation of the Phonographic Industry) and national industry organisations as RIAA (Recording Industry Association of America) and the MPAA (Motion Picture Association of America) have taken increasingly stronger measures to protect their property and preserve copyright in cyberspace.

[3]CEN is an acronym for European Committee for Standardization, ETSI is an acronym for European Telecommunications Standards Institute, and IEC is the International Electrotechnical Commission.

There are reasons to ensure compensation for expended resources that may be important for the circulation of ideas central to liberal democratic society. However, the problem seems to be that in cyberspace it is difficult in practice to apply the longstanding principles of protection of copyright, and that the measures taken seem to have a number of unintended consequences, among these restrictions on creativity and self-expression. However, what is most concerning for democracy is the Digital Millennium Copyright Act (DMCA), an act passed by US Congress on October 28th 1998, which has laid down that:

> 'No person shall circumvent a technological measure that effectively controls access to a work protected under this title'. (Sec 1201.a.A1)

and that:

> 'No person shall manufacture, import, offer to the public, provide, or otherwise traffic in any technology, product, service, device, component, or part thereof, that – '(A) is primarily designed or produced for the purpose of circumventing a technological measure that effectively controls access to a work protected under this title ...' (Sec 1201.b; see http://thomas.loc.gov/cgi-bin/query/z?c105:H.R.2281.ENR:)

In short, it is prohibited to circumvent programs and/or hardware that protect copyright, and it is prohibited to develop programs with the purpose of doing this. This act hands over legislative, judicial and executive power to the business sector, and the role of the classical legal system basically just becomes to ensure this delegation of power.

It has been shown in a study by the Electronic Frontier Foundation that the DMCA has been employed as a tool for anti-competition, that it has stifled legitimate research into cyber-security and encryption technologies, and that it is undermining 'fair use' of products. It has also impinged on academic databases and electronic journals restricting their use, and many believe that the act will put restrictions on academic work in the public domain (see: www.law.duke.edu/pd/papers.html#history).

On 22nd May 2001 the EU passed similar rules in the Infosoc directive:

1. Member States shall provide adequate legal protection against the circumvention of any effective technological measures ... (which protect copyright, JH & FB)
2. Member States shall provide adequate legal protection against the manufacture, import, distribution, sale, rental, advertisement for sale or rental, or possession for commercial purposes of devices, products or components or the provision of services which:
   (a) are promoted, advertised or marketed for the purpose of circumvention of ... any effective technological measures'. (Art. 6; see http://europa.eu.int/smartapi/cgi/sga_doc?smartapi!celexplus!prodCELEXnumdoc&numdoc=301L0029&lg=EN).

So, most of the West has demonstrated that 'code is law' in the strongest sense. Also, the US is pushing the DMCA in bilateral trade negotiations, and many of its elements are manifest in treaties administered by the World Intellectual Property Organization (WIPO).

From a democratic perspective it is bothersome that these technical devices include the development of so-called digital rights management systems (DRM-system), which are general programs that protect the copyright of information. This has led BEUC, Bureau Européen des Unions de Consommateurs, to warn against the perspectives of DRM backed up by law. DRM creates a 'new relationship between right holders and consumers, with altered consumer rights, freedoms and expectations. (The development is) ... towards the general replacement of copyright law with contract law and codes'. This means that law concerning access to information is privatised to contracts, which are realised in computer programs.

BEUC also hold the point of view that this restricts consumers' rights concerning private copying and fair use, which means loss of access to information. It should be noted also that Lessig has argued that the restriction of 'fair use' is detrimental to creativity. Furthermore, according to BEUC, DRM-systems threaten to undermine freedom of speech and privacy due to control of the user's behaviour in the interest of right holders. Also, BEUC points to the fact that right holders are free to require such control in contracts with consumers. http://www.beuc.org/Content/Default.asp?PageID=103 2004-09-15.

4. Trusted computing

However, even more concerning are the measures currently being taken to protect intellectual rights by integrating software and hardware in the computer in order to enforce DRM. Most notable in this respect is Microsoft's NGSCB (Next Generation Secure Computing Base) system, and the work going on in the so-called Trusted Computing Group (TCG); an organisation set up by Intel, IBM, Microsoft, HP and Compaq that today comprises more than 100 IT-firms. (https://www.trustedcomputinggroup.org).

NGSCB[4] is a further development of Microsoft's existing DRM-system, which works for sound and video files in Microsoft's Media Player. A recording company or a video producer, who wishes to control the use and copying of their product on the buyer's computer, can use Microsoft's Media Player. With software from Microsoft, the producer can change the sound or video files to encrypted files, which can only run on the Media Player if the user has a digital key, which he/she has to buy. The producer can regulate the number of times a tune can be listened to or a video can be shown, and whether the sound or video file can be copied or burnt on a CD. This system is very similar to other DRM-systems, e.g. the project initiated by Real Player (https://devicedrm.helixcommunity.org). However, a major difference is that NGSCB generalises the DRM-system, so that the whole operating system on the PC will be controlled by a system of rights, where not only sound or video files, but also e-mails, databases, text, pictures and other programs, are protected against unauthorised use.

If things turn out as Microsoft expects, NGSCB will be the standard operating system on the next generation of computers. Seen in the context of the market dominance of central Microsoft products like the Office package and Internet Explorer, Microsoft will be able to decide which programs it is possible to run together with its dominating products. If Microsoft programs are used on the big majority of the citizens' computer, it means that Microsoft will obtain the possibility of denying other programs access to data protected by Microsoft programs. Thus, Microsoft will have a crucial influence on which programs it will be possible to run on the computers. If, therefore, the most important information/content providers in society accept NGSCB, it may force citizens also to use NGSCB if they want access to text, sound, video files, or if they want to send and receive protected e-mails and other information from public authorities, for example. Microsoft claims that one of NGSCB's big advantages is that the user can avoid viruses etc. because only accepted programs can run under NGSCB. However, the same functionality can be obtained on the basis of IBM's TCG-system for Linux. The crucial difference is that while IBM gives the owner of the PC a possibility to protect himself against 'foreign' attempts to change the software on the computer, Microsoft is protecting the 'foreign' content providers against the owner if he/she attempts to make changes to his/her PC. (http://www.research.ibm.com/gsal/tcpa/why_tcpa.pdf, p. 5).

[4]The following information on Microsoft's Next Generation Secure Computing Base (called 'Palladium' at an earlier stage) system are all from [26].

5. Digital rights management systems and software patents

In December 2001 Microsoft obtained a US-patent on a 'Digital Rights Management Operating System', which is likely to be used to block competing DRM operating systems, ensuring Microsoft is the only provider of DRM-operating-systems. Microsoft has also filed WIPO patent applications to patent their DRM systems. Thus, the coming of the DRM-systems should be seen in connection with the development in the area of software patents, *and it is exactly the combined development that makes the situation problematic from a democratic point of view*. To cut a long story very short, there has for some time been some difference in the American and the European approach to software patents. Whereas it was not possible to patent software in Europe before 1986, software patenting had been made possible in the USA since 1981. In 1985 the EPO (European Patent Office) changed its practice, and made a reinterpretation of the European Patent Convention making it possible to patent most software that can be run on a computer and offers a technical contribution to the state of the art. However, 'technical' is not defined, and therefore it is completely unclear which software is patentable, and which is not. This has created an unclear legal situation in Europe, which has incited the European Commission to propose a software patents directive that will force the EU countries to pass legislation that widens the field for software patents even more than the dubious practice of the EPO. If the Directive is passed, this will bring the European situation very close to conditions in the USA.

The *ratio* of patent law is that *society* shall benefit from patents. When the disadvantages by giving privileges outweigh the advantages stemming from higher incentives for innovation, patents should not be given. A number of economic investigations and analyses from different authors have convincingly shown that software is a special type of product, the patenting of which will have a number of negative consequences [24–28]:

Firstly, software patents seem primarily to protect the market position of dominating firms rather than stimulating innovation. Secondly, software patents will hamper the development of free, open source software that offers the only important competition to Microsoft's dominance. The continuous development of free, open source software is crucial because citizens and institutions may then opt for knowing what is going on in their ICT-infrastructure. An example of this effect is that the patent on mp3-files has been used to stop the development of a free, open source mp3-encoder. Thirdly, the proposed patent regime allows patenting digital standards or even broad ideas about standards. In general, exchange of information between programs and computers requires common standards, and patenting of standards therefore offers good opportunities for dominance. Fourthly, since software patents are patents on certain ways of changing information, such patents may cover information processing within politics and democracy. An example is the Acacia patent, which covers streaming of sound or video on the Internet, notwithstanding the technology. This patent is just a broad idea about information exchange, but it could be used to interfere with the freedom of speech. It has been used to demand a payment of 3–5% percent from small internet companies. Fifth, institutions, also public institutions, will lose the right to know about what is going on in their ICT-infrastructure, as most of the programs they will be using will have closed code. Sixth, access to the Internet and other forms of digital exchange of information requires common standards. With the new patent regime it will be possible to patent such standards. Also, this could mean that it will be difficult to protect oneself against eavesdropping.

All these six perspectives becomes paramount when it is taken into consideration that those who control the new software ideas, may control the development of software; that is, they control how information is handled in future. The case of DRM clearly shows the potential for dire consequences that this may have.

Returning to NGSCB, through the next generation of Windows, Microsoft is likely to have a crucial influence on the type of programs required to read the lion's share of the information on the Internet due to the combination of patented Microsoft standards, and the dominance of Microsoft programs on many citizens' computers. A worst case scenario is that also search engines will have to be certified by Microsoft before citizens can make use of them. Thus, Microsoft has already launched a first version of a Microsoft search engine, which one could fear will have the same effects on other search engines as Internet Explorer had on Netscape. In this way Microsoft and its partners may obtain crucial power to decide about what it is possible (or impossible) to distribute over the Net – a power that closely resembles a censuring function.

Furthermore, to use NGSCB on a computer and to obtain access to information encrypted by NGSCB, the computer must be certified by a 'third party' that, in practice, will often be Microsoft. The installation of Windows XP already requires certification by Microsoft. This offers Microsoft a unique opportunity to tap information from citizen's computers. So, even though citizens, businesses and public authorities will have better possibilities of controlling their internal communication with NGSCB, and be able better to avoid hacking, it also enables access to citizens' data. Since also the information activities of criminals and terrorists will be protected by NGSCB, both police and intelligence services will be likely to obtain information through collaboration with Microsoft. It is a complex matter how this will be handled, but most observers agree that such questions are a matter of public concern, and not something that should be left Microsoft to decide through the design of their operating system. Therefore, alternatives to Microsoft's NGSCB should be available [see for example [29]). The US patent on digital rights management operating systems prohibit others making similar systems unless Microsoft allows it. If the EU Commission's pending software patent directive is passed, Microsoft will probably be able also to obtain the patent in Europe. In itself, this should be reason enough to seriously reconsider the Directive on software patents, and make sure that open source alternatives to NGSCB are developed.

To conclude, DRM systems, in combination with Infosoc and DMCA, delegate legislative power (control over access to information), judicial power (the right to judge about violations), and executive power (the right to block access to information) to a few multinational companies and industry organisations. If Microsoft is enabled to install NGSCB on most computers and combines this with patenting the DRM operating system in Europe, this will give Microsoft a legislative, judicial and executive power of enormous dimensions, in a world where computers and the Internet, at least in the rich part of the world, are increasingly citizens' access to news, entertainment, information, political discourse, products of various kinds, jobs, private communication, etc. This power, which is furthermore highly automated, will set Microsoft up as a decisive *political* authority in the information society.

Thus, what we see from these examples of commercial censorship backed up by political decisions, is a serious undermining of the Internet as an open, liberal and free public arena (a 'commons' [20]), and a likely change of the internet to a medium that is characterised by global control. Gradually, limitations on access in the widest sense, as both free access to different kinds of hardware/software and information, on privacy, on diversity and on openness is about to be imposed. This infringement on the Internet as a symbol of liberal democracy is happening in the shadow of 'the war on terrorism' (cf. the new security discourses described in [23]), and the Internet could easily become one of the bigger casualties of this war if no action is taken to avoid it.

6. Conclusion

Media citizenship concerns the rights to seek, receive and impart information through any medium and, as described in the introduction, the Internet has been seen as an important lever for media citizenship and democracy more generally. However, what we have shown in this article is that the development of digital rights management (DRM) systems, in combination with current developments in the right to take out patents, constitutes a serious undermining of the freedom for anyone to seek, receive and impart information on and through the Internet. It is particularly Microsoft's DRM operating system that threatens to change the architecture of the Internet so that information in the future may not be acquired without password and payment. This implies an unprecedented degree of control over citizen's behaviour on the Internet in respect of their private computers. In this connection it is also very concerning that private companies may use these systems to curb freedom of speech on the Internet and to monopolise creativity due to the reduced rights associated with the fair use of information.

One might claim that this development only concerns the Internet, and therefore has marginal consequences for 'real' democracy. However, as we have also tried to describe above, we have, at least in the Western world, taken a significant and irreversible step into the information society; to a world where computers and the internet are increasingly citizens' access to news, entertainment, information, political discourse, products of various kinds, jobs, private communication, etc. Politics, political discourse, and thus democracy today are unthinkable without computers and the Internet, which is why we should be extremely concerned about the development of regulation in the virtual world. As computers and the Internet have become part and parcel of political practices and the exercise of democracy, any attempts to curb or restrict uses of computers and the Internet in relation to such practices is a threat to democracy.

In the final analysis we can say that Lessig is right: code is law, or becoming law, maybe in an even more literal sense than Lessig meant. What we see is that the world's largest information providers as well as software and hardware producers are preparing a basic change in the architecture of the Internet. We do not seem to be far away from a situation where these companies control the development of hardware and software, including software that automatically controls parts of human's actions and their access to and use of information. And, augmenting these concerns, the political systems both in Europe and the USA seem to be prepared to enforce this control. This development seems unavoidable if no countervailing power organises a resistance against the new 'security and control regime'. We have recently seen such resistance towards for example EU's software patent directive. This resistance comes from many corners of society: a) from small software companies concerned about the increasing dominance of the big multinational players in the field, b) from consumer interests, like for example BEUC, concerned about the 'privatisation' of consumer rights (here copyright law), c) from open source groups concerned about the autonomy of programmers and computer users, and d) from civil rights advocates, concerned about the possibilities of seeking, receiving and imparting information on and through the internet, and about individual privacy. Whether such resistance will gain momentum or not remains to be seen, and the fate of EU's software patent directive will be an interesting showcase in this respect.

References

[1] B. McNair, *An Introduction to Political Communication*, Routledge: London & New York, 2002.

[2] J.G. Blumler and D. Kavanagh, The Third Age of Political Communication: Influences and Features, *Political Communication* **16** (1999), 209–230.

[3] J. Corner and D. Pels, eds, *Media and the Restyling of Politics*, Sage: London, 2003.

[4] J. Habermas, *Between Facts and Norms*, The MIT Press: Cambridge, Mass., 2001

[5] N. Fraser, *Justice Interruptus*, Routledge: London, 1997.

[6] J. Habermas, *The Structural Transformation of the Public Sphere*, The MIT Press: Cambridge, Mass., 1989[1962].

[7] W.B.H.J. van de Donk et al., *Orwell in Athens. A Perspective on Informatization and Democracy*, IOS Press: Amsterdam, 1995.

[8] J. Hoff, K. Löfgren and S. Johansson, *Internet og demokrati, Erfaringer fra kommunalvalget 1997*. DJØF Forlag: København, 1999.
[9] I. Hutchby, *Conversation and Technology, From the Telephone to the Internet*, Polity: Cambridge, 2001.
[10] M. Castells, *The Power of Identity*, Blackwell Publishers: Oxford, 1997.
[11] C. Barnett, *Culture and Democracy. Media, Space and Representation*, The University of Alabama Press & Edinburgh University Press, 2003.
[12] WSIS, http://www.itu.int/wsis/documents/doc_single-en-1161.asp., 2003.
[13] Th.H. Marshall, Citizenship and social class in: *Class, Citizenship and Social Development: Essays*, T.H. Marshall, ed., Cambridge: Cambridge University Press, 1950.
[14] M. Schudson, *The Power of News*, Harvard University Press: Cambridge, Mass. and London, 1995.
[15] R. Deibert, *Black Code: Censorship, Surveillance, and the Militarization of Cyberspace*, Paper prepared for the International Studies Association Conference, Portland, Oregon, USA, February 2003.
[16] D. Lyon, *The Electronic Eye, The Rise of the Surveillance Society*, Polity: Cambridge, 1994.
[17] C. Raab, Connecting Orwell to Athens?: Information Superhighways and the Privacy Debate, in: *Orwell in Athens. A Perspective on Informatization and Democracy*, W.B.H.J. van de Donk, ed., IOS Press: Amsterdam, 1995, pp. 195–211.
[18] M. Monmonier, *Spying with Maps*, The University of Chicago Press: Chicago, 2002.
[19] L. Lessig, *Code and other Laws of Cyberspace*, Basic Books, New York, 1999.
[20] L. Lessig, *The Future of Ideas, The fate of the commons in a connected world*. Vintage Books: New York, 2001.
[21] Y. Benkler, From Consumers to Users: Shifting the Deeper Structures of Regulation, *Federal Communications Law Journal* **52** (2000).
[22] J. Hoff and F. Bjerke, Politik, magt og demokrati i informationssamfundet. En teoretisk ramme, in: *Danmark som informationssamfund. Muligheder og barrierer for politik og demokrati*, Jens Hoff, ed., Aarhus Universitetsforlag: Aarhus, 2004, pp. 22–70.
[23] R. Deibert, Circuits of Power: Security in the Internet Environment, in: *Information Technologies and Global Politics*, J. Rosenau and J.P. Singh, eds, State University of New York Press: New York, 2001.
[24] J. Bessen and R. Hunt, *An empirical look at software patents*, http://www.researchoninnovation.org/swpat.pdf, 2003.
[25] J. Bessen and E. Maskin, *Sequential Innovation, Patents and Imitation*, Working Paper. Department of Economics. Massachusetts Institute of Technology, 2000.
[26] F. Bjerke, Softwarepatenter og magt, in: *Danmark som informationssamfund. Muligheder og barrierer for politik og demokrati*, Jens Hoff, ed., Aarhus Universitetsforlag: Aarhus, 2004, pp. 105–139.
[27] Hart, Holmes and Reid, *The Economic Impact of Patentability of Computer Programs*, Section III, pp. 28–38. http://europa.eu.int/comm/internal_market/en/indprop/comp/studyintro.htm, 1999.
[28] FTC (Federal Trade Commission) Report, To promote innovation: the proper balance of competition and patent law and policy. Chapter 3.V. http://www.ftc.gov/os/2003/10/innovationrpt.pdf, 2003.
[29] OpenOffice.org, The office pack OpenOffice is free and open software, which can be downloaded from: http://www.openoffice.org.